ROUTLEDGE LIBRARY EDITIONS: ART AND CULTURE IN THE NINETEENTH CENTURY

Volume 8

THE LAST TROUBADOURS

THE LAST TROUBADOURS
Poetic Drama in Italian Opera,
1597–1887

DEIRDRE O'GRADY

LONDON AND NEW YORK

First published in 1991 by Routledge

This edition first published in 2019
by Routledge
2 Park Square, Milton Park, Abingdon, Oxon OX14 4RN

and by Routledge
711 Third Avenue, New York, NY 10017

Routledge is an imprint of the Taylor & Francis Group, an informa business

© 1991 Deirdre O'Grady

All rights reserved. No part of this book may be reprinted or reproduced or utilised in any form or by any electronic, mechanical, or other means, now known or hereafter invented, including photocopying and recording, or in any information storage or retrieval system, without permission in writing from the publishers.

Trademark notice: Product or corporate names may be trademarks or registered trademarks, and are used only for identification and explanation without intent to infringe.

British Library Cataloguing in Publication Data
A catalogue record for this book is available from the British Library

ISBN: 978-1-138-35894-2 (Set)
ISBN: 978-0-429-42671-1 (Set) (ebk)
ISBN: 978-1-138-36512-4 (Volume 8) (hbk)
ISBN: 978-1-138-36513-1 (Volume 8) (pbk)
ISBN: 978-0-429-43090-9 (Volume 8) (ebk)

Publisher's Note
The publisher has gone to great lengths to ensure the quality of this reprint but points out that some imperfections in the original copies may be apparent.

Disclaimer
The publisher has made every effort to trace copyright holders and would welcome correspondence from those they have been unable to trace.

THE LAST TROUBADOURS

Poetic drama in Italian opera 1597–1887

Deirdre O'Grady

London and New York

First published 1991
by Routledge
11 New Fetter Lane, London EC4P 4EE

Simultaneously published in the USA and Canada
by Routledge
a division of Routledge, Chapman and Hall, Inc.
29 West 35th Street, New York, NY 10001

© 1991 Deirdre O'Grady

Typeset in 10/12pt Garamond by
Input Typesetting Ltd, London
Printed and bound in Great Britain by
TJ Press (Padstow) Ltd

All rights reserved. No part of this book may be reprinted or reproduced or utilized in any form or by any electronic, mechanical, or other means, now known or hereafter invented, including photocopying and recording, or in any information storage or retrieval system, without permission in writing from the publishers.

British Library Cataloguing in Publication Data
O'Grady, Deirdre
The last troubadours: poetic drama in Italian opera, 1597–1887.
1. Opera in Italian, history
I. Title
782.10945

Library of Congress Cataloging in Publication Data
O'Grady, Deirdre.
The last troubadours: poetic drama in Italian opera 1597–1887/
Deirdre O'Grady.
p. cm.
Includes bibliographical references.
1. Libretto. 2. Librettists—Italy. 3. Opera—Italy. I. Title.
ML2110.04 1991
782.1'026'80945—dc20   90-32869

ISBN 0-415-05459-1

To my mother

CONTENTS

List of illustrations   ix
Introduction   xi
Acknowledgements   xiii

Part I   Baroque, Arcadian and Enlightenment influences

1 ARISTOCRATIC BEGINNINGS IN FLORENCE, MANTUA AND ROME   3
2 POPULAR SUCCESS AND MATURITY IN VENICE: BUSENELLO, BADOARO AND CICOGNINI   28
3 INNOVATION AND REFORM: ZENO, METASTASIO AND CALZABIGI   42
4 OF SERVANTS AND MASTERS: FEDERICO, GOLDONI AND DA PONTE   64

Part II   The expression of individualism

5 A CRY FOR FREEDOM: HIGH PRIESTS AND PATRIOTS   99
6 OF REASON AND DELIRIUM   128
7 JESTER, TROUBADOUR AND COURTESAN   152
8 THE DEVIL'S ADVOCATE: EVIL IN THE WORKS OF ARRIGO BOITO   180

Notes   202
Select bibliography   223
Index   228

LIST OF ILLUSTRATIONS

1 Jacopo Peri singing the role of Orfeo in *Euridice* (1600)	15
2 Gian Francesco Busenello (1598–1659)	32
3 Apostolo Zeno (1668–1750)	47
4 Pietro Metastasio (1698–1782), portrait by Rosalba Carriera (Gemäldegalerie, Dresden)	51
5 Carlo Goldoni (1707–93)	70
6 Lorenzo Da Ponte (1749–1838)	78
7 Felice Romani (1788–1865)	107
8 Temistocle Solera (1815–78)	121
9 Salvatore Cammarano (1801–52)	144
10 Francesco Maria Piave (1810–76)	169
11 Antonio Ghislanzoni (1824–93)	183
12 Arrigo Boito (1842–1918)	185

INTRODUCTION

The present study traces the history of the Italian operatic libretto from its courtly origin, through the crisis of the aristocracy and the struggle for independence, to the rejection of traditional values in favour of a realistic assessment of being and behaviour. The poetic world of heroic valour, cunning servants, revolutionary ardour and romantic tenderness is captured, while the historical and cultural significance of such expressions is stressed. The role and achievement of the librettist are probed. As poet, dramatist and mouthpiece for political propaganda, he in turn echoes and mocks social convention. He thus demonstrates both the cultural climate and social taste of his times.

A further aspect of the function of the libretto, however, demands attention. This is its contribution to the diffusion of European culture. The interdisciplinary nature of such an approach to the text carries libretto studies into the realm of comparative literature and translation techniques. The historical pursuit and analysis of the operatic word thus provide a literary and linguistic dimension that ranges from the provincial to the national, and from the national to the European.

I have divided the book into two main parts, each containing four chapters. Part I treats the opera from its birth at the beginning of the baroque period to the advent of the French revolution. Innovations and reforms are discussed. A historical and chronological approach is applied throughout. With the dawning of the romantic movement the European dimension in opera was clearly demonstrated. For that reason my approach in Part II pursues a thematic and selective vision of the nineteenth century. Opera is considered as a purveyor of European culture. Themes of ardour, delirium and philosophical experimentation are discussed.

The European popularity of Shakespeare, Scott, Schiller, Guttierez and Dumas the younger during the nineteenth century owes much to the adaptive ability of the librettist. Hugo's *Le Roi s'amuse* achieved wide recognition as a result of Francesco Maria Piave's version of it, at a time when it was under censorship ban in France. It can also be argued that realism was introduced into the Italian theatre not with Verga's *Cavalleria rusticana* and its operatic adaptation by Menasci/Targioni-Tozzetti with music by Mascagni, but with Piave's librettos for *Rigoletto* and *La traviata*, adapted from Hugo and Dumas the younger respectively.

This study of texts for music concludes with a consideration of the poetic projection of evil in the works of Arrigo Boito. By common consent the librettos of Verdi's two final masterpieces *Otello* and *Falstaff* are the finest in Italian opera. Here poet and composer achieved an affinity of comprehension and expression, so bringing the art of artistic collaboration to its highest point. What began as 'drama for music' in the hands of Rinuccini in the sixteenth century became 'music drama' towards the end of the nineteenth century, so preparing the way for twentieth-century *verismo* and a complete break with the romantic idiom.

This in no way claims to be a complete study of a fascinating genre. Many great works have been accorded merely a passing glance, or in some cases have been totally ignored. Rather, it is an assessment of an art-form, and an attempt to prove its significance, not merely as the servant of a more illustrious master, but as a historical expression of literary trends and tendencies from 1597 to 1887.

The textual quotations are, if not otherwise stated, from the Ricordi, Milan, editions of the librettos. The translations are my own.

Deirdre O'Grady
March 1989

ACKNOWLEDGEMENTS

I wish to take this opportunity to thank most sincerely all those who offered help, advice and moral support in the course of the preparation of this book. In particular I acknowledge the assistance of the staff of the following libraries and institutes: the Biblioteca Nazionale Braidense, Milan; the Biblioteca del Conservatorio Giuseppe Verdi, Milan; the Biblioteca Nazionale Marciana, Venice; the Fondazione Giorgio Cini, Venice, and the Arts Library, University College, Dublin. I must also express my thanks to Maria Teresa Muraro, Secretary of the Fondazione Giorgio Cini, Venice, for permission to reproduce the portraits and photographs of Italian librettists in their collection.

I owe a special debt of gratitude to my Head of Department, Professor John Barnes of University College, Dublin, for facilitating my research in every respect and for coming to the rescue with aid and advice at crucial points along the way. Thanks are also due to my two patient typists, Carene Comerford and Judy Barnes, for their never-failing efforts to decipher my longhand.

Finally, a special word of appreciation to my mother for her constant encouragement. This book is dedicated to her.

Part I

BAROQUE, ARCADIAN AND ENLIGHTENMENT INFLUENCES

1
ARISTOCRATIC BEGINNINGS IN FLORENCE, MANTUA AND ROME

I

The origin and development of opera have proved tantalizing and fascinating topics since the beginnings of the genre at the end of the Italian Renaissance. That Italy should be its birthplace is in no way surprising: for centuries a source of cultural inspiration to the civilized world, its name evokes images of beauty and taste. The association of poetic expression with songs of love and lamentation had been established much earlier at the medieval court of Frederick II, at Palermo, centre of the Sicilian school of poetry. Here Jacopo da Lentini[1] is credited with having invented the sonnet, a form perfected by Petrarch[2] in his collection of poems entitled *Rerum vulgarium fragmenta*, more usually called the *Canzoniere*, meaning 'Song-book'. Through the figure of his beloved, Laura, the poet succeeds in associating the poetic laurel, classical mythology, nature, love and beauty. Such associations and identifications are among the devices employed by poets following in the wake of Petrarch. This poetic tradition, as absorbed into the pastoral dramas, alongside a desire to perpetuate the classical theatre, forms the literary basis of the new art-form which developed at the courts of Florence and Mantua at the close of the sixteenth century, and in the early years of the seventeenth century.

The *melodramma* or early opera is a child of the Renaissance, and came into its own during the baroque period. It reflected the literary climate of the time, but in addition added a new and extra dimension: words were set to music to assist the dramatic situation. The belief that this artistic fusion added authenticity to the classical revival originated from a collective opinion that the ancient Greeks and Romans had sung throughout their tragedies, and had used solos, not choruses. Opera is a result of the pursuit and rediscovery of the Greeks, and the dramatization of their myths. Daphne and Apollo, Orpheus and Eurydice, and Ariadne and Bacchus as operatic protagonists faced a new aristocratic public in sumptuous settings designed by the leading baroque artists and architects of the day. Since the performances were originally associated with marriage festivities, the strength and enduring power of love was a favourite theme. As interest spread from Florence to neighbouring towns and cities, principally Mantua, the association and co-ordination of words and music became increasingly significant. Later the operatic activities at the papal court in Rome marked a shift from pagan mythology to Christian doctrine as subject-matter of the libretto. However, the Florentine, Mantuan and Roman court operas were at all times aristocratic affairs, initiated and organized for the instruction and entertainment of the invited nobility.

Up to the publication of Claude V. Palisca's extensive research on the origins of Italian opera in 1962,[3] it was believed that all initial activity and operatic experimentation was concentrated around what was known as the Camerata dei Bardi. This was a group of artists and scholars who met at the house of Count Giovanni Bardi in Florence, with the object of reviving Greek drama. Yet what early historians of opera called the Camerata was really, to quote Palisca, 'two different and separate, indeed even opposed, social and intellectual circles'.[4] One was Bardi's group, which advocated discussion of learned topics and amateur music making. The second group was sponsored by Jacopo Corsi, and was a semi-professional music and dramatic workshop, which was directly responsible for the first musical pastorals. Thus Bardi and Corsi were rivals, as also were the musicians Peri and Caccini. Members of Bardi's group included Vincenzo Galilei (1529–91; the father of Galileo), the composer Giulio Caccini (c.1545–1618) and Pietro Strozzi. Vincenzo Galilei expounded the theories of the Camerata in the preface to his musical treatise *Dialogo sulla musica antica e moderna* (1581). He explained that the object of the group was to free music from polyphony by rediscovering the songs of the Greeks which were as spontaneous as the songs of shepherds. Galilei's experimentations first surfaced in the form of a musical version of the Ugolino episode in Dante's *Inferno*,[5] followed by the *Lamentations of Jeremiah* for solo voice.

ARISTOCRATIC BEGINNINGS

In contrast to the informality of this little-documented group, the activities of the official literary academies of the second half of the sixteenth century are profusely recorded. The one, according to Palisca, which contained the greatest number of musical amateurs was the Accademia degli Alterati. By 1571 it had twenty-one members, among whom are listed Jacopo Corsi (d.1604), a musician; Alessandro and Ottavio Rinuccini, poets; Gabriello Chiabrera (1552–1638), a poet; and Don Giovanni dei Medici, son of Duke Cosimo I. Even a superficial consideration of the members of both groups and their later operatic activities will indicate that what is usually associated with the Camerata took place outside it: the creation of the early Italian operas was effected in spite of artistic difference, and could be regarded as the outcome of a divergence of musical opinions, experiments and results. In other words, there was no single catalyst. Rather, it was the flourishing artistic life of sixteenth-century Florence that provided, as a result of its diverse activities, the climate in which opera was born.

It must, however, be borne in mind that it was the literary element that initially was the most highly developed. Since Bardi himself was responsible for the organization of festival performances at the court of the Grand Duke of Tuscany, it was inevitable that the activity of the Florentine amateurs should eventually have been given a high profile. In preparation for the performances, two distinct elements, drama and *stile recitativo* (the new form of musical declamation), were combined. What resulted was sung recitative and aria based on the tone, pitch and punctuation of human speech. Just as the voice assumes a mournful, melancholic tone to express sadness, so the musical line became grave and low pitched, with *legato* or smoothness of emission alternating with shorter expressions denoting sighs in the communication of sorrow. Happiness on the other hand, associated with a quickening heartbeat, was rendered by an acceleration of the tempo, demanding greater vocal agility on the part of the singer.[6] The introduction of the solo, at a time when madrigal choruses had always performed dramatic enactments of individual emotion, represented a stylistic revolution. The solo recitative bore no relation to the old liturgical chant or monotone setting of the psalms which had ignored the dramatic content of the words recited. The recitative of the early operas had instrumental chord accompaniments: violins, violas, basses, harpsichord, lyre, lutes and flutes.

The printed scores, however, do not reveal the distribution of instruments, but presumably it was in keeping with the various situations. In fact the overture to Monteverdi's *Orfeo* (1607) consists of a fanfare followed by an elegiac *ritornello*, which set the contrasting moods of the opera.

Musical *intermedi* on mythological subjects preceded the emergence of operatic performances proper. A number of brilliant festivals were held in Florence towards the close of the sixteenth century to celebrate the marriages of members of the Medici family.[7] As part of the novelty, a drama with musical accompaniment was performed in 1586 to honour the marriage of Eleonora dei Medici and Vincenzo Gonzaga, who became Duke of Mantua the following year. Three years later, in 1589, there followed another musical tableau to mark the wedding festivities of the Grand Duke of Tuscany and Christina of Lorraine, the niece of Catherine dei Medici. The mythological scenes were introduced by colourful pageantry, with Jacopo Peri (1561–1633) and Giulio Caccini providing the vocal entertainment. Such *intermedi* captivated the aristocratic Florentine court. Yet these spectacles were a far cry from the performances which introduced the final result of the experiments undertaken by poets, musicians and artists. With the presentation of *Dafne* (Florence, 1597), the theories of Emilio de' Cavalieri (1550–1602) who advocated a sung declamation (*recitar cantando*), Jacopo Peri who aimed at song imitating speech (*imitar col canto chi parla*) and Giulio Caccini who used the term harmonious speech (*in armonia favellare*), finally brought mythology to life in a unique fashion.

II

If the entire operatic venture can be regarded as revolutionary, the early poetic content of the Florentine melodrama reflects the influence of Renaissance pastoral drama alongside Petrarcan symbolism representing poetry, love and beauty. With regard to the literary pastoral drama, the earliest significant work was the *Favola d'Orfeo* of Angelo Ambrogini of Montepulciano, known as Il Poliziano. Although several conflicting dates have been put forward for its first performance at Mantua, leading critics including Mario Apollonio[8] and Nino Pirrotta[9] agree that the most likely date is 1480. The work tells the story of Orpheus, the singer and son of Apollo, god of music, and his bride Eurydice. Significant features are the establishment of Orpheus in a humanist rather than medieval setting, and the praises of Cardinal Gonzaga of Mantua, patron of the poet, contained in the Latin verses forming the song of Orpheus. The juxtaposition of good and evil is conveyed in terms of a conflict between the god of music, on the one hand, and Pluto, Proserpina and Minos, the infernal deities, on the other, rather than between any symbols of vice and virtue as in the medieval morality plays. Another salient aspect of the work is the fact that it was presented with incidental music. The musician is often erroneously referred to as Pietro Germi. The latter, however, as is pointed out by Pirrotta,[10] was an obscure nineteenth-century musician, who wished to establish himself by writing music to accompany Poliziano's work, four centuries after its first presentation! The original music has disappeared without trace, but we can be sure that the first enactment of this pastoral drama at Mantua cultivated a taste for musical accompaniment for such a genre. When Tasso's *Aminta* was first presented in 1573 we are aware that several sections were set to music by various composers.[11] The pastoral theatre was not based on Aristotelian principles, but merely allowed to develop in order to meet public taste. Mythological figures performed allegorical functions. The musical accompaniment served to heighten the spectacle, while the historic and artistic surroundings in which the works were performed made for the creation of a unique atmosphere.

The pastoral tradition, then, is preserved in the world of the melodrama where muses and gods appear in a new guise: that of singers projecting harmony. What is now accepted as the 'first' Italian opera, although none of its music survives, is *Dafne* (1597)[12] by Ottavio Rinuccini, a disciple of Tasso, the music being provided by Peri and Caccini. The work was performed in Florence, in the home of Jacopo Corsi, with great success; it was equally successfully reset in 1608 with music by Marco da Gagliano.[13] Three years later, in October 1600, the same trio, Rinuccini, Peri and Caccini, collaborated on *Euridice* which was performed before a splendid gathering to celebrate the marriage of Maria dei Medici to King Henry IV of France. Its success was unprecedented, and when it was performed again in 1602, at the Pitti Palace, the entire musical score was reset by Caccini. Both versions have survived. Rinuccini[14] also provided a libretto on the Narcissus myth, entitled *Narciso*, in addition to the text for both Monteverdi's *Arianna* (Mantua, 1608) and *Il ballo delle ingrate* (Mantua, 1608). Three famous poets who also played an essential part in the development of the libretto were Gabriello Chiabrera (1552–1638), author of *Il pianto d'Orfeo* (1608), Alessandro Striggio who wrote *La favola d'Orfeo* for Monteverdi (1607), and Stefano Landi who in 1619 provided yet another poetic version of the Orpheus legend with the title *La morte d'Orfeo*. These classical compositions written for musical accompaniment dramatize the cult of the poetic laurel (*Dafne*), the triumph of music and harmony (*Euridice, La favola d'Orfeo, La morte d'Orfeo*), the power of love and the projection of self-love (*Arianna* and *Narciso*). Together they can be seen to set a vogue for the ceremonial presentation of mythology, shortly before Gian Lorenzo Bernini created his mythological masterpieces and brought the pagan deities to the Roman piazza, marking the triumphant entry of baroque splendour into the art of town planning.

Rinuccini's *Dafne* has been frequently dismissed as unimportant in comparison to the poet's later and more mature *Euridice*, because of the former's structural weakness and lack of dramatic immediacy. Ulderico Rolandi finds little dramatic development, and a simplicity of dialogue, more in keeping with pure pastoral drama than with true melodrama.[15] Professor Pirrotta sees it as a preliminary attempt by the famous poet.[16] The libretto comprises twenty-four pages, of which pp. 3–19 are taken up with the text, and pp. 20–2 contain a *canzone* in praise of Jacopo Corsi, who had assumed the position of leader and co-ordinator of the organizing group. The text of the drama itself consists of 445 lines without division into acts or scenes. Its popularity can be gauged by the fact that on the occasion of the visit of the Duke of Parma to Florence, on 26 October 1604, *Dafne* was once again presented, and lines 19–20 were replaced by a tribute to the Duke's host. The edition from which I quote is that of 1608 entitled *La Dafne di Marco da Gagliano nell'Accademia degl' Elevati, L'Affannato, rappresentata in Mantova, in Firenze appresso Cristofano Marescotti, MDCVIII*. I feel it deserves attention as Rinuccini's first attempt at melodrama and the first true operatic treatment of the poetic laurel, since the drama of 1484 with music by Della Viola cannot be regarded as opera. Rinuccini's *Dafne* so marks the entry of Petrarchism into the world of the baroque theatre.

The plot is derived from the first book of Ovid's *Metamorphoses*, and the figure of Ovid appears in a twenty-eight-line prologue to the entire work. Rinuccini's intention is obviously to pay tribute to poetry and to classical mythology, symbolized by the figure of Dafne who, according to the myth, on her rejection of the love of the god Apollo was transformed into a laurel, the symbol of poetic inspiration. The work begins:

> Da' fortunati campi, ove immortali
> Godonsi a l'ombra de' frondosi mirti
> I graditi dal ciel felici spiriti,
> Mostromi in questa notte a voi, mortali.
> (*Dafne*, Prologue, 1–4)[17]

(O mortals, I show myself to you tonight, from the fertile fields, where immortal and happy spirits make merry in the shade of leafy myrtles.)

Rinuccini proceeds to stress the achievement of Ovid which rendered him immortal:

> Quel mi son io, che su la dotta lira
> Cantai le fiamme de' celesti amanti,
> E i trasformati lor vari sembianti
> Soavi sì ch'il mondo ancor m'ammira.
> (*Dafne*, Prologue, 5–8)

(I am he who on the learned lyre sang so melodiously of the ardour of the heavenly lovers, and of the transformation of their forms that the world still admires and honours me.)

The third scene introduces the dialogue between Dafne and Apollo which consists of a series of brief exchanges. The transformation of Dafne is narrated by a messenger in Scene 5:

> et ecco in un momento
> Che l'uno e l'altro leggiadretto piede,
> Che pur dianzi al fuggir parve aura o vento,
> Fatto immobil si vede
> Di salvatica scorza insieme avvinto,
> E le braccia e le palme al ciel distese
> Veste selvaggie fronde:
> Le crespe chiome e bionde
> più non riveggo e 'l volto e 'l bianco petto;
> Ma dal gentile aspetto

Ogni sembianza si dilegua e perde;
Sol miro un arboscel fiorito e verde.
(*Dafne*, Scene 5)

(And in an instant each of her graceful feet, that previously like a breeze or wind seemed to carry her in flight, was made immobile, and bound together in the form of a rugged tree bark. And her arms and hands, stretched to heaven, are now unruly branches. I no longer see her thick golden hair, or her face and white breast. Every trace of her comely form vanishes. I only now see a leafy green tree.)

Rinuccini achieves the instantaneous transformation by illustrating what is and what is not, while providing an image of the act of transformation by indicating the movement of the nymph in flight. 'Arms', 'hands', 'feet' and 'hair' preserve the physical image, while the poetic symbol 'arboscel fiorito e verde' is placed at the end of the line. The work closes with a hymn to the laurel, sung by a chorus. It consists of forty-eight lines – lines 398–445. The opening is as follows:

Bella Ninfa fuggitiva,
Sciolta e priva
Del tuo mortal velo,
Godi pur pianta novella
Casta e bella
Cara al mondo, e cara al cielo.
(*Dafne*, Scene 6)

(Beautiful, nimble, fleeing nymph, deprived of your mortal body, take pleasure in your new, plant form, chaste and beautiful, dear to heaven and earth.)

Rinuccini's *Dafne* is of historical and poetic interest since between the years 1600 and 1866 there were 400 operatic librettos written on the same subject. As the precursor of these it merits consideration as a possible source for later poet–librettists. As a piece of baroque sophistication it takes its place alongside the works of Chiabrera and Striggio, representing a new fashion and an age whose verse was soon to become overladen with linguistic incongruities.

Euridice is generally regarded as Rinuccini's masterpiece, in which both words and music are concentrated on a poetic appraisal of harmony. It embodies the first operatic presentation of the Orpheus legend. In the first performance Orfeo was sung by Peri himself, while Euridice was sung by Vittoria Archilei who was famous far beyond Florence as a singer and lutanist. Contemporary engravings representing court festivals provide us with some idea of the kind of stage setting that was used. The stage was raised, framed by a large impressive proscenium, with wide steps leading to the auditorium. Scenery was quite primitive and location was indicated by painted scenes on a backdrop. The classical landscapes were presented as seen through the eyes of the baroque artist, and Arcadian exteriors were complemented by baroque interiors, furnishing and attire. So the baroque stage combined the classical and the contemporary, mingling them in a manner which, though anachronistic, became the accepted territory on which opera was born and flourished. The success of Rinuccini's *Euridice* established opera as an art-form, and soon the fashion began to spread to other Italian towns.

The *Euridice* manuscript consists of twenty pages: sixteen of text, without divisions into scenes or acts, and four of dedications by Rinuccini, Peri and Caccini. The work consists of 790 lines. In the dedication *Alla Cristianissima Maria Medici Regina di Francia e di Navarra*, Rinuccini refers to the success of *Dafne*, which he says gave him the courage to rework it and allow it to be heard not only by the Florentine nobility but also by the Grand Duchess and by Cardinals Dal Monte and Montaldo. Realizing that such music-dramas give pleasure, he continues now to write two more, excusing himself for daring to provide a happy ending for the Orpheus legend by stressing the felicitous occasion for which it was written. He finds consolation, however, in the fact that Dante in his reference to Ulysses' voyage provided facts contrary to those found in Homer and other poets.[18] *Euridice* could be called a tribute to music through the medium of poetry. Orfeo, son of the god of music, laments, rejoices and finally exalts the power of harmony. In keeping with the central theme of the libretto, Rinuccini aims at creating a felicity of diction and images, so that the final outcome in the plot is in the form of the triumph of love, beauty and harmony over physical pain. Poetry and music are constrasted with evil and death, and song renders the lovers immortal. Here Rinuccini shows greater maturity than in his earlier *Dafne*. He provides twelve characters as opposed to six, and 790 lines as opposed to 445.

The protagonist is at once established as a figure rejoicing in song and dance, in an idealized world. Euridice's words are:

> Ma deh, compagne amate,
> Là tra quell'ombre grate
> Moviam di quel fiorito almo boschetto,
> E quivi al suon de' limpidi cristalli
> Trarrem liete carole e lieti balli.
>   (*Euridice*, Scene 1)[19]

(But, beloved friends, let us proceed to the shade of those kind trees, to that sweet flowery glade. And there to the sound of limpid streams, let us sing and dance happily.)

It is immediately clear that Rinuccini was concerned with creating groups of vowel sounds in order to accommodate the human voice: 'compagne amate' and 'ombre grate' contain transitions from 'o' to 'a', 'fiorito almo boschetto' provides four vowels which makes for clarity of diction. An idyllic Arcadian world is at the same time evoked. The chorus, some lines later, repeats the 'song' and 'dance' of Euridice, as the light merrymaking gathers momentum:

> Al canto, al ballo, a l'ombre, al prato adorno,
> A le bell'onde e liete
> Tutti, o pastor, correte
> Dolce cantando in sì beato giorno
> Al canto, al ballo. . . .
>   (*Euridice*, Scene 1)

(All hasten, o shepherds, to singing, to dancing, to the shady meadow, to the graceful happy waves, singing sweetly on such a joyful day.)

The joyful sound is replaced by the groan of Euridice, bitten by a serpent, which in turn yields to Orfeo's lamentation:

> E dal profondo core
> Con un sospir mortale
> Sì spaventoso, ohimè! Sospinse fore
> Che, quasi avesse l'ale
> Giunse ogni Ninfa al dolorose suono.
>   (*Euridice*, Scene 2)

(And from the depths of her heart, there issued such a deadly sound, so terrifying, that every nymph, as though on wings, came at the sorrowful call.)

There follows in lines 418–47 what can be regarded as the first surviving operatic lament to enter the popular operatic repertoire. Orfeo rejects the beauty of nature, painting a picture of the pastoral world shrouded in darkness. Imagery and light are extinguished for him, yielding to eternal night, identified with sounds of anguish, brought to music in his lament:

> Funeste piaggie, ombrosi orridi campi,
> Che di stelle o di sole
> Non vedeste giammai scintill'e lampi,
> Rimbombate dolenti
> Al suon de l'angosciose mie parole,
> Mentre con mesti accenti
> Il perduto mio ben con voi sospiro;
> E voi, deh, per pietà del mio martiro,
> Che nel misero cor dimora eterno,
> Lagrimate al mio pianto, Ombre d'Inferno.
> *(Euridice,* Scene 4)

(Dismal shores, horrendous, gloomy fields that never have seen the sparkling light of the stars or of the sun, you resound in sorrow to my words of anguish, while I with you sigh for my lost love. And you, infernal shades, pitying my suffering, which dwells eternally in my wretched heart, weep on account of my woe.)

Rinuccini allows the beauty of Orfeo's expression to penetrate the Underworld and it becomes a poetic plea for the effectiveness of harmony:

> Senti, mia vita, senti
> Quai pianti e quai lamenti
> Versa il tuo caro Orfeo dal cor interno.
> *(Euridice,* Scene 4)

(Hear, my beloved, hear what sorrow and lamentation your dear Orfeo expresses from the depth of his heart.)

Pluto, the god of the Underworld, is finally moved and the lament becomes a song of joy in which Orfeo invites all nature to celebrate with him the restoration of light:

Gioite al canto mio, selve frondose,
Gioite amati colli, e d'ogn'intorno
Eco rimbombi da le valli ascose.
Risorta è il mio bel sol di raggi adorno.
                              (*Euridice*, Scene 6)

(O leafy forests, rejoice at my song, rejoice beloved hills, and every surrounding quarter. May an echo resound from the hidden vales. My beloved sun has risen adorned with rays of light.)

The work concludes with a hymn to Apollo (father of Orfeo and god of music), exalting poetry and the power of music. No small measure of the triumphant success of the first performance of the work is due to the fact that Peri, in the role of Orfeo, was praised for his beautiful and expressive voice. The instruments also played an important part in the opera. They included a harpsichord played by Caccini behind the scenes.

Among the visiting dignitaries attending *Euridice* was the Duke of Mantua, Vincenzo Gonzaga, whose interest had been aroused by the Florentine experiments. The success of the venture clearly excited the jealousy of the rival court, and soon the *melodramma* was cultivated at Mantua. The talents of Claudio Monteverdi[20] were secured for this purpose. Monteverdi was born in Cremona in 1567 and died in Venice in 1643. From 1604 to 1613 he resided in Mantua, holding the position of court musician. He was the first great composer to write opera. Before his participation in this new musical activity, he had studied at Cremona with Marcantonio Ingegneri, who had acquainted him with the composition techniques of the Venetian composers. By the time he began writing opera for Mantua he had already published several books of madrigals, some of which were regarded as daring and revolutionary on account of his use of a free play of harmonic modulations and progressions. This represented a move away from the church modes in favour of an approach which led to freedom of expression. Monteverdi's *Favola d'Orfeo* was presented at the court of Mantua, during the carnival of 1607. The libretto is by Alessandro Striggio (c.1535–95) who, unlike Rinuccini, uses the entire classical legend. Orfeo disobeys Pluto's command that he should not look back during his ascent from Hades, and so loses his beloved once more.

Mantua was then to be the scene of Monteverdi's early operatic

ARISTOCRATIC BEGINNINGS

1 Jacopo Peri singing the role of Orfeo in *Euridice* (1600)

triumphs before his departure for Venice in 1613. *La favola d'Orfeo* and *Arianna* carry the mythological opera to a new dimension, marking the introduction of elaborate machines, spectacular sets and scenic effects. Elaborate décor and flying objects helped to bring about an increase of interest in the productions. The splendour of baroque artistry was not merely reflected in the musical innovations. The slogan *far stupire* (to amaze) was also applied to the theatrical presentation. Leading designers and architects were called upon to devise a system of transportation for gods, devils and muses. With the collaboration of Striggio and Monteverdi at the court that had witnessed the first hearing of Poliziano's *Orfeo*, surrounded by Mantegna's fresco of the Gonzaga family, the stage was set at Mantua for the second important phase in the development of the early Italian opera.

III

With Striggio's *Favola d'Orfeo* the Italian melodrama takes a step nearer the consolidation of music-drama, with the division of the text of 687 lines into a prologue and five acts and the emphasis constantly on the humanity of the characters. Ironically, it also marks a move towards the acceptance of the priority of music over words. The opera is now credited to the composer of the music – Monteverdi – while the librettist has always lurked in the shadow of the first great Italian operatic composer's success. Striggio, in presenting Orfeo's journey through the Underworld, conveys a more convincing sense of descent than his predecessor Rinuccini. In keeping with the classic concept of the journey, the traveller is accompanied by a guide who, at a certain point, must retreat and vanish. Orfeo then encounters Caron, the infernal ferry-man, before confronting Pluto or Proserpina. In addition to the classical influence, Striggio has, however, assimilated the medieval allegorical journey of Dante's *Divina commedia* (*Divine Comedy*), which was widely read by intellectuals of the time. In the *Commedia*, Dante, the traveller, was guided by Reason, in the form of the Latin poet Virgil. Orfeo in search of Euridice is guided by Speranza or Hope, who is unable to proceed beyond the gate of the city of Dis. Both figures are in search of beauty, truth and love, symbolized by a woman whose virtue shines from her eyes. Orfeo will attempt to carry her from the Underworld. Dante's Beatrice has no place in hell, but will be reunited with her lover in paradise. Finally Orfeo is united with his Euyridice in a Christianized adaptation of the pagan myth. Striggio's libretto marks the progression from *dramma pastorale* to *dramma* proper. Its effect is created to a great extent by the chorus and its function throughout the opera. The dramatic recitatives of the nine soloists immediately reveal a new power of expression which has often been attributed to Monteverdi's influence.[21] Musically the opera incorporates a number of innovations including the introduction of an overture, the invention of the tremolo and the use of pizzicato to add a further degree of dramatic expressiveness to the orchestral colouring.

Rinuccini's *Dafne* and *Euridice*, although of historical importance as the earliest examples of operatic librettos, are in reality pastoral poems. Key acts or actions are seldom played out on stage, since tales of catastrophic happenings are carried by nymph messengers or the chorus. With the division into acts, the dramatic content becomes more structured. In both of Rinuccini's works the exaltation of the Muse was the prime intention of the poet, and the adventures of the mythological couples provided a vehicle for this. While Striggio[22] also provides a poetic allegory in a prologue with a personified Music praising Orfeo, the characters are the source of their own dramatic consistency. Unlike his predecessor Rinuccini, Striggio also cultivates a universal dimension. Having dramatized the misfortune on earth of the son of the god of music, he proceeds to depict Hades. The work concludes with Orfeo borne by his father Apollo to the heavens, where he will be united with Euridice for all eternity. *Dafne*, then, depicted the eternal separation of the lovers Dafne and Apollo, and the triumph of the poetic laurel. *Euridice*, with its happy ending, is the story of the reunion of the couple through the power of harmony. Striggio, as can be seen, is working on a grander scale and dealing with greater complexity of situation. For this reason his personae, although more convincing, are somewhat lacking in the qualities which render Rinuccini's poetic miniatures memorable.

The drama opens with the Prologue, Music, singing the praises of Orfeo and the powers of music:

> Io la Musica son, ch'a i dolci accenti
> So far tranquillo ogni turbato core.
> Et or di nobil ira et or d'amore
> Posso infiammar le più gelete menti.
> (*Favola d'Orfeo*, Prologue)[23]

(I am Music, who, with sweet harmony can placate every troubled heart. Sometimes with noble anger, sometimes with love, I can enflame the most icy spirits.)

> Quinci a dirvi d'Orfeo desio mi sprona,
> D'Orfeo che trasse al suo cantar le fere.

> E servo fe' l'Inferno a sue preghiere,
> Gloria immortal di Pindo e d'Elicona.
> (*Favola d'Orfeo*, Prologue)

(Thus desire presses me to speak of Orfeo, of Orfeo who induced the wild beasts to listen to his song, and made hell servile as a result of his prayers. The immortal glory of Pindo and of Helicon.)

The drama develops as an appraisal of love as the marriage of Orfeo and Euridice is solemnized, and Orfeo blesses the day when he first saw his beloved. It is interesting to compare Rinuccini's and Striggio's accounts of the death of Euridice. Striggio has the nymph Silvia narrate the tale:

> In un fiorito prato
> Con l'altre sue compagne
> Giva cogliendo fiori
> Per farne una ghirlanda a le tue chiome
> Quando angue insidioso
> Ch'era fra l'erbe ascoso,
> Le punse il piè con velenoso dente:
> Ed ecco immantinente
> Scolorirsi il bel viso e ne' suoi lumi
> Sparir quei lampi, ond'ella al sol fea scorno.
> (*Favola d'Orfeo*, Act 2)

(In a flower-covered meadow, with some of her companions, she went plucking flowers in order to make a garland for your hair. A threatening serpent hidden in the grass bit her foot with its poisonous fang. And look! Her face immediately grew pale and the sparkle, on account of which she held the sun in contempt, disappeared from her eyes.)

Rinuccini has the nymph Dafne tell the tale of woe:

> Prendea dolce diletto
> Con le compagne sue la bella sposa
> Chi violetta o rosa
> Per far ghirlande al crine
> Togliea dal prato e da l'acute spine,
> E qual posando il fianco
> So la fiorita sponda
> Dolce cantava al mormorar de l'onda,

ARISTOCRATIC BEGINNINGS

> Ma la bella Euridice
> Movea danzando il piè su 'l verde prato,
> Quando ria sorte, acerba!
> Angue crudo e spietato
> Che celato giacea tra' fiori e l'erba
> Punsele il piè con sì maligno dente,
> Ch'impallidì repente
> Come raggio di sol che nube adombrè.
> *(Euridice,* Scene 2)

(The beautiful spouse rejoiced in the company of friends. Some plucked violets and roses from the meadow and from sharp thorns, to make garlands for their hair. And reclining on the flower-covered bank, she sang sweetly to the murmur of the waves. But the beautiful Euridice was dancing in the green meadow, when, oh bitter fate, a cruel and pitiless snake, which had been lying among the flowers and grass, bit her foot with so poisonous a fang that she grew pale, as a ray of sun eclipsed by a cloud.)

One is at once aware of a similarity of situation and vocabulary: in Rinuccini's text the garland is for Euridice's own hair, in Striggio's it is for Orfeo's. In each case Euridice is in the company of friendly nymphs. Rinuccini's snake is 'crudo' and 'spietato' ('cruel and pitiless'), Striggio's is 'insidioso' ('treacherous'). Both bite with 'dente' ('tooth' and 'fang'). In *Euridice* it is 'maligno', in the *Favola d'Orfeo* it is 'velenoso' ('poisonous'). Rinuccini's Euridice merely pales, while Striggio's loses the light of the eyes that competed with the sun. It is clear that the texts are extremely close, as though Striggio was avoiding an exact repetition of Rinuccini and so provided alternative vocabulary. In attempting to pass critical judgement, however, I believe Rinuccini's lines, if slightly simplistic, are the more lyrical, idyllic, in a word the more beautiful. His is the world of Arcadian Utopia, of unblemished classical perfection. Rinuccini's Dafne narrates the death of Euridice in thirty-two lines, Striggio's Silvia in nineteen lines. Striggio's then is shorter, more factual, more restrained. Rinuccini was clearly writing a refined and beautifully projected pastoral. Striggio was projecting fast-mounting drama.

Orfeo's first lament is built out of a series of opposites, reconciling themselves in the persona's decision to join his beloved in death if all else fails. One is touched by the note of immediacy and almost modern rationalizing:

> Tu se' morta, mia vita, ed io respiro?
> Tu se', tu se' pur ita
> Per mai più non tornare, ed io rimango?
> No, che se i versi alcuna cosa ponno
> N'andrò sicuro a più profondi abissi.
> E intenerito il cor del Re de l'Ombre
> Meco trarrotti a riveder le stelle:
> E se ciò negherammi empio destino
> Remarrò teco in compagnia di morte.
> A dio, terra; a dio, cielo, o sole a dio.
> *(Favola d'Orfeo*, Act 2)

(You, my life, are dead and I breathe? You have departed never to return, and I remain? No, for if my poetry is of any effect, I shall go safely to the deepest abyss, and I will bring you with me, to see the stars once again, the heart of the King of the Shadows being moved. And if impious destiny deny me this, I shall remain with you in the company of death. Farewell earth; farewell heaven, o sun farewell.)

Striggio succeeds in restraining his emotions, and thus in conveying dignified sorrow, against the backdrop of a world of poetic convention. The three-dimensional universality of the piece is here touched on with the final line: 'A dio terra; a dio, cielo, e sole a dio'. The Dantesque 'a riveder le stelle'[24] is the only piece of light imagery in the lament. It contrasts with 'profondi abissi', and 'Re de l'Ombre'. In his later address to Hope, Orfeo states his intention of proceeding to the Underworld with the allegorical figure as his companion and guide. Here the Dantesque parallels are again in evidence:[25]

> Tu, mia compagna e duce,
> Per così strane e sconosciute vie
> Reggesti il passo debile e tremante
> Ond' oggi ancora spero
> Di riveder quelle beate luci
> Che sole a gli occhi miei portano il giorno.
> *(Favola d'Orfeo*, Act 3)

(You, my companion and leader, you supported my weak

and trembling passage through such strange and unknown paths. For that reason today I still hope to see again those blessed eyes that alone bring daylight to my eyes.)

The situation is indeed Dantesque. Striggio's model is Dante's *Inferno*, Canto II. The sorrowing lover, guided by an allegorical figure, makes his way through the Underworld in search of his beloved, the light of whose eyes symbolizes beauty, light of day and truth. The dependence of Orfeo on Hope, or Speranza, is reminiscent of Dante the traveller's dependence on his guide Virgil in the early cantos of *Inferno*. The allegorical persona Hope is denied entry to the 'city of sorrow'. The inscription, taken from Dante *Inferno*, Canto III, line 9,[26] is in evidence over the gate: 'Lasciate ogni speranza o voi ch'entrate' ('Abandon hope all you who enter here'). Striggio, in keeping with Dante's conception of the Underworld, also refers to the 'città dolente' or 'city of sorrow'.

By way of conclusion after Orfeo has lost Euridice for the second time, Striggio departs slightly from the pagan nature of the pastoral, to allow him to enjoy eternal happiness, as a result of his suffering and prayers. Once again, as in *La divina commedia*, what is theologically impossible is artistically feasible. Orfeo in the footsteps of Dante, the traveller, proceeds to heaven, having already witnessed infernal torment:

> Vanne, Orfeo, felice a pieno
> A goder celeste onore,
> Là 've ben non vien mai meno,
> Là 've mai non fu dolore,
> Mentr' altari, incensi e voti
> Noi t'offriam lieti e devoti.
>
> Così va chi non s'arretra
> Al chiamar di nume eterno,
> Così grazia in ciel impetra
> Chi qua giù provò l'inferno,
> E chi semina fra doglie
> D'ogni grazia il frutto coglie.
> (*Favola d'Orfeo*, Act 5)

(Go there, Orfeo, completely happy, to partake of celestial honours, where there is never shortage of good, where there was never sorrow, while we, happy and devout, offer you altars, incense and prayers.

Thus goes he who does not hesitate when the eternal lord calls. Thus he who down here experienced hell, obtains celestial favour. And he who sows with sorrow and pain, gathers the fruit of every grace.)

Striggio, then, in his libretto for Monteverdi provided eloquent and restrained drama drawing on Dantesque situations, conventional poetic images, while touching on the themes of mortality and immortality, the physical and the spiritual, and salvation and damnation. Physically he has embraced the kingdoms of the living and the dead and has juxtaposed temporal and physical separation with eternal and celestial union.

The year following the first production of the Striggio/Monteverdi *Favola d'Orfeo*, the Gonzagas commissioned two more melodramas as part of further wedding festivities. These were *Arianna*, and a short festival piece *Il ballo delle ingrate*. *Arianna* soon become popular and was heard in many neighbouring towns. Both texts were by Rinuccini, the poet of *Dafne* and *Euridice*. Unfortunately the music of the exceptionally successful *Arianna* has been lost and all that remains is the lament 'Lasciatemi morire'. The story is that of the Greek Ariadne, who was abandoned by Theseus, and as a result tried to drown herself. She is consoled by the god of wine Bacchus, and all concludes in felicitous celebrations. The subject, then, is the immortality of love and the fortune of being loved by a god.

The magnificence of spectacle surrounding the first performance is recorded in the first edition of the text, *Compendio delle sontuose feste fatte l'anno MDCVIII nella città di Mantova* by Federico Follino. It reads:

> On Wednesday last, there was performed in the theatre built for this purpose, the tragedy *Arianna* set to music, which [on the occasion of these marriage celebrations] Sig. Ottavio Rinuccini had composed, having been called to Mantua for this purpose, with the leading poets of our time. There were present at that performance the invited princes, princesses, ambassadors and ladies and as many visiting nobility as the theatre could hold, its capacity being over 6,000. The Duke had refused admission to his own entourage and to all the nobility of the place. None the less, the theatre could not

accommodate all the visitors that sought admission, and congregated at the entrance in such numbers that neither the efficiency of Captain Camillo Strozzi, the Deputy Lieutenant of the Duke's bodyguard, nor the authority of Sig. Carlo Rossi, General at Arms, succeeded in controlling such confusion. It was necessary for the Duke himself to return several times to hold back the crowd.

The opera was very beautiful on its own account and on account of the public that attended it, in attire more ostentatious than appropriate, and on account of the setting, which showed an Alpine rock in the midst of waves which from the furthest point of the scene could be seen to move most charmingly. When one adds the strength of the music of Sig. Claudio Monteverdi, the Duke's choir-master, a man whose ability is known to the world and who on that occasion surpassed himself; when one adds to the melodiousness of the voices, the harmony of the instruments assembled behind the scenes that accompanied, varying the sound to meet with the demands of the music, and when one considers that both men and women excelled in the art of singing, its every part was most wonderful, especially in Arianna's lament, which she sang on the rock, after being abandoned by Teseo. The latter was sung with such tenderness and in such a pathetic manner, that there was not one present who was not moved nor was there a Lady who did not shed a tear or two on account of her suffering.[27]

The tragedy is entitled *Arianna, Tragedia Rappresentata in Musica, Nelle Reali Nozze del Serenissimo Principe di Mantova e della Serenissima Infanta di Savoia*. During 1608 it was published in Mantua, Florence and Venice. It consists of 114 lines divided into a prologue and eight scenes, and lasts two and a half hours. *Arianna* marks the progression of melodrama from the world of the pure pastoral to human tragedy. A glance at the list of personae reveals that the nymphs and shepherds of Arcadia have been replaced by fishermen and soldiers. The pastoral aura and the idealized golden age have yielded to a society in which humans suffer and are sometimes compensated for their sufferings. The drama is a tale of the sufferings of an abandoned lover. Despair and happiness in love are the subjects of the piece. This is declared in the final four lines of the prologue:

> Odi: Sposa real, come sospiri
> Tradita amante in solitari riva:
> Forse avverrà che de la scena argiva
> L'antico onor ne' novi canti ammiri.
> *(Arianna,* Prologue)[28]

(Listen, Royal Bride, how a betrayed lover may sigh on a solitary shore. Perhaps you will come to admire the ancient honour of the Hellenic episode in my new lines.)

The drama begins with the celebration of love by Venus and Love, and closes with the jubilant lines of Bacchus as he ascends into the eternal heights with Arianna. The most famous aria of the opera, the lament, occurs at Scene 6. Its outstanding feature is its simplicity. Even today, it is among the most popular of the operatic *arie antiche*:

> Lasciatemi morire,
> Lasciatemi morire;
> E che volete voi che mi conforte
> In così dura sorte,
> In così gran martire?
> Lasciatemi morire.
> *(Arianna,* Scene 6)

(Leave me to die, leave me to die. And what do you believe could be of comfort to me in such cruel fate, in such great suffering? Leave me to die.)

Rinuccini also wrote a further libretto for *melodramma, Il Narciso* (1616), based on the classical legend of Narcissus and Echo. The work was offered to Monteverdi, who by this time was resident in Venice, but it never became an opera. The text was finally published in the nineteenth century. Its prologue was rediscovered by Angelo Solerti in 1903.[29] The classical myths continued to prove popular as subjects for opera, but soon the artform could no longer be contained within aristocratic circles. Nor could it be limited to the cultured members of society. Soon, the comic, popular element was introduced. This derived partially from classical comedy, but to a greater extent from the improvised comic Italian theatre of the day, the *commedia dell'arte*. Before this can be considered in any detail, attention must be focused on the third centre in which opera flourished, after Florence and Mantua: the papal court of Rome.

IV

Florence had initiated the movement leading to the birth of opera. Its courtly splendour, patronage and abundance of poets and musicians, allied to financial prosperity, all contributed to an atmosphere in which artistic innovation flourished. Rome, however, was a city of a different nature. The home of the papal court, its dramatic endeavours were cast in a didactic framework. Florence, birthplace of the Renaissance and its operatic offspring, appeared positively provincial in comparison to the seat of the papacy. It is therefore not surprising that Rome should be associated at an early stage with the early opera, as, however, a form of moral instruction.[30]

The first evidence of musical drama in Rome is the performance of Emilio de' Cavalieri's (c.1550–1602) *La rappresentazione di Anima e di Corpo* (1600), with words by Agostino Manni, at the Oratory of Santa Maria. It is a medieval morality play set to music, in which allegorical figures such as Body, Soul, Intelligence and Pleasure personify the moral conflict between the spirit and the flesh. Cavalieri died shortly afterwards, but soon the innovations of the Florentine musicians began to interest the Roman hierarchy, and in 1619 the Roman opera *La morte d'Orfeo*, with words and music by Stefano Landi, was performed. The text was published the same year in Venice. This work reached a more exalted public than the Florentine and Mantuan melodramas, since it was produced at the pontifical court, before the Borghese pope, Paul V. In 1621 Filippo Vitali's *Aretusa* was staged, with Caccini's son Pompeo participating as singer and scenographer. The patronage of cardinals soon became an important factor. The first of these was Cardinal Pietro Aldobrandini, who employed such music directors as Palestrina, Marenzio and Frescobaldi. Also among the members of his household were Domenico Mazzocchi and his brother, a choir-master at the Lateran. These were to become extremely influential figures in the short life span of Roman opera. In 1626 Domenico Mazzocchi's opera *Le catene di Adone* (The Chains of Adonis) attracted the attention of the Florentine Prince Barberini and his brothers, who were the leading drama patrons in Rome. It was owing to the enthusiasm of this family, a member of which had been elected pope in 1623 with the name of Urban VIII, that the spectacular extravagances of the next twenty years were staged. They financed the construction of the Barberini Theatre which had a capacity of 3,000.[31] This became a centre of experimentation. Pageants were brought indoors. The introduction of oratorio in the presence of the upper classes and the clergy paved the way for the Venetian and French opera. (Antonio Barberini was the papal legate to France.)

The high literary standard of the Roman libretto underlines the didactic purpose of the allegorical Roman opera. In addition to the traditional pastoral plots, a moral dimension was introduced into the texts derived from the best-known literary pieces of the day. The chivalric romance *Gerusalemme liberata* by Tasso appeared in new guises, with the titles *Il ritorno di Angelica dalle Indie* (1628), *Erminia sul Giordano* (1633) and *Il palazzo incantato d'Atlante* (1642).[32] The most famous Roman librettist was Cardinal Giulio Rospigliosi, in 1667 to become Pope Clement IX.[33] In addition to being a poet, he was a keen lover of music. He wrote the librettos for most of the operas produced by the Barberini. He showed a sense of the dramatic and a capacity for character drawing which led to the introduction of peasant types and comic figures. Didactic Christianity was proclaimed in *Sant'Alessio* (1631 and 1634), *Santa Teodora* (1635) and *San Bonifatio* (1638). In these works there are for the first time comic scenes illustrating the difference between the social classes. The most memorable of them is *Sant'Alessio*, which tells the story of the saint's life. Interesting is the librettist's emphasis on the protagonist's crisis of identity, and his posing as a beggar in his own home. The subtle conflict between status and identity, with religious and moral undertones, is for the first time treated dramatically. It marks the establishment of the Christian legend, in place of classical mythology. It also inaugurates the operatic prayer of which there are no less than three examples in the text: (i) an invocation to death; (ii) the chorus beseeching divine protection for Alessio; (iii) the salutation of death. The musical score was provided by Stefano Landi. It was, however, somewhat eclipsed by the spectacular settings and the dramatic declamation. The artistic director was the sculptor and architect Gian Lorenzo Bernini. Enormous sums of money were spent on machinery, settings and costumes.

With the architectural achievements of Bernini, that is the tombs, the chair of St Peter and the *baldacchino* (canopy), all in St Peter's Basilica, the Italian baroque expressed Catholicism triumphant. In the era of the Spanish occupation, the Index, the Counter-Reformation and the prominence of the Jesuit Order, the sombre reality of everyday life was counteracted by the visual extravaganzas giving artistic expression to miracles and mysteries of religion. With Bernini's designs adding weight and pomp to the communication of religious doctrines, the Roman opera staged at the papal court represents a statement of the social climate of seventeenth-century Rome. Yet the ostentatiousness of the Barberini family offended some of the Roman nobility. On the death of Pope Urban VIII in 1644, they fled to France. In 1653 they returned and their theatre was reopened, again with a libretto by Rospigliosi, *Dal male al bene* (From Evil Comes Good), set to music by Marazzoli. The final Barberini production was staged in honour of Queen Christina of Sweden in 1658 after which the theatre closed for good.[34]

The achievement of the Roman opera is considerable. Apart from the departure from mythology to Christianity and the introduction of a comic, popular element deriving from the improvised *commedia dell'arte* of the day there was also an important musical /dramatic dimension. Rome introduced the *recitativo secco*, a half-sung, half-spoken type of dialogue, which was first heard in Rospigliosi's *Chi soffre speri* (Let the Sufferer Hope). Moreover, the composers Virgilio Mazzocchi and Marco Marazzoli added a highly original chorus describing a fair scene, in which the cries of the vendors were imitated. John Milton, the English poet, was present in 1639, and states that the performance was given 'with true Roman magnificence'. All was directed, however, towards intellectual and academic activity in the presence of princes, poets and cardinals. There was no public participation, and although in both *Sant'Alessio* and *Chi soffre speri* (Act 2, Scene 4) there was a lighter element, the advent of opera as a popular form of entertainment belongs to Venice. There with the opening of the first opera house, and the admission of a paying public, opera as we know it today was born.

2

POPULAR SUCCESS AND MATURITY IN VENICE: BUSENELLO, BADOARO AND CICOGNINI

I

Venice, that unique city, the home of the carnival, in which there is a constant swing between the real and unreal, is a natural setting for disguise, mask and masquerade. The scene of pomp and splendour, its pageantry and processions are recorded in the panel paintings of Carpaccio and the Bellini brothers, and the music that developed in the fifteenth and sixteenth centuries reached its climax in the compositions of Claudio Merulo[1] and the two Gabrieli.[2] These composers conveyed in their music the sense of vivid colour that distinguishes the works of the great Venetian painters. In 1612, the year before Monteverdi arrived in Venice, Giovanni Gabrieli died. This marked the end of an era, and the beginning of a new fashion in taste and entertainment. All preceding musical traditions were superseded by the melodrama, which captured the interest of the people and the patricians alike, and marked a shift in taste from the sacred to the profane.

With its arrival in Venice the melodrama underwent a series of transformations, which carried it closer to the art which we call opera. In fact, it was in Venice that the term opera came into common usage. The first 'opera house', the San Cassiano Theatre,[3] was inaugurated in 1637 by the librettist and musician Benedetto Ferrari,[4] and the term libretto or small book, with which this study is primarily concerned, referring to the text of the work, was adopted. Venice, then, introduced a popular form of entertainment, which allowed for the coexistence of mythology and romance but which also embraced historical drama reflecting a key moment in the evolution of poetic taste.

Before any detailed study of poetry and drama in the Venetian opera can be undertaken, some reference must be made to the libretto and its function and format in early Italian opera.[5] Before opera became open to the public, the printed text was not small, but of a good size, with engravings and often dedications, in order to appeal to the cultural aristocracy attending a performance in a courtly setting. As opera grew in popularity the book became smaller, in order that it could be handled more conveniently, until it reached pocket size. To facilitate reading during a performance, small candles or *cerini* were sold. These often left wax stains on the libretto, and so such texts became known as the 'cerini librettos'. Most of the early texts were signed by the librettist, the impresario and sometimes the printer. Often the composer was not mentioned. A prominent position was accorded, however, to the scenographer, who, in an age of baroque extravagance, was responsible for the sophisticated settings and machinery.

The early libretto frequently contained stage directions not found in the musical score. It provided explanatory notes, a list of personae, and the date when the opera was first performed. Most seventeenth-century librettos also had set out an *argomento*, or plot synopsis, and a summary of events which had taken place before the opera began. It can therefore be stated that the libretto established the social and cultural atmosphere surrounding the performance, and provided practical information regarding the plot, while in essence being the literary dimension of the melodrama. Therefore in terms of society, culture and art it occupies a unique position. It demonstrates the relationship between the various disciplines, it reflects poetic taste, and in some cases can be approached as drama in its own right, since it often pre-dates the music. As Professor Bruno Brizi declares, the libretto reflects a specific moment in the evolution of taste, in the course of the development of literary civilization.[6]

Recent studies by Wolfgang Osthoff,[7] Simon Townley-Worsthorne,[8] Nino Pirrotta,[9] Bruno Brizi,[10] Thomas Walker[11] and Gianfranco Folena[12] have clarified many misconceptions and misunderstandings regarding the Venetian opera during its early development. Above all the reliability of sources such as Ivanovich's *La Minerva al tavolino*[13] has been questioned, and this has in turn led to further research in the field of the identification of librettists and composers, and a renewed interest in such figures as Gian Francesco Busenello, Benedetto Ferrari, Francesco Guitti and Giacomo Badoaro.

The principal sources for the operatic performances presented in Venice during the seventeenth century are: Cristoforo Ivanovich, *La Minerva al tavolino* (Venice, 1681) which was reprinted in 1688 along with a second volume; Giovanni Carlo Bonlini, *Le glorie della poesia e della musica contenute nell'esatta notizia de' teatri della città di Venezia e nel catalogo purgatissimo de' drami musicali quivi sin 'hora rappresentati ... de 1731*; Antonio Groppo, *Catalogo di tutti i drammi per musica recitati ne' teatri di Venezia dall'anno 1637 ... sino all'anno presente 1745*; Livio Niso Galvani (Giovanni Salvioli), *I teatri musicali di Venezia nel Sec. XVII (1637–1700), memorie storiche e bibliografiche ... del 1879*. Apart from dated correspondence, often difficult to trace, Ivanovich is the principal source for a considerable amount of data concerning Venetian performances. His reliability has, however, been questioned by Thomas Walker,[14] who has demonstrated that out of forty-eight librettos considered, only twenty-three provided the name of the composer. We are therefore relying on Ivanovich's memory, judgement and generosity for a precise catalogue of titles, poets and musicians. In 1730 Bonlini set about providing a corrected account but was successful only in so far as the librettos consulted provided the necessary detail. For that reason, even to the present day surprising information is coming to hand, as correspondence of composers, scenographers, librettists and general observers comes to light. According to Ivanovich for example, the poetry of *Le nozze d'Enea con Lavinia*, of which no printed libretto has been traced, was by Badoaro. An *argomento* or explanation of the plot of 1640 also contains a letter from the author to his friends. This demonstrates that the poetry of *Il ritorno di Ulisse in patria* (music by Monteverdi) and of the above-mentioned *Le nozze d'Enea con Lavinia* are by two different people.[15] However, in two articles[16] Professor Wolfgang Osthoff has proved beyond doubt that Badoardo is the librettist for *Il ritorno di Ulisse in patria*. It is therefore clear that *Le nozze d'Enea con Lavinia* is by another. This is merely one small example illustrating the difficulty of identifying poets and dramatists.

The outstanding Venetian librettist of the seventeenth century is Gian Francesco Busenello.[17] Born into the 'secondary' Venetian nobility, he was excluded from the higher public offices. His family enjoyed a certain affluence, and on completion of his legal studies in Padua in 1619, he established himself in Venice as a successful legal adviser. In 1620 he married Barbara Bianchi by whom he had five children, the eldest of whom, Faustina, entered the convent of Corpus Domini in 1642. Her father celebrated the occasion with a poem in her honour. Busenello is present in the legal records of the Venetian state on account of his defence of the Marquis Pio Enea Obizzi of Padua, following the criminal murder of his wife Lucrezia Orologio.[18] Despite professional success he never abandoned his literary pursuits. At the age of 25, enthused by the success of Giovanni Battista Marino, he addressed a eulogy to the poet, which appeared prior to the publication of the Venetian edition of Marino's *Adone* in 1623.[19] It would appear that the young lawyer, with literary leanings, and perhaps more than a little stagestruck, was attempting to cultivate the outstanding poet of the era. He was in fact able to count on the friendship and loyalty of that other prominent Venetian librettist Giacomo Badoaro,[20] who introduced him into theatrical circles, making him known, to quote De Grada,[21] to Monteverdi, for whom he wrote his most celebrated and successful libretto *L'incoronazione di Poppea*, for the Grimani Theatre in 1642.

A consideration of the titles of the librettos written by Busenello reveals that he did not abandon the pastoral drama which made the Florentine and Mantuan melodrama a success. Rather he gives proof of his versatility by providing mythological and historical plots, shifting from the sacred to the profane, while underlining destiny and human weakness. Throughout his works, however, is witnessed the triumph of the word, which expresses full-blown concepts, metaphysical conceits, incongruous metaphors, striking similes and strange antitheses. Works by the Venetian librettist for the operatic stage, the authorship of which has been authenticated, are: *Gli amori di Apollo e di Dafne*, written for the San Cassiano Theatre in 1640, with music by Francesco Cavalli; *La Didone*, also written for the San Cassiano in 1641 and set to music by Cavalli; *L'incoronazione di Poppea*, produced at the Grimani Theatre in 1642, with music by Monteverdi; *La prosperità infelice di Giulio Cesare dittatore*, written for the Novissimo Theatre in 1656, with music by Cavalli; *La Statira, principessa di Persia*, for the SS. Giovanni e Paolo Theatre, first presented in 1655; *La discesa d'Enea all'Inferno* which remains unpublished. Busenello then was assured of prominence in Venetian society, writing for the two outstanding and innovative composers of the day, and reproducing the new literary media for which the public clamoured:

2 Gian Francesco Busenello (1598–1659)

the historical drama and the world of the classics, brought to life in the manner of the *marinisti* or followers of Marino.

Gli amori di Apollo e di Dafne would appear to follow in the poetic footsteps of Rinuccini's *Dafne*. Yet the source is clearly Tasso's *Aminta* rather than the Florentine librettist. Busenello's work is essentially a happy one – the text concludes with a hymn to the laurel, symbol of art and intellect. Busenello, while preserving the artistic symbolism, provides dramatic agitation which mounts in the course of a five-strophe aria.[22] In this way the progression of the character's thoughts is conveyed, while a relationship between the two protagonists is established. It is interesting to note the manner in which Rinuccini's Dafne dissuades Apollo, as opposed to Busenello's more complex and expansive figure:

> Altra preda non bramo, altro diletto
> Che fere e selve; e son contenta e lieta
> Se damma errante o fer cignal saetto.
>   (*Dafne*, Scene 3)[23]

(Besides beasts and forests I do not desire any other prey or joy. And I am both happy and joyful if I shoot a wandering deer or a fierce wild boar.)

Dafne's aria in *Gil amori di Apollo e di Dafne* consists of thirty lines and occurs in Act 2, Scene 4. It develops in terms of a series of opposites; night versus day, light versus darkness, brightness versus dullness, and strength as opposed to weakness. Dafne, in the second strophe, is the successor of Tasso's *Silvia*, as the symbol of constancy and chastity:

> Lascia Apollo ogni speranza,
> Torna in Ciel, se tu sei Dio;
> Non tentar la mia costanza,
> Ch' ascoltar non ti vogl'io:
> Porta in pace i tuoi martir
> Verginella io vuò morir.
>   (*Gli amori di Apollo e di
>   Dafne*, Act 2, Scene 4)[24]

(Apollo, abandon all hope, go back to heaven, if you are a God. Do not test my constancy, because I do not wish to listen to you. Bear your suffering with patience. I wish to die a virgin.)

In the second strophe Dafne becomes the symbol of light, honour and goodness. Apollo, on the contrary, assumes the quality of a tempter to evil:

> Se dei giorni il lume sei
> L'occhio destro di natura,

> Non voler, che gl'honor miei
> Sian sepolti in notte oscura;
> Nato sei per illustrar.
> E me sola vuoi macchiar.

(If you are the light of the day, nature's right eye, do not wish that my virtues be buried in dark night; You are born to illuminate, and you wish to soil me alone.)

Dafne here appeals rhetorically and poetically to Apollo, concluding with a decisive statement. All sensuousness of expression is avoided until the final two lines of the aria:

> Se nel labro hò dolce il miele
> Non vò darlo a te crudel.
> (*Gli amori di Apollo e di
> Dafne*, Act 2, Scene 4)

(If in my lips I have sweet honey, I do not wish to give it to you, cruel one.)

Her final refusal contains a further temptation, providing a taste of her favours which she declines to confer. This aria is the emotional climax of the libretto, preparing for her transformation, which is seen as a voluntary act of despair. It is an illustration of Busenello's and Cavalli's use of the aria or set-piece to establish relationships between the various operatic personae. It is also significant in terms of dramatic projection and development, in that the relation between various arias can be seen to illustrate dramatic development within 'smaller dimensions of scene groups and even single scenes'.[25] Above all, and I believe this to be a most crucial point when regarding the dramatic libretto as a reflection of the literary climate of the time, the poetic images of Dafne's aria are clearly created for effect. The juxtapositions carry the contrasts far beyond the pastoral simplicity of Rinuccini's Arcadian world. They assume an active, thematic and visual function and provide a pattern for Busenello's later librettos where effective contrast is achieved between personae, between the principal plot and the sub-plot, and between the serious and comic characters. The Venetian librettist's works are concerned with conveying aspects of love and ambition such as: pursuit, possession, conquest and rejection, all shrouded in a voluptuousness of expression. The theme of love is seen as an active force, operating with a total disregard for the wishes of the less passionate and opposed to social and moral conventions. In the words of Adriano Cavicchi, the sensuality of the operatic drama in the 1630s and 1640s supports the claim of many historians, that the period witnessed a decline in public morality at every level.[26] In Busenello's drama there emerges the figure of the female protagonist, i.e. Dido, Poppea and Statira, each of whom comes to identify the gratification of the senses with social acceptance.

In order to confer dramatic reality on such figures, Busenello subtly fuses and juxtaposes the fact with the legend, the real with the unreal. This statement can be supported by a quick reference to the personae and the settings of the operas under discussion. Apollo and Dafne are familiar mythological figures, but they are instilled with emotions and linguistic expressions unknown in Arcadia. Dido rejects her lover Jarba by destroying his false hopes: she appears as a legislator of amorous expectations, a realistic force in a legendary setting. Poppea as projected in *L'incoronazione di Poppea* is one versed in statecraft, who manages to fulfil her ambitions and her desires. The plot is historically accurate, as told by Tacitus. Poppea's lascivious outburts often border on the indecent. By the time Busenello wrote *La Statira, principessa di Persia*, the artifice of expression which he had acquired stilted the character delineation and development. The lovers are reduced to a series of sighs and lamentations, and the only figures with any real spark of life are the comic characters.

Busenello's poetic inspiration reaches its high point in *L'incoronazione di Poppea*. At this stage in his career the librettist achieved successful characterization, while allowing serious and comic elements to mingle, providing a variety of scenes and situations. The voice of honour is heard in the figure of Seneca, who linguistically is identified with the world of the pastoral, while expressing a multi-faceted image of life and death:

> Brev'angoscia è la morte
> Un sospir peregrino esce dal core,
> Dov'è stato molti anni
> Quasi in ospizio come forestiero,
> E sen vola all'Olimpo
> Delle felicità soggiorno vero.
> (*L'incoronazione di Poppea*, Act 2, Scene 3)

(Death is brief anguish. A vagrant sigh issues from the heart, where it has been for many years, almost as a guest in residence. And it flies away to Mount Olympus, the true seat of happiness.)

The lightness conveyed by the 'vagrant sigh' from the mouth of Seneca is complemented by the less successful physical image of the sun and Poppea:

> Per capirti negli occhi
> Il sol s'impiccioli,
> Per albergarti in seno
> L'Alba dal ciel partì
> E per farti sovrana a donne e a Dee
> Giove nel tuo bel volto
> Stillò le stelle e consumò le idee.
> *(L'incoronazione di Poppea*, Act 3, Scene 8)

(In order to dwell in your eyes, the sun became small. To dwell in your breast, the dawn left heaven. And Jove, in order to make you sovereign and goddess above women, poured stars into your beautiful countenance and perfected knowledge.)

The subtle progression of ideas in the above passage is a good example of Busenello's uses of imagery in order to fuse light (*occhi*, 'eyes'; *il sol*, 'the sun'), physical attributes associated with nature (*seno*, 'breast'; *alba*, 'dawn'), the concept of conquest of the human and superhuman (*sovrana*, 'sovereign'; *donne*, 'women'; *Dee*, 'Goddesses'), and finally the association of beauty and intellectual prowess (*stelle*, 'stars'; *idee*, 'ideas'). In the course of the closely knit lines beauty is given a physical and intellectual dimension, which finds its climax in the concept of sovereignty. In his choice of verbal conceits Busenello proves to be a disciple of Marino. He has introduced into melodrama a series of elements hitherto the property of poets. The language can so be defined as both metaphysical and lyrical, providing a myriad images, followed by academic word-play.

The philosophical dimension is introduced at the opening of the opera, in the prologue spoken by the figure of Virtue:

> Può dirsi senza adulatione alcuna,
> Il puro incorrottibile esser mio

Termine convertibile con Dio.
(*L'incoronazione di Poppea*, Prologue)

(To my pure and incorruptible being, there can be applied, without a trace of flattery, a term interchangeable with God.)

From the opening the poet has clarified that a drama of the flesh and intellect would follow. He has succeeded in putting on stage an example of the strengths and weaknesses of *Seicentismo*. By adapting it to dramatic needs he has allowed for an objective assessment of *concettismo*, before its final decline. For this reason, Busenello can be regarded as a representative poet in the history of Italian literature, and a highly successful writer of dramas for music.

II

Busenello demonstrated an interest in historical drama, reflecting further common ground between the operatic and straight theatre of the day. The year 1604 saw the first production of Ruggeri's *Reina di Scozia*. Bonarelli's *Solimano* was presented in 1619, while the celebrated tragedian from Asti, Piedmont, Federigo Della Valle wrote his *Reina di Scozia* in 1628. The plots of opera during the first half-century of its existence had consisted of pastoral dramas in Florence, Mantua and Venice. Sacred presentations with comic interludes were popular in Rome, while mythology and historical drama coexisted in Venice. Giacomo Badoaro (1602–54) wrote principally librettos based on classical plots. He collaborated with Monteverdi, Cavalli and Sacrati, and was a member of the Accademia degli Incogniti. Works of his which have been authenticated are: *Il ritorno di Ulisse in patria* (1641) with music by Monteverdi; *L'Ulisse errante* (1644) with music by Sacrati; *Helena rapita da Theseo* (1653) with music believed to be by Cavalli. It has been established beyond doubt that the libretto *Le nozze d'Enea con Lavinia* is not by Badoaro.

Monteverdi, Cavalli and Cesti were the outstanding composers of the Venetian school of opera. As William C. Holmes states in his article 'Giacinto Andrea Cicognini's and Antonio Cesti's *Orontea* (1649)',[27] the term 'Venetian School' is misleading and equivocal. With the passing of time Florentine, Roman and Venetian operas were performed in all Italian cities and towns, by singers trained for the most part in Rome.[28] Of the great musicians mentioned above, only Cavalli was born in Venice. Antonio Cesti (1623–69) achieved fame in Venice and later as *maestro di cappella* to the Archduke Ferdinand of Austria. His most celebrated works are: *Orontea* (1649), *Cesare amante* (1641), *La Dori* (1661) and *Il pomo d'oro* (1666). Cesti's first opera was one of the most widely performed works in the seventeenth century. It was written for the Venetian stage by a composer from Arezzo, who studied with Roman teachers, and its libretto was by Giacinto Andrea Cicognini (1606–51), a Tuscan who had spent some years in Venice. Most of Cicognini's works had been for the straight theatre, but towards the end of his life he wrote four opera librettos: *Celio* (Florence, 1646), *Giasone* (Venice, 1649), *Orontea* (Venice, 1649) and the posthumously published *Gl'amori di Alessandro Magno* (Venice, 1651). In collaborating with both Cesti and Cavalli he assured himself a prominent position in the history of the Venetian opera. However, towards the end of the seventeenth and in the early eighteenth centuries his work was generally derided, as critics clamoured for a reform of the literary side of opera. G.M. Crescimbeni, in his *Dell'istoria della volgar poesia* (1698), decries what he sees as the rise of popular opera and a pandering to popular taste. As an example of this he cites Cicognini's *Giasone*, in which he claims the arts of comedy and tragedy are destroyed. Cicognini's work stands out as a reflection of public taste of the time, and of the growing popularity in Italy of Spanish drama. As early as 1641 Busenello, in the preface to his *Didone*, had stated that his drama did not follow the rules prescribed by the ancients, but was written in the Spanish tradition, in which the action developed over a period of years. Structurally the Spanish drama differed from that advocated by humanist tradition: it consisted of three rather than five acts. In addition, both noble and common people were constantly depicted.

Cicognini actually recorded in writing the changing aesthetics of opera in his own time. In the preface to *Celio* (1646) he wrote that he composed for the sheer fun of it! This statement was amplified in 1649, in the preface to *Giasone*: he claimed that his intention in writing operatic librettos was to entertain, which in turn meant satisfying the taste of the reader and the listener. If he succeeded in doing so, he commented, then he would have achieved his aim.[29] William C. Holmes[30] considers such intentions as the manifesto of Italian opera for at least a century afterwards.

In *Orontea* we have an example of romantic comedy, which

borders on the fairy-tale. There are personae from all walks of life: queen, painter, courtier, servant. The happy ending shows the queen marry her handsome painter only when his true identity, that of a noble prince, is revealed. They live happily ever after. Orontea's most famous aria occurs in Act 2, Scene 16. She sings it to her lover Alidoro as he lies unconscious. It is an address to the breeze and sweet dreams to assist him. Cicognini has achieved here a gentility of expression absent from the amorous expressions of Busenello. A subtle sensuality is conveyed by the repeated use of the letter *s* in order to convey the impression created by the breeze:

> Intorno all'idol mio,
> Spirate, pur spirate
> Aure soavi e grate.
> E nelle guance elette
> Baciatelo per me – cortesi aurette.
>
> Al mio ben, che riposa
> Su l'ali della quiete,
> Grati sogni assistete.
> E il mio racchiuso ardore
> Svelategli per me – larve d'amore.
>   (*Orontea*, Act 2, Scene 16)

(Blow, sweet gentle breezes, please blow around my beloved, and kiss him on my behalf on his desired cheeks, kind breezes. Sweet dreams, assist my beloved who reposes on the wings of tranquillity. Spirits of love, reveal my restrained ardour to him.)

Cicognini has allowed ample dramatic space for the inclusion of arias at the opportune moment, adding lyricism and effective pauses. This feature is also a significant innovation.

At this point in the consideration of the Venetian libretto, some comment must be made on the comic scenes, which, although not present in all works, are of historical interest, as they were to prove most influential on the eighteenth-century libretto, notably on da Ponte's *Le nozze di Figaro*. Comic episodes were first introduced into opera by the Roman composers. One of the first examples is a drinking song sung by Caronte in Stefano Landi's *La morte d'Orfeo* (1619).[31] Rospigliosi's libretto for Landi's *Sant'Alessio* (1632) is enlivened by the antics of the comic pages

Martio and Curtio. Iro, the comic page in Badoaro's *Il ritorno di Ulisse in patria* (1641), is another example. The drunken servant Gelone and the old nurse Aristea in *Orontea* are type figures found in the classical Roman theatre and the *commedia dell'arte*. Aristea woos a handsome young man who in reality is a woman servant Giacinta. This scene is full of grotesque humour and parody. A further significant example is the comic scene in Apolloni's *La Dori*, first performed in Florence in 1663, with music by Antonio Cesti. These are examples of the typical comic scenes which occurred in the Venetian opera, and formed part of the sub-plot, between 1650 and 1670. After this time such scenes were dropped from the Venetian operas, but added in the Neapolitan versions. In *La Dori*, Act 1, Scene 4, Dirce, an old nurse, attempts to force her attentions on Golo, a servant. The scene concludes in a rapid series of insulting exchanges:

Che vecchia maledetta!	What a cursed old hag!
Che buffone insolente!	What an insolent clown!
Perfida!	Treacherous one!
Dispettoso!	Disrespectful one!
Arrogante!	Arrogant one!
Furfante!	Rogue!
Empia!	Impious one!
Vituperoso!	Abusive one!
Maliarda!	Witch!
Spione!	Spy!

It can be argued that this exchange is the source of the conversation between Susanna and Marcellina in *Le nozze di Figaro*, Act 1, Scene 4, in which the two women, the soubrette and the elderly housekeeper, abuse one another.

In the mid-seventeenth century at the time when the Neapolitan opera was beginning to attract attention, the Venetian librettist found it increasingly necessary to write for purely commercial theatres whose audiences demanded pure entertainment, tuneful music and virtuoso performances. Soon the librettist had little influence over opera as an art-form, and set about voicing his complaints to the public. Little happened until the librettist decided to take the situation into his own hands. In an attempt to reform the literary side, he returned to the theatre of the ancients and restored opera as a literary proposition. In the meantime, as the star of Venice had begun to set, Naples blazed forward in musical triumph, providing outstanding musicians, singers and virtuosi, and so becoming the musical capital of Italy.

3

INNOVATION AND REFORM: ZENO, METASTASIO AND CALZABIGI

I

The Italian operatic libretto in the late seventeenth century and throughout the eighteenth century was an art-form crying out for a singular and individual identity, as opposed to that of the literary dimension and partial component of a form of theatre, in which the musical element held undisputed supremacy. Since its inception it had been in the hands of academicians, musical and dramatic theorists and literary reformers. It was not until the nineteenth century that it could develop as the autonomous voice of a new society in the making. The romantic cry for freedom broke all institutional barriers, allowing for individuality of declamation in a non-stylized framework, which reached a working as well as a ruling class. It spoke for social and political reform, in addition to satisfying the romantic yearnings of Lombardy under Austrian occupation. In other words, in breaking away from 'schools' and erudite traditions, it at last spoke directly to all willing to listen. At the same time it made a unique contribution to romantic literature and thought.

Before this process could take place, however, the libretto was derided, reformed, acclaimed and reformed again during the eighteenth century. *Melodramma*, which was the child of the Renaissance, and which reached general audiences during the baroque period, was redirected by the anti-baroque school, seeking to eliminate its 'tastelessness'. The formation in Rome in 1690 of the *Istituti della Ragunanza degli Arcadi*, which was commonly known as Arcadia, was the first step in the direction of freeing literature from baroque conceits and incongruities. It advocated a return to pastoral simplicity, and was to have a profound effect on the texts of opera, giving rise to the theories and reforms of members such as Silvio Stampiglia, Apostolo Zeno and Pietro Metastasio, each of whom occupied the position of poet laureate at the court of Vienna. These attempted to re-establish the libretto as classical drama, projecting taste and heroism and cultivating moral behaviour. To this, in order to add a further degree of complexity, was added philosophical instruction. The result was that heroes in Roman togas spouted Cartesian ideology, providing a didactic element which in some respect compensated for the lack of dramatic conviction. So, in the operatic convention reason and rococo became synonymous, and in time became the two diverse poles of the *opera seria* or heroic opera. The classical reform of Metastasio was carried further by Calzabigi, who effected the return to mythology, the reduction of the number of personae, and the addition of spectacular ballets and choruses.

It was pointed out at the end of the last chapter that Naples soon superseded Venice as the centre of opera.[1] Such composers as Leonardo Vinci (1690–1730), Giovanni Battista Pergolesi (1710–36) and Alessandro Scarlatti (1660–1725) were the principal representatives of the new school. Soon Italians in other musical centres of Europe furthered the acclaim of the Neapolitan opera: among others, Niccolò Jomelli (1714–74), Tommaso Traetta (1727–79) and Giovanni Battista Bononcini (1670–1755). But as Naples basked in its musical supremacy and the talent of its performers, the literature, poetry and drama of the pieces very soon began to occupy second place. The operas were tailored to fit the singers. They became a series of arias, conceived in order to display the vocal endowments of the artist as well as the creative fluency of the composer. The recitatives perished as opera developed as a selection of songs. It is in this light that the reforms of Stampiglia, Zeno and Metastasio must be considered, and as our task is to follow the literature of this form of theatre, the musical achievement of the Neapolitan masters is not our primary concern.

It is also significant that it was in Naples that the definite division between heroic and comic opera was established.[2] The latter developed along lines directed by the *commedia dell'arte* and was reformed and revitalized towards the mid-century by the father of Italian comedy, the Venetian lawyer, actor and dramatist Carlo Goldoni. This chapter discusses the Neapolitan *opera seria*, and the reforms of the poet laureates Stampiglia, Zeno, Metastasio and Calzabigi.

As a close examination of the Neapolitan school of the late seventeenth and eighteenth centuries reveals, there were few Neapolitan librettists of note. Furthermore, the Neapolitans did not appear interested in controlling the literary trends of their own or any other Italian operatic centres. Yet mention must be made of some memorable contributions and theories, before we pass on to trace the various reforms which emanated from Rome. In connection with Neapolitan opera, Andrea Perrucci (1651–1704) is significant as the author of a review of theatrical forms entitled *Dell'arte rappresentativa premeditata ed all'improvviso* (1699). In addition he wrote several librettos, including *Stellidaura vendicata* (1674) for Provenzale, and *Chi tal nasce, tal vive, o vero l'Alessandro Bala* (1677–8). The best-known librettist of the early eighteenth century was Sebastiano Bianchi, otherwise known as Domenico Lalli (1679–17??). He spent most of his career in northern Italy, and began writing librettos for Venice in 1710. Most of his subsequent works first appeared in that city, although three of his texts are known to have been first presented at the San Bartolomeo Theatre, Naples. These were *Il gran Mogol* (1713, music by Mancini), *Tigrane* (1715, music by Alessandro Scarlatti) and *Cambise* (1719, music by Alessandro Scarlatti).

Throughout the peninsula during the early half of the eighteenth century, the aristocracy enjoyed an affluent existence, punctuated by banquets, receptions, carnivals and galas. Wealth was in the hands of the few, while the masses experienced untold misery. It was the period of the gavotte, minuet, powdered wig, worldly clerics and the pomp of the papacy. The day of an aristocrat allowed time for a ceremonial service of morning coffee, the lady was visited by her hairdresser, dancing-master and finally *cicisbeo* or gallant, from whom she would accept service and indulge in erudite conversation, while her own husband pursued the same practice in the service of another lady. French customs and fashions were in vogue, but there was also a profound interest in English literature. The most popular foreign poet was Alexander Pope: *The Rape of the Lock* was read enthusiastically throughout the length and breadth of Italy.[3]

In such an atmosphere the salons of the aristocrats flourished. The circle in Rome of ex-Queen Christina of Sweden was in fact the precursor of the Accademia dell'Arcadia.[4] After her death the Academy was founded with its prime intent the expulsion of bad taste as exemplified in the baroque movement. Its founder members included Crescimbeni, Gian Vincenzo Gravina and Stampiglia, to whose ranks soon were added Redi, Menzini, Magalotti and Maggi. In a short time Arcadia became the most prestigious academy in Italy. Its membership embraced almost all eighteenth-century writers of note, from Muratori and Vico to Parini and Alfieri. Taking its name from the home of the shepherds in pastoral Greece, its insignia depicted the god Pan, crowned with laurel and pine. Its primary aim, having restored naturalness and simplicity after the verbal extravagances of *marinismo*, was to give new impulse to form. The two principal sources of inspiration were Petrarch and Berni, seen as the contrasting poles of pure Italian civilization. The Christian spirit was incorporated with the adoption of the infant Jesus as the protector of the academy. Its principal achievements were, however, in the fields of the evolution of literary theory, theatrical reform and the creation of an animated poetic world in miniature. From the exaggerated extravagances of baroque literature, with the projection of images on a grand scale, the poets of Arcadia opted for rococo miniatures and linguistic diminutives which, apart from providing novelty, cannot be said to have brought poetry any closer to 'nature' or the 'natural'. They did, however, make a large contribution to the eighteenth-century history of ideas. It is in this respect that their relationship to the *melodramma* is of special significance.

Critics of the time had coined their own definitions of *melodramma*. To Muratori[5] and Gravina,[6] it was a failed tragic form. The former aspired towards rendering the theatre 'a delightful school of fine customs and a seat of moral lessons'. The latter, in so doing, advocated, in his *Ragion poetica* (1708), the observance of the classical unities in a search for new simplicity. In point of fact the first 'reformer' to purge the opera of unnecessary comic scenes and simplify the action was one of the founder members of Arcadia, Silvio Stampiglia (1664–1725). Yet most critics dismiss his contribution:

> The dialogue in his early dramas written for Naples in the period 1696–1702 contains a great many short staccato sentences which characters toss around between themselves, or pass, as asides, to the audience. The language is bold in the extreme and only attempts to rise above the ordinary when extreme emotions are aroused or gallant feelings expressed.[7]

Stampiglia collaborated with the greatest composers of the day.

The dramas to which Robinson refers in the above quotation are *La caduta dei decemviri* (1697), *Eraclea* (1700) and *Tito Sempronio Gracco* (1702), all of which were set to music by Alessandro Scarlatti. His *Il trionfo di Camilla* (1696) was set by Bononcini, and *Partenope* by Manzi. From 1706 to 1714 he was court poet at Vienna, a post held later by both Zeno and Metastasio. It has indeed been argued that it was by virtue of this appointment that his name became associated with theirs, and their reform of the libretto. Stampiglia returned to Naples in 1722, three years after Pietro Metastasio had taken up residence there. Stampiglia, it appears, did not write any new librettos for Naples at this time, but merely brought some older ones up to date, for new productions at the San Bartolomeo Theatre.

The second poet laureate to owe his fame to his reform of the *melodramma* was a Venetian by birth. Apostolo Zeno[8] (1688–1750) based his vision of theatrical revival on the philosophical conflict between reason and emotion, which would later be the subject of all of Vittorio Alfieri's tragedies of *libertà*. The love theme, seen as an 'effeminate passion',[9] passed to second place, giving way to a theatrical presentation of valour, the hallmark of an essentially didactic art-form. The exemplary heroes and heroines of Zeno, and especially Griselda in the melodrama of the same name, exemplify the stoic domination of the passions by the rational principle, obedient to the moral law. Zeno began his career in 1695, with *Gli inganni felici*. In 1710 he, together with his brother Pier Caterino, founded the journal *Giornale de'Letterati d'Italia*, to which both Scipione Maffei and Antonio Vallisnieri contributed. Between 1718 and 1729, his principal works were written in Vienna. These comprised thirty-six melodramas, seventeen sacred dramas and fourteen librettos in collaboration with Pietro Pariati.

The outstanding feature of Zeno's theatre is his treatment of the aria. Rather than developing as a self-contained expression of love, hatred, tenderness or fear, it assumes the form of a logical comment on events or situations already dramatically unfolded in the course of the action. It so develops as a logical assessment of reality, containing comparisons, syllogisms, descriptions and assessments. Theatrically, then, it functions as a contemplative section, alternating with the dramatic movement and introducing the philosophical.

Structurally the aria developed as three parts, A, B and C, and

3 Apostolo Zeno (1668–1750)

became known as the *da capo aria*, that is one containing a preliminary passage leading to a new movement which finally yielded to the tone and form of the opening. In other words, A and C were similar in form. The C section could consist of *musical* decoration and ornamentation, which could also convey further dramatic meaning to the initial expression. From the poetic viewpoint the aria developed in two sections. The following example from *Andromaca* (1724) serves to illustrate the point. It forms part of Andromaca's lament:

>   Vedova tortorella
>   piange così'l suo fido,
>   ma della cara prole
>   vola d'intorno al nido
>   e abbandonar nol sa.

> Timida de suoi danni
> guarda qua e là, ma resta,
> nè spiega lungi i vanni,
> tanto in quel picciol core
> può di materno amore
> la natural pietà.
> (*Andromaca*, Act 1, Scene 4)[10]

(Gentle widowed dove, in this way weeps for her faithful [departed] one. But she flies around the nest of her dear family, and cannot bring herself to leave it.

Shy on account of her misfortune, she looks around, but remains. Nor does she spread her wings far afield, so strongly in that little heart does natural pity inspire maternal love.)

Zeno is here also establishing the aria in sharp contrast to the recitative, which is gauged in rhetorical terms, illustrating the dual linguistic nature of Arcadian poetry: the classical, drawing on traditional images and figures, and the 'natural' deriving from Petrarcan inspiration.[11] This is an aspect of the aria, and of the *melodramma* in general, which will be perfected by Metastasio. Andromaca's recitative, inspired by the French classical theatre, begins:

> O fortunate voi che non mai foste
> madri nè spose e insieme
> con l'alta Troia rimaneste oppresse;
> quanto v'invidio.

(O fortunate you, who were never mothers or wives, and were oppressed along with great Troy. How I envy you.)

In addition to its contrast to the recitative, the variation within the aria itself necessitated the use of fewer set-pieces, and these were usually relegated to the end of a scene or act. By Metastasio's time, the aria has become the dramatic *conclusion* of the scene, rather than merely one of its constituent parts.

The introduction of the concept of the strength of will, and the domination of the individual by the will to virtue, is already apparent in Zeno's *Griselda*. Deriving from Boccaccio, the drama tells of the heroic constancy of a wife in the face of cruel repudiation by her husband. It shows in heroic terms the loyalty, faithfulness and virtue of the woman. Metastasio later identifies heroic virtue with patriotism and loyalty to Rome, personified by the figure of Attilio Regolo. Griselda is assured of her own constancy. Her words represent the unchanging force of will:

> Ne la crudel mia sorte
> non ti lusinghi il cor
> vana speranza.
> Più stabile e più forte
> vedrai del tuo rigor la mia constanza.
> (*Griselda*, Act 1, Scene 5)[12]

(On account of my cruel fate, do not allow vain hope to touch my heart. You will find my constancy stronger than your demands.)

II

Zeno's reworking of the melodrama prepares the way for its total transformation by Metastasio. It must be conceded that the third of the poet laureates under discussion owes much in terms of aria structure and philosophical content to Zeno, who, it is true, lacked the ability to confer dramatic conviction on his personae. His figures lack psychological finesse, his poetry falls short of the lyrical fluency and precision of vocabulary found in Metastasio. Metastasio finally succeeds in rendering the melodrama convincing theatre, and in so doing paves the way for the greatest of Italian tragedians, Vittorio Alfieri. Zeno was not capable of viewing the text as pure theatre as such, as is revealed in a letter to his brother Pier Caterino.[13] He considered the music as the necessary icing on the cake, a concession to public taste, but nevertheless contrary to the serious nature of classical drama. It was left to Metastasio to provide texts for music which could find their place in Italian literature, by virtue of their dramatic content, poetic diction and didactic nature.

Pietro Trapassi[14] was born in Rome in 1698, and died in Vienna in 1782. His lifetime spans almost the entire eighteenth century, and so he witnessed the flourishing Arcadian tradition, the birth of the Enlightenment and the undercurrent of revolutionary zeal. His career falls into three main divisions: his Neapolitan, Roman and Viennese periods. His life contained two major influences which determined the direction of his artistic and personal affiliations. These were Gian-Vincenzo Gravina, poet, philosopher and dramatic theorist, and Marianna Benti Bulgarelli, a leading singer of the day, at whose instigation Metastasio would write some of his major melodramas. In 1708 Trapassi first met Gravina, who at once undertook responsibility for his classical education. At the same time he adopted the Greek equivalent of his name, and so Trapassi became Metastasio. In 1712 he was introduced by Gravina to his cousin Gregorio Caloprese, a philosopher of the Cartesian school. This was a crucial meeting as it fired the young poet's enthusiasm for the writings of Descartes, and brought about his own association of Stoicism, heroic valour and the eighteenth-century cultivation of enlightened reason. On the death of Gravina in 1718, Metastasio became a member of Arcadia, having presented *La strada della gloria* (The Path of Glory), a work in praise of his late patron. The following year he left Rome for Naples where he became popular, gracing aristocratic salons, largely due to the protection of the singer Benti Bulgarelli.

The writer's early Neapolitan period is characterized by a series of poems which would have assured him success during his lifetime,[15] but amount to little in the eyes of posterity. He was drawn towards the melodrama because he believed it to be an art-form which encapsulated the poetic, theatrical and ideological trends of the era. He believed that this form of theatre could contain the unifying element of diverse disciplines, as well as objectively projecting life in its purest form. He so endeavoured to become, to quote De Sanctis, 'the poet of the melodrama, of which Zeno was the architect'.[16]

Metastasio's first dramatic effort was a tragedy, *Giustiniano*, written when he was 14 years old. It is based on *Italia liberata dai goti* by Trissino. It was published in Naples in 1717, in a volume containing idylls, epics and mythological poems. His first melodrama was *Didone abbandonata*, the tale of Dido's abandonment by Aeneas. With its production in 1718, Metastasio's Neapolitan period came to an end. He returned to Rome, where he wrote a series of melodramas for the Roman and Venetian public including *Siroe* (1726), *Catone in Utica* (1728), *Ezio* (1728), *Semiramide riconosciuta* (1729), *Alessandro nelle Indie* (1729) and *Artaserse* (1730). The latter is generally regarded as the most successful work of this period. It marked his last Italian composition. In 1730, he set out for Vienna to take up the post of poet laureate

INNOVATION AND REFORM

4 Pietro Metastasio (1698–1782), portrait by Rosalba Carriera (Gemäldegalerie, Dresden)

which had been held by Zeno. At the imperial court, he found yet another protector, the Countess Marianna Pignatelli Belmonte. He proceeded to write melodramas, mythological and sacred poems. The period 1730–40 is regarded as his most fruitful and artistically rewarding. To it belong *Demetrio* (1731), *Demofoonte* (1733), *Adriano in Siria* (1732) and his classical masterpiece *Attilio Regolo* (1740, but not produced until 1750 in Dresden). The same year saw a number of changes in Metastasio's life and outlook, which contributed in no small measure to his artistic decline. In place of theatrical works the poet concentrated on poetic treatises and observations: *Note all'arte poetica di Orazio* (1749, completed in 1773), *Estratto della 'poetica' d'Aristotle e considerazioni sulla medesima* (1773) and *Osservazioni sul teatro greco* (published posthumously in 1795).

In 1740 Charles VI was succeeded on the imperial throne by his daughter Maria Teresa, whose reign was characterized by the War of the Austrian Succession and the Seven Years War. Such continued unrest heralded a change not only in the atmosphere at court, but also in Metastasio's own financial situation and the general high standard of living which he had always enjoyed. He had associated and identified the royal court with the guardianship of aristocratic values, and the protection of those committed to those values. With the diffusion of Enlightenment theory, Metastasio, who belonged to the older generation, felt all that had nurtured his poetic output was being threatened. He feared that approaching anarchy might destroy established public order. In fact Metastasio could be defined the last poet of aristocratic Arcadia, in so far as his entire social ambience and poetic vision was contained in a pre-revolutionary society, which along with its artistic endeavours fell to the guillotine.

In taking a closer look at some of Metastasio's librettos, it becomes obvious that the poet laureate was writing in order both to appeal and instruct. A significant feature of Metastasio's librettos is the fact that they were not written specifically for any one composer, and indeed were set to music by various musicians. There are several versions of each of his melodramas.

Metastasio's social vision extends in two directions: it looks back to the world of classical Greece and Rome and outwards to a cultured élite that sought instruction alongside entertainment. Metastasio provides both by dramatizing the doctrines of antiquity in the light of Cartesian interpretations, and so contributes to eighteenth-century philosophical thought. His heroes do not point towards any desired political structures, nor do their sacrifices provide messages for the statesmen and rulers of the day. His projection of abstract heroism exists on an academic rather than on any practical level. For this reason his heroes, while at all times interesting creations, are generally lacking in dramatic conviction. Writing for a cultured audience, he provided felicity of diction, alongside heroic deeds. The result is that Greek and Roman heroes provide the rhetorical recitatives expected of them, while the arias (in this respect Metastasio had much in common with Zeno) are cast in Arcadian conceits and eighteenth-century Petrarchism. Metastasio's poetic diction thus comprises both the heroic and the contrived: classical rhetoric and rococo elegance. This tends, from the linguistic viewpoint, to fragment his characters, which at times verge on the grandiose, and at other times appear as graceful vignettes. Even his accepted masterpiece *Attilio Regolo* is a piece of Arcadian elegance, in which Roman consuls expound Cartesian doctrines, all the time to the accompaniment of the music of the leading composers of the day.

In attempting to analyse the content of Metastasio's thought, the most outstanding feature is his dependence on Stoic, Renaissance and Cartesian philosophy.[17] In striving to create the 'pure classical being', Metastasio attempts to recreate the ideological world in which it resided. His figures rationalize their own behaviour, in adherence to the ethical doctrines of the ancient world. While dramatically conforming to their codes, their convictions are further explained in the course of the drama. The brave Stoic pleads indifference to external influences, and stresses that virtue resides in the will. In the course of the juxtaposition of freedom and servitude it emerges that freedom is characteristic of consciousness. As a result there develops a series of dramas on the subject of rationalization, devoid of psychological considerations. There emerges from the mouth of Attilio Regolo a doctrine of abstract absolutism. Metastasio arrives at 'figuration' as opposed to characterization. Personae become symbolic of abstractions: Didone (*Didone abbandonata*) of a passionate personality constantly given to emotional expression, Aeneas of Cartesian doubt which is the essence of his being, Megacle (*Olimpiade*) of loyalty and Attilio Regolo of heroism.

Didone, in *Didone abbandonata*, in an impassioned outburst at the conclusion of Act 1, Scene 17, enforces her personality on the public with the force of her dramatic expression. Metastasio has achieved his effect by providing alternating interrogatives and statements. In the first section of the aria Didone asks of Enea if her abandoned heart has not the right to express its condemnation. The central movement consists of two contrasting passages: the first is addressed to lovers, the second is a further condemnation of her lover. The final section consists of a second address to lovers, in the form of an interrogative. Here then is the *da capo aria* with a new subtlety, in terms of contrast and alternation of statements and questions. The variation of metre within the aria provides for the unexpected, and yet allows for a rhyme between the lines at the conclusion of each section:

> Non ha ragione
> un core abbandonato
> da chi giurogli fè?
> Anime innamorate,
> se lo provaste mai,
> ditelo voi per me!
> Perfido! tu lo sai
> se in premio un tradimento
> lo meritai da te.
> E qual sarà tormento
> anime innamorate
> se questo mio non è?
>   (*Didone abbandonata*, Act 1, Scene 17)[18]

(Is not a heart justified when abandoned by one who swore fidelity to it? Spirits in love, if you ever have such experience, speak of it on my behalf. Unfaithful one! You know whether or not I merited betrayal by you. And spirits in love, what is torment if this my [suffering] is not?)

At first reading this is merely an impassioned condemnation of Enea's abandonment. On closer linguistic analysis it is clear that it is the rationalistic expression of anger: emotion justified by reason. In other words the spontaneous expression of dismay or despair conforms to reason: it is reasonable to indulge in anger. Metastasio chooses the terms 'ragione', 'meritai'. Rather than love being opposed to reason it in fact is portrayed as rational.

Most significant in relation to the above is Maria Grazia Accorsi's illuminating article 'Metastasio e l'idea dell'amore'[19] in which she analyses the contradiction and necessary elements of love, as seen in Metastasio's librettos. Highlighting the rational, irrational and uncertain aspects of the theme, she concludes that the librettos contain, in addition to the battles between protagonists, the drama of existence, punctuated by uncertainty of conviction and a voluntary blinding of the self, in order to find refuge in hope, illusion and fantasy. This thesis can be carried a step further when one considers that the above statement is also true for the Alfierian concept of love, in particular as applied to Clitennestra in his *Agamennone*. Clitennestra, symbolizing heroic weakness, blinded by passion, flees from the momentary flashes of reason, which finally yield to the *funesta fiamma* (sad flame) of ardour. This in turn in Alfieri's imagery gives way to blood, representing violence, anarchy and an absolute abandonment of reason.

Enea's aria in the following scene is a theatrical analysis of indecision or Cartesian doubt. The second section of the piece could be defined as contemplative as opposed to dramatic:

> Se resto sul lido,
> se sciolgo le vele,
> infido crudele
> mi sento chiamar
> e intanto, confuso
> nel dubbio funesto,
> non parto, non resto,
> ma provo il martire,
> che avrei nel partire,
> che avrei nel restar.
> (*Didone abbandonata*, Act 1, Scene 18)

(If I remain on the shore, if I untie the sails, I hear myself called cruel, unfaithful one. And in the meantime, confused by distressing doubt, I neither leave nor stay. But I experience the anguish of both departing and remaining.)

The first, shorter section is an exposition of a hypothesis of alternatives. Enea hears accusations of cruelty, whatever his action. The second section sets out the effect of such a hypothesis on the mind and on the body. Confusion caused by doubt results in physical immobility, and actual suffering, the equivalent of that which would have been felt if either alternative had been accepted. In *Didone abbandonata* indecision has taken control of Enea. As one who doubts, his predicament exists in terms of the defeat of the will by the emotions, resulting in an abandonment of reason. Didone, then, paradoxically, while indulging in emotional expression, is the symbol of the rational being. Her drama is played out against the plight of one who, even when taking decisive action, has not succeeded in philosophically resolving his own dilemma.

The critic Franco Gavazzeni regards *Didone abbandonata* as the first step in a journey towards the resolution of the conflict of opposites, that is between reason and nature.[20] He points out that in *Ezio* (1728) the drama is played between duty and inclination, while in *Adriano in Siria* (1732) the dilemma is resolved by the defeat of the passions and the triumph of virtue. At this point Metastasio is occupied with a violent or rather forceful conclusion: he provides a victor and a vanquished. Later, in *Il re pastore* (1751), affection replaces reason, leading to the peaceful reconciliation of opposites.

The patriotic theme is one that allows Metastasio to explore public and private affiliations, and allows for the conversion of the fainthearted to heroic dedication to public duty. This is the case in *La clemenza di Tito*, *Attilio Regolo* and *Temistocle*. While it can be argued that in *Il re pastore* peaceful reconciliation of opposites is achieved, the various conflicting ideas expressed in the early dramas are present in *Attilio Regolo*. This classical melodrama depicts the choice of a heroic death by a Roman consul. The love theme occupies a subordinate position. The heroic *virtù* of the Romans is complemented by an *anti-virtù*, or lack of comprehension by the Carthaginian representative. In other words the basic conclict between Rome and Carthage incorporates such opposites as good/evil, valour/cowardice, knowledge/ignorance. Regolo's will to good acts as a challenge to all Romans. The dramatic conclusion is seen in terms of the triumph of absolute endurance and strength of will, in both abstract and physical terms.[21]

In cultivating classical concepts Metastasio, in addition to the pursuit of the philosophy of the ancients and the unities of time, place and action, allows the theme of unity to surface in relation to many aspects of the drama of *Attilio Regolo*. Regolo is seen as a leader who can unite all Rome, and with whom the will of all can be identified. Yet paradoxically Regolo seeks self-gratification. In the final scene Regolo's tragic end is celebrated. Regolo, as the representative of Rome triumphant, sheds all his individuality:

> La patria è un tutto
> Di cui siamo parti

> Al cittadin è fallo
> Considerarsi se stesso
> Separato da lei.
> (*Attilio Regolo*, Act 2, Scene 1)[22]

(The fatherland is an entity of which we are elements. It is wrong for the citizen to consider himself as separate from it.)

At the opening of the melodrama Attilio's daughter Attilia pleads for her father's safety, but as the drama develops, she too is educated to the significance of being Roman:

> REGOLO: Io giurai perché volli,
> Voglio partir perché giurai.
> (*Attilio Regolo*, Act 3, Scene 5)

(I wish to leave because I swore to go. I swore because I wished [it so].)

In further stressing the magnanimity of Regolo, Metastasio associates him with not only the grandeur of Rome, but also with its physical features: its walls, its streets, the Forum, the temples and the Campidoglio. A visual impression of his popularity is provided with the description of the attempt to prevent his departure and death:

> Per impedirvi
> il passaggio alle navi, ognun s'affretta
> precipitando al porto, e son di Roma
> già l'altre vie deserte.
> (*Attilio Regolo*, Act 3, Scene 6)

(Each one makes haste to block your passage to the ship by rushing to the harbour. And the other streets in Rome are already deserted.)

The concerted will of the citizens, attempting to persuade their hero to remain, is specially communicated. When eventually Regolo succeeds in prevailing on all to clear his passage the crowd parts to allow him to pass. Once again, and this time dramatically, the effect of Regolo's will is physically conveyed:

> REGOLO: Più non tardate il corso, al mio trionfo
> o amici, o figli, o cittadini. Amico

	favor da voi domando,
	esorto, cittadin, padre comando.
ATTILIA:	(Oh Dio! Ciascun già l'ubbidisce.)
PUBLIO:	(Oh Dio?
	ecco ogni destra inerme.)
LICINIO:	Ecco sgombro il sentier.

(Attilio Regolo, Act 3, Scene 10)

REGOLO:	O friends, O children, O citizens, do not delay any longer the course of my triumph. As a friend, I ask a favour of you. As a citizen I exhort. As a father, I command.
ATTILIA:	(O gods! each one already obeys him.)
PUBLIO:	(O gods! behold every right hand defenceless.)
LICINIO:	Behold the path is clear.

Metastasio's reform of the melodrama may be summed up as follows: he restored tales of magnanimous deeds, set in the framework of the classical structure, to the theatre for music. The content of the pieces was the result of the combination of dramatic theory and philosophical analysis of human behaviour. On this account the tragedies, viewed as a whole, contain an intellectual progression, constituting a theatrical experimentation of the conflict between reason and emotion, heroism and tyranny, freedom and servitude. In this respect he laid the foundations for Alfieri's tragic theatre, which dispensed with the musical dimension and belongs to the *teatro di prosa* tradition. Although Metastasio was forward-looking in his abstract projection of society, because his conviction remained at the level of the theoretical, he is representative of an age of contemplation and meditation as opposed to action. To posterity he stands out as the leading exponent of Arcadia, bringing to the theatre of the eighteenth century the refined intellectual exercises of the Academy. His verse belongs to the world of the rococo, poetic miniature expressed in melodious quatrains. Yet he defies easy definition: an Arcadian poet with aspirations beyond the capacity of his own poetic medium; a figure, generally regarded as opposed to Enlightenment doctrines, whose dramas are a *mise-en-scène* of enlightened reason. Above all, a poet who carried the melodrama to the level of straight theatre which can be appreciated, studied and enjoyed with or without the company of its fellow muse.

With the advent of Stampiglia, Zeno and Metastasio, Italian

heroic opera ceased to be associated with any particular Italian city or province. Its centre was the court of Vienna, and its topics provided a contribution to European thought. While the librettists continued to be Italian, and operate in the field of Italian literature, Austrian, Prussian and French composers wedded their scores to the Italian texts. Italy had provided the impetus, while the discerning Viennese audiences had prompted the reforms. Yet another attempt at renewal emanated from Vienna in the middle of the eighteenth century. It came in the form of the Calzabigi/Gluck collaboration and its effect was felt throughout musical Europe.

III

Although Metastasio's librettos held sway both inside and outside Vienna, the city had long been associated with a taste for new forms and experiments which favoured the spread of Enlightenment doctrines and ideals. Rousseau's idea of a return to nature and the cult of the noble savage, and the discoveries of Newton, encouraged a re-examination of sentiments and spontaneity. Poetry was no longer seen as a refined academic exercise, but rather as a means of communicating truth. Metastasio's form of melodrama to many seemed antiquated on account of its sophisticated artifice and its reliance on stereotyped situations. The final impetus for reform was given when the Italian poet Ranieri de' Calzabigi[23] (1714–95) was introduced to the Bohemian composer Christoph Willibald Gluck (1714–87). The 'reform', however, was in reality no more than a revival – a revival of the classical, mythological opera which had characterized the works of the Florentine academies, and in which the emphasis was clearly placed on the poetic as opposed to the musical medium. When one considers the intentions and achievements of Calzabigi and Gluck, it becomes more and more apparent that their neo-classic compositions constituted a revitalization of the drama based on Grecian models, to which was added chorus, song and dance. The reason that such a revival did not enjoy the success that many believe it deserved was primarily because it contained no real innovation, nor did it reflect any social and intellectual change or crisis. The comic medium, long regarded as of an inferior nature, finally at this time gained the upper hand. This was because it contained vestiges of the popular comedy but yet succeeded in applying comic situations to the social climate of the day. In this respect it heralded the romantic opera which, stripped of theories and tradition, spoke directly to a public hungry for spontaneous expression.

The most important result of the Calzabigi/Gluck reform was the relaxing of the existing rigid forms. The *da capo aria* gave way to short passages closely connected with the drama. And the *recitativo secco* was completely eliminated in favour of a continuous, unified musical line. Calzabigi concentrated entirely on the main action. In *Orfeo ed Euridice* (1762) there are only three characters, and the chorus and the ballet take an important part in the plot throughout. In the second collaboration of the two artists, *Alceste* (1767), there are seven characters. Gluck's last opera, which was also written with Calzabigi, was *Iphigénie en Tauride* (1779). For the first performance in Paris Calzabigi's text was translated into French. The poetic aspect of the work was highlighted. In the preface to *Alceste* Calzabigi wrote the following, which was later signed by Gluck:

> pensai di ristringere la Musica al suo vero ufficio di servire alla poesia per l'espressione, e per le situazioni della Favola, senza interromper l'Azione, o raffreddarla con degli inutili superflui ornamenti.[24]

> (I thought of restricting the Music to its true office of serving poetry, for the expression and situations of the Fable (plot) without interrupting the Action, or rendering it cold, with useless and superficial ornaments.)

Orfeo ed Euridice by Calzabigi is a poetic work of nobility and statuesque beauty. Here the legend made music–drama by Rinuccini and Striggio is produced on a far grander scale. It contains nothing of the miniature elegance and idyllic atmosphere of the early melodrama, but is an example of the purity of the poetic form, aided by music, mime, ballet and chorus. The work opens with a chorus of nymphs and shepherds lamenting the death of Euridice.

> Ah! se intorno a quest'urna funesta,
> Euridice, ombra bella, t'aggiri,
> Odi i pianti, i lamenti, i sospiri
> Che dolenti si spargon per te.
> Ed ascolta il tuo sposo infelice
> Che piangendo ti chiama e si lagna;

Come quando la dolce compagna
Tortorella amorosa perdè.
(Orfeo ed Euridice, Act 1, Scene 1)

(Beauteous shade of Euridice, ah, if you are present near this gloomy urn, hear the cries, the laments and the sighs which in sorrow are uttered for you. And hear your unhappy spouse, he who in tears calls you and mourns, like the loving dove when he lost his sweet companion.)

The work concludes with Orfeo, Euridice and Amor (Love) joining with the chorus in the celebration of the triumph of love. Throughout the development of the action, the chorus is omnipresent, providing a poetic comment on the situation and plight of the lovers. But it must be stressed that in *Orfeo ed Euridice*, and indeed also in *Alceste*, the chorus does not merely relieve the monotony of the piece, or fill the space between recitatives and arias. It performs the function of a persona, entering directly into the dialogue and performing a bridge between Orfeo and the Furies. It also provides an amount of poetic variety, ranging from mere comments on a situation to celebratory hymns, from rhetorical questions (at the beginning of the second act) to the provision of essential information (Act 2, Scene 2).

The work develops through a series of laments, finally turning to joy when Orfeo and Euridice are united. Calzabigi has provided a happy ending. Orfeo's first lament which consists of fifty lines falls into three main sections: his plea to be left alone, an address to Euridice and a denunciation of the gods, which moves Amor to pity:

Assisterà
Pietoso Amor l'infelice consorte!
A te concede Giove in sua pietà,
Varcar le pigre onde di Lete. Va!
Euridice a trovar nel tetro regno!
Se il dolce suon de la tua lira,
Al cielo, Orfeo, saprà salir,
Placata fia dei Numi l'ira
E resa l'ombra cara
Al primo tua sospir!
(Orfeo ed Euridice, Act 1, Scene 2)

(Compassionate Love will assist the unhappy consort. In his

pity Jove permits you to cross the dull waters of Lethe. Go! Go the find Euridice in the dark kingdom. If Orfeo succeeds in raising the sweet sound of his lyre to heaven, may the anger of the gods be placated, and the beloved shade returned at your first sigh.)

The most famous aria of the opera occurs in Act 3, Scene 1 when Orfeo loses Euridice for the second time and is about to take his own life when he is disarmed by Love, and Euridice is restored to him for all eternity:

>Che farò senza Euridice?
>Dove andrò senza il mio ben?
>Euridice! ... Oh Dio. Rispondi!
>Io son pure il tuo fedele!
>Euridice ... Ah! non m'avanza
>Più soccorso, più speranza
>Nè dal mondo, nè dal ciel!
>(*Orfeo ed Euridice*, Act 3, Scene 1)

(What shall I do without Erudice? Where shall I go without my beloved? Euridice, oh god, answer! I am indeed faithful to you. Euridice, neither help nor hope comes to me from heaven or earth!)

The clarity and simplicity of diction carry the listener straight into the protagonist's dilemma. Language in its most essential and pure form is here communicating human tragedy and eternal justice. The moral theme of both *Orfeo ed Euridice* and *Alceste* centres on human relationships and marital fidelity. Both dramas consist of the bare essentials; the key moments in *Orfeo ed Euridice* are: the death of Euridice (Act 1); the descent of Orfeo into hell and his recovery of Euridice in the Elysian Fields (Act 2); the second death of Eruidice and the intervention of Amor (Act 3).

Similarly *Alceste* develops with the dramatic pinpointing of emblematic moments: the illness of Admeto; the Oracle; the decision of Alceste to die for her husband; the death of Alceste and the intervention of Apollo. Both dramas illustrate the same theme. Both tales derive from mythical antiquity. One tells of a husband deprived of a wife, the other of a wife deprived of a husband. Both bereaved confront the spirits of the Underworld, and the tale closes with the reunion of the lovers. *Paride ed Elena* (**Paris and Helen**) written in 1770 is an example of a piece of pure classicism in which the nobility of expression, movement, gesture is carried to the point where there is little or no physical action. All is concentrated on the psychological juxtaposition of the characters. The conflict, then, is an internal one, with virtually no externalization of the dilemma.

After a cool reception in Vienna, Gluck decided to move to Paris. This brought an end to his collaboration with Calzabigi. The Italian librettist's text for *Iphigénie en Tauride* appeared in Paris, in translation by François Guillard.

The Calzabigi 'reform' was then merely a revitalization of the Italian melodrama in its most essential form. It can be regarded as a neo-classic experiment, and an example of the idealistic yearnings of those engaged in theatre for a renewal and return to noble structures and values.

This revival, however, looked to the ideal, which had little contact with life of the day, or indeed of any day.[25] The remoulding of the *commedia dell'arte* by Carlo Goldoni, and the new comic opera librettos of Casti and da Ponte, provided the essential element missing from the work of both Metastasio and Calzabigi: in a word, truth. Goldoni did not stop at a mere projection of aesthetic values, but provided opera true both to nature, and the social milieu of the day.

4

OF SERVANTS AND MASTERS: FEDERICO, GOLDONI AND DA PONTE

I

Up to this point in the present study total attention has been focused on the *opera seria*, and with the exception of a brief reference to comic scenes in the Venetian historical opera, the emphasis has been placed on the academic orientation of the heroic melodrama and the structured framework in which it flourished. *Opera seria* was the property of academicians. It was born in an attempt to add authenticity to the classical revival. Its development was punctuated by a series of reforms, revivals and renewals. As theorists forced it into a rigid framework which made it the mouthpiece of idealized behaviour, it became increasingly stereotyped and stylized. The heroic opera so found its inspiration in art and artifice. Life, livelihood and the projection of the times had little place on the 'serious' operatic stage. On the contrary, the comic opera, which, it can be argued, developed from the comic intermezzos[1] and short light scenes within the serious opera, evolved both freely and naturally. Its subject was the people, their ups and downs, fun and games, and social ills.

The sources of the comic scenes in the Venetian opera and all eighteenth-century comic texts is the *commedia dell'arte*,[2] born as a reaction to the classical theatre, but which, as a result of instantaneous success, gained an entry not only to the Italian courts but also to those of Europe. It became an influential aspect of European drama, and long before its reform by Goldoni it had been adopted by such diverse comic masters as Shakespeare and Molière.

The principal stimulus for the emergence of a comic popular theatre in Italy during the Renaissance was the need for a form of entertainment in which all classes could share. The classical theatre, tailormade for the erudite, and centred on a social élite, made no concessions to the masses. From medieval times the latter had indulged themselves at carnival time, a period before the beginning of Lent, when the social order was overturned. The word carnival derives from the Latin *carnem levare*, meaning to abandon the use of meat. During the celebrations which preceded forty days of austerity and abstinence, servants became masters, elaborate parades took place and athletic feats were staged. The carnival, with its festive atmosphere, brought forth the free expressions of the people, their local dress and native traditions, which during the remainder of the year went unobserved. When the same masses sought to found a type of spectacle reflecting their daily lives, it was to this form that they returned, which in time became an extravaganza of colour, buffoonery, sketches and songs.

The essential aspect of the *commedia dell'arte* was the fact that its dialogue was improvised. There was no text, and the success of the performance depended on the skill of the actor to invent and entertain. There did, however, exist a loosely woven plot, or *canovaccio*, and characters were assigned their own *formulario* of expressions and tricks of the trade. The plots reflected the day-to-day problems of the masses: the discrepancy between young and old, the attempts of avaricious elders to marry young heiresses, and the ability of the cunning servant to foil such efforts. Often the plots were a skit on the erudite theatre. The Latin comedies of Terence and Plautus were parodied and rendered in the various Italian dialects and set in diverse provinces. Certain characters quickly became popular with the public, and so appeared again and again in repetitive *scenarios*. Soon, with the introduction of masks, the character became fixed, providing little opportunity for psychological expression or development. This in turn rendered the figures both familiar and predictable, making them both loved and accepted throughout the peninsula. Thus, every play presented the same stock characters, playing out their life patterns with the 'sameness' of approach and technique as demanded by the public.

By the end of the seventeenth century the term 'mask' was applied to the entire character, as opposed to indicating merely a covering for the face, or disguise. The principal stock mask figures were Pantalone, Dr Balanzone and Captain Spavento, and the servants Arlecchino, Brighella, Colombina, and Pulcinella. Pantalone was a Venetian merchant whose name derives from *piantaleone* (propagate the lion), a term applied to Venetian merchants trading in the east. He wore a long black cloak and skull-cap, and is usually depicted holding a money-bag, a symbol of his avarice. He may well have been Shakespeare's model for Shylock, the Jewish money-lender in his comedy *The Merchant of Venice*. Dr Balanzone is a skit on the educated class. Wearing the toga of the University of Bologna, he gave forth in garbled gibberish, carrying a stick which provided protection from the plague, and sporting an artificial pointed nose. He found his way into the comic theatre of Goldoni in a more refined and less grotesque form. Captain Spavento was a symbol of foreign occupation. Speaking Italian with a Spanish inflection, he introduced a military dimension. His striped tassel-trimmed uniform, plumed hat and brandished sword make him a cross between a dashing hero and court jester.[3]

Since the *commedia dell'arte* originated from the need of the lower classes to see their own milieu dramatized, the social rifts and discriminations were enacted as seen through the eyes of the masses. The true heroes were the clever servants who overturned the social order and resolved the problems of their masters, while providing a variety of tricks and acrobatics. The three most famous *zanni* or servants were Arlecchino, Brighella and Pulcinella. The female servant Colombina, Arlecchino's companion, was sometimes known as Arlecchina. Arlecchino (Harlequin) originated from the character Hellecin in Anglo-Saxon folklore, a devilish figure or spirit of the dead. The Italian Harlequin was first presented speaking the bergamasque dialect and wearing a patched costume. He wore a black mask, barely revealing the stumps of two small horns, indicative of his devilish origins. Later, the patches on the costume became diamond-shaped. Being rather dim-witted, he was aided by the cunning Colombina, who does not wear a face mask and was identified by the style of her apron. These two characters, remoulded by Carlo Goldoni, became the basis for Beaumarchais's characters Figaro and Suzanne, and were given operatic life by the Da Ponte/Mozart collaboration. The servant Brighella, usually a trickster and often an innkeeper, in the hands of Goldoni likewise underwent a transformation. Apart from emerging as an honest servant, he is fused with Colombina in order to create what many consider Goldoni's greatest female comic creation: the figure of Mirandolina, the crafty innkeeper of *La locandiera*.[4]

The success of the *commedia dell'arte* was instantaneous. By 1577 it had been introduced into England. In the same year Henry III of France employed his own players at court. In 1645 Molière had set about studying this form of theatrical presentation which was unfortunately degenerating into a ragbag of vulgar jokes, forced situations and clownish acts. It had, however, formed the basis of the comic intermezzo and the comic operatic interludes. Before Carlo Goldoni's remoulding and reform of the improvised comedy, the *commedia dell'arte* types were flooding the comic operatic stage. A good example of the servant versus master situation, with its subtle social implications, can be seen in G.A. Federico's *La serva padrona* (Naples, 1733) with music by Pergolesi.[5] This intermezzo is played out in terms of a battle of wits between an elderly gentleman Uberto and his maidservant Serpina, who finally establishes herself as mistress of all situations and overturns the social order by marrying her employer and superior.

This is a *commedia dell'arte* plot *par excellence*. Serpina, whose name meaning 'little snake' implies guile, is Colombina, while the grumpy gentleman is a fusion of the Doctor and Pantalone. The plot develops through a succession of recitatives, five arias, and two duets. The arias, rather than providing moments of reflection, are integrated into the dramatic action which proceeds at a rapid pace. The juxtaposition of service and command is introduced straight away with the emphasis on the maid's refusal to serve:

> Son tre ore che aspetto, e la mia serva
> Portarmi il cioccolatte non fa grazia,
> Ed io d'uscire ho fretta.
>   (*La serva padrona*, Part 1)

(I have been waiting for three hours and my maidservant does not deign to bring me my chocolate. And I am in a hurry to go out.)

Serpina's refusal to serve the chocolate indicates a total rejection of eighteenth-century convention. This beverage, associated with social pretence, is denied to this master as it merely served to emphasize the difference between the classes. Similar complaints are expressed by Despina in *Così fan tutte*. Serpina highlights the plight of the downtrodden maid and her need of respect:

> Adunque
> Perch'io son serva, ho da esser sopraffatta,
> Ho da essere maltrattata? No signore.
> Voglio esser rispettata,
> Voglio esser riverita come fossi
> Padrona, arcipadrona, padronissima.
> (La serva padrona, Part 1)

(So, because I am a servant, must I be walked on? Must I be treated badly? No, Sir, I want to be respected, I wish to be honoured as though I were mistress, the highest mistress, very much the mistress.)

The first section of the intermezzo closes with Serpina relating her charms:

> Non son io bella,
> Graziosa e spiritosa?
> Su, mirate, leggiadria,
> Ve' che brio, che maestà.
> (La serva padrona, Part 1)

(Am I not beautiful, elegant and full of spirit? Go on, observe what grace, what vivaciousness, what majesty.)

Serpina proves to be the first of the many operatic heroines to win her man and her own game, in the demonstration of feminine guile. She will be Goldoni's model for artful widows, astute landladies and contriving opportunists. In addition, the librettist Federico makes use of a direct and basic form of expression, not at all in keeping with the poetic genre previously associated with the operatic theatre. Yet in this naturalness of dialogue, a rationalistic approach to society and status is communicated, and the academic question of being and becoming is debated in a comic rather than a philosophic guise. As Professor Gianfranco Folena so eloquently points out,[6] all is clear to the public from the very beginning: Serpina, from the rank of servant, will rise to mistress. It will happen because she wills it so – 'Serpina vuol così' ('Serpina so wishes'). We are therefore face to face with a comedy of neither character nor action, but one of situation. Federico has succeeded in inventing a colloquial Italian for the charming intermezzo scored in a spoken register, and verging on Neapolitan usage with frequent dialectal syntax. It is, however, the language of both servant and master. Equality has been achieved linguistically, as the two voices alternate in the final duet in an expression of contentment. It is on a note of 'godimento' – *sol tu mi fai goder* (only you provide diversion) – that the short work closes. The strength of will of the crafty *servetta* has won the day, but, in the final context, both fun and games triumph.

II

The father of Italian comedy, the so-called 'reformer' of the *commedia dell'arte*, was born in Venice in 1707. Carlo Goldoni, the son of a doctor, was destined for the legal profession. Never an assiduous student, his fascination with the theatre caused him to stow away with a group of *commedia dell'arte* strolling players, when a student at Rimini.[7] The experience opened up for him a whole new approach to actors and their craft, which in time was reflected in his comedies. As a result, 'the Venetian lawyer' is now credited with the restoration and development of the comic character. This process consisted of his stripping his characters of their masks in order to reveal the expressiveness of the face and the resonances of the voice, so allowing for the further development of the character. Rather than eliminate the stock figures, he transformed them. In bringing on stage the world of the Venetian *campiello* or square, in addition to the inn and gambling house, he returned to the written word. A realistic portrait of avaricious lawyers, elderly tutors and corrupt *cicisbei* (cavalier servants) emerged. In the process he can be said to have provided social, psychological, historical and economic truth. Far from being a simplistic writer of social comedy, Goldoni humorously provides gentle satire on eighteenth-century manners and mannerism. Reason, intuition and general 'know-how' paradoxically exist among the servant class which, although winning its successive battles, none the less retains its social identity.[8]

Goldoni, then, is the principal writer of comedies during the eighteenth century in Italy. He is also the most influential humorist of his time. His influence on the operatic libretto can be seen far beyond his own century. Sterbini's *Il barbiere di Siviglia* for Rossini, Ruffini's *Don Pasquale* in collaboration with Donizetti, and Felice Romani's *L'elisir d'amore* for the same composer can all be said to be cast in the Goldonian tradition. Yet the Venetian writer cannot merely be seen as an important influence on the

5 Carlo Goldoni (1707–93)

literature of the libretto. He in fact made a significant contribution to this art-form, as the author of fifteen intermezzos and fifty-five comic operatic plots.⁹

Goldoni's reform of the *commedia dell'arte*, which is manifested in a return to the written theatre and a projection of comedy once again as literature, did not constitute an immediate abandonment of the *scenari* and *formulari* of stage managers and actors. Rather, it took the form of a gradual dependence on a text, and a playing down of the inventive freedom of the actor. But whereas their liberty to improvise diminished with the passing of time, their freedom of expression increased. The result was a new form of creativity, based on imitation as opposed to exaggeration. By the age of 40, Goldoni had abandoned the financial and social security of the legal profession to dedicate himself to the most precarious of careers – that of comic writer. By that time, however, his formation was in fact almost complete. He no longer wrote sketchy *scenari*. The year 1743 marked the appearance of his first completely written comedy, *La donna di garbo*. Six years later he began his collaboration with Galuppi, and his most successful comedies, *Le femmine puntigliose*, *La bottega del caffè*, *Il bugiardo*, *La Pamela* and *La locandiera*, were to follow in quick succession.¹⁰

Goldoni's development as a librettist can be assessed in relation to three periods: that of the early intermezzos; the period of his dedication to the *opera seria*; the beginning of his collaboration with Galuppi and his combination of both serious and comic figures, so providing a clear-cut vision of eighteenth-century society.¹¹ While Goldoni was writing sketches and *scenari* for the comic theatre, he was in fact practising his craft as a satirical humanist, providing complete comic operatic entities for the San Samuele Theatre in Venice. Thus the theatrical reform of the *commedia dell'arte* can be traced to Goldoni's comedies for music, in which he was providing rounded comic figures, conforming to typical Venetian types. At the same time he was still practising his profession as a lawyer. This is the period of *Pupilla* (1734), *Birba* (1735), *Filosofo* (1735), *L'amante cabala* (1736) and *Monsieur Petiton*. In the latter work Goldoni provides a skit on *cicisbeismo*, holding to ridicule the *cavaliere servente* and the social convention of the aristocratic lady being served by a nobleman, never her husband. At this stage in his career Goldoni is touching on a social usage later to be the subject of many of his comedies, including *Il cavaliere e la dama*, and of Parini's satirical poem, *Il giorno*. The aforementioned intermezzos provide a mixture of Italian, Italianized Venetian, Bolognese and French. A close analysis illustrates how the reform of the *commedia dell'arte* and the subsequent development of eighteenth-century comedy cannot properly be assessed without reference to the drama for music.

By the time Goldoni has begun his collaboration with Galuppi it is apparent that the librettist was aiming at the creation of coexisting comic and serious types in order to provide a lighthearted lesson on human behaviour. In the works one finds traces of the classical Metastasian approach appearing in the form of the *da capo aria*. While the slick buffoonery of the *commedia dell'arte*[12] is still omnipresent, yet another dimension is becoming evident: the *commedia lacrimosa*, or comic wallowing in sentiment, preparing for the emotional extravagances in both comic and serious matters of the nineteenth century. The significant works in this direction are: *L'Arcadia in Brenta* (1749), which marks the start of Goldoni's collaboration with Galuppi; *Il Conte Caramella*; *Il filosofo di campagna* (1754), with music by Galuppi; *La buona figliuola* (1757) with music by Piccini; and *Il mondo della luna* (1777) with music by Haydn. The libretto *L'Arcadia in Brenta* is a satire on eighteenth-century academies, and the aristocratic obsession with leisure and relaxation in the country villa. It paves the way for Goldoni's later amusing theatrical comedies *Momolo cortesan* and *Momolo sulla Brenta*. *Il mondo della luna* is a parody on Italian serious opera, with a combination of both comic and serious characters, buffoonery and eloquent expression. Goldoni has in fact summed up, in an exaggerated manner, the operatic world of the day. The two most significant works from a theatrical viewpoint are *Il filosofo di campagna* and *La buona figliuola*. In each of these dramas Goldoni demonstrates his dependence on Metastasio, in his projection of the classically conceived aria, and his leaning towards a rationalization of behaviour through the astute reasoning of the servant class. Since Paolo Gallarati in his study, *Musica e maschera, il libretto italiano del Settecento*, has already provided an illuminating analysis of the latter, my points are best illustrated by providing some information on the comic libretto, *Il filosofo di campagna*.

Il filosofo di campagna was first produced at the San Samuele Theatre, Venice, on 26 October 1754. Divided into three acts, it tells the tale of the aristocratic Eugenia, in love with Rinaldo but destined for marriage to Nardo, a rich farmer. With the aid of her servant Lesbina, Eugenia succeeds in marrying her lover, while the crafty *servetta* claims Nardo for herself. The success of the ruse hinges on Lesbina's masquerading as her mistress.

The conclusion takes the form of a lesson in a new philosophy of life: the rank of the lady is of little consequence. Be she servant or mistress, her merits may be enumerated in the following order: honesty, beauty, politeness, means and virtue. As Nardo the enlightened farmer states:

> per me nel vostro sesso,
> serva, o padrona sia, tutto è lo stesso.
> (*Il filosofo di campagna*, Act 3, Scene 2)

(It makes no difference to me, as far as your sex is concerned, whether you are maid or mistress.)

In spite of the simplicity of the tale, the lack of complication in the plot and the clarity of dialogue, the libretto points towards Goldoni the upholder of the Enlightenment, and the propagator of natural philosophy. The opening scene takes the form of a clear-cut conflict between nature and art. The art in question is, however, ingenuity, personified by Lesbina, who, in finally winning *sapienza* or knowledge, in the form of Nardo, represents the combination of wit and intelligence, which in its turn points to a new social order. The two female protagonists are introduced in terms of diverse creations of nature: the refined and the rustic. Eugenia opens the comedy with the following words:

> Candidetto gelsomino
> che sei vago in sul mattino
> perderai vicino a sera
> la primiera tua beltà.
> (*Il filosofo di campagna*,
>   Act 1, Scene 1)

(Pretty white jasmine that is beautiful in the morning, coming up to evening time, you will lose your first beauty.)

Lesbina's self-identification with nature is expressed in popular terms, linguistically creating common ground between the servant and the country philosopher.

> Son fresca, son bella
> cicoria novella,

> mangiatemi presto
> coglietemi su.
> Se resto nel prato
> radicchio invecchiato,
> nessuno si degna
> raccogliermi più.
> (*Il filosofo di campagna*,
> Act 1, Scene 2)

(I am fresh, I am beautiful, a sprouting chicory. Eat me up fast. Pluck me. If I remain in the meadow, an aged chicory, no one will deign to gather me any longer.)

As part of a lighthearted lesson on reason, wit and contrivance, the more serious aspect of Goldoni's message comes across: truth can surface with the aid of pretence, and the artful prank functions towards dispelling anger and allowing all to conclude on a note of gaiety. Reason, understanding and explanation are associated and expounded by Don Tritemio in Act 1, Scene 3.

> La mia ragione è questa,
> mi par ragione onesta:
> La figlia mia chiedeste
> e la ragion voleste.
> La mia ragion sta qui.
> (*Il filosofo di campagna*,
> Act 1, Scene 3)

(My reason is as follows. It seems to me an honest one: you ask for the hand of my daughter and you want satisfaction. This is my reason. It is as follows.)

Lesbina in order to capture the rich countryman prepares to use every act of deception at her disposal: 'Tutta l'arte ci vuole, tutto l'ingegno' ('All cunning must be employed, every guile') (*Il filosofo di campagna*, Act 2, Scene 1).

The device adopted by Lesbina to captivate the wealthy farmer is to disguise herself as her mistress. This falsification of person is one of the stock situations in the *commedia dell'arte* and the early comic opera. Later, Lorenzo Da Ponte in the libretto *Le nozze di Figaro*, adapted from Beaumarchais's *Le Mariage de Figaro*, uses change of costume for a different purpose. In Goldoni's libretto the servant masquerades as the mistress for the mere purpose of aiding both Eugenia and herself: 'Servo me stessa e servo la padrona' ('I serve myself and I serve the mistress') (*Il filosofo di campagna*, Act 3, Scene 3).

In Da Ponte's *Le nozze di Figaro* the lady's maid Susanna dons her lady's cloak in a plot to foil an unfaithful husband. Yet the change of garb has social and political implications. In a pre-revolutionary social comment, Da Ponte points to a time when the social order shall be reversed. The masses will don the garment of government while the aristocracy will be deposed and sent into exile. In both librettos, however, love emerges victorious. In *Il filosofo di campagna*, it is celebrated thus:

> Noi diciamo: così sia,
> stiamo dunque in allegria,
> ché la cosa – minacciosa
> tosto in ben si muterà,
> e l'amore – in ogni core
> con piacer trionferà.
> (*Il filosofo di campagna*,
> Act 2, Scene 3)

(Let us say: so be it. We are now full of merriment, since the matter, although perilous, soon will change for the better. And love with pleasure will triumph in every heart.)

Goldoni's librettos cannot be regarded as so politically orientated as *Le nozze di Figaro* by Lorenzo Da Ponte. The Venetian lawyer never the less attacks the insufferable arrogance of the overbearing aristocracy in *La contessina* (1743). In point of fact Goldoni above all strikes at the difference between the two outstanding ideologies of the eighteenth century: the growing acceptance of an individual for his honour, disposition and social conscience, and the ideological approach to birth, title and manners, soon to fall to the guillotine. It rests to Lorenzo Da Ponte, however, also a native of the Italian Veneto region, to present the two classes in harmony, while upholding moral behaviour and social decorum.

III

The eighteenth-century comic libretto developed as an attempt to give musical life and expression to the *commedia dell'arte*, itself both a parody on the erudite theatre and an outlet for the common folk. Yet, as has been seen, the comic intermezzos and early librettos of Carlo Goldoni were themselves instrumental in paving the way for a comic Italian theatre capable of standing comparison with its European counterparts. In both music and prose Italian comedy made its mark all over Europe, and with Goldoni's self-imposed exile in France in 1762, Venice's loss became the French capital's gain. Goldoni wrote several plays in French for the French theatre. Amid gentle satire and playful jests, however, there harboured in the world of Goldoni the voice of social reform, the influence of which cannot be ignored since it became apparent in the works of the French dramatist Caron de Beaumarchais. The latter's trilogy *Le Barbier de Seville* (1775), *Le Mariage de Figaro* (1778) and *La Mère coupable* (1791) reflects the popular servant versus master situation of the *commedia dell'arte*. The type characters are carried to a new degree of French sophistication, and their antics carry social, political and moral overtones. It is not, however, surprising that the characters invented by Beaumarchais and cast in the mould of the Italian *commedia* figures were to attain popularity, not only in the straight French theatre but in the Italian operatic medium, as a result of the Da Ponte/Mozart and Sterbini/Rossini collaboration.

The intrigues associated with the Beaumarchais Figaro and his associates are in fact no less audacious than those of his creator.[13] Caron de Beaumarchais was by profession a watchmaker, and a dramatist in his spare time. As clockmaker to Louis XV of France, he became the friend and confidant of his four daughters, to whom he gave music lessons. As a result of his musical talents – he was a fine harpist and singer – he managed to accumulate sufficient wealth to provide himself with a title. His diplomacy and social know-how resulted in his being enlisted to advise and assist kings and princes. He even provided Charles III of Spain with a French mistress – his own! By the time he reached the age of 38, he had been twice widowed, and twice suspected of having poisoned his wives. In London he bought off a notorious blackmailer who was casting aspersions on the past of Madame du Barry. It is to a dramatist of such social experience, wit and versatility that Da Ponte owes his acquaintance with the Almaviva household, the source of his adaptation which became *Le nozze di Figaro*.

Although critics have been slow to accept the political implications of Da Ponte's libretto *Le nozze di Figaro*, the French comedy was regarded as subversive from its inception. It was condemned by the king of France and although it had been read at social gatherings, it was not performed until 1704. Even in its final accepted form, however, the Beaumarchais drama can be seen to combine the traditional comic buffoonery with sophisticated satire, so providing a contained attack on the aristocracy of the day with more than a veiled prediction of open revolt. As servants hankered after being masters in the old comic tradition, Figaro proved a perfect example of the clever civil servant, so carrying the social conflict to a new dimension, while providing an entirely modern approach to the dramatis personae. It is indeed true to say that after the advent of Caron de Beaumarchais the European comic tradition was never again the same.

If Beaumarchais can be regarded as one who lived by intrigue and resourcefulness, it can equally be claimed that his adaptor, Lorenzo Da Ponte, did likewise.[14] Born Emmanuele Conegliano, of Jewish parents, in Cenada, north of Venice, in 1749, he soon converted to Catholicism, took the surname of the local Catholic bishop and began to study for the priesthood. After tiring of pious practices he set about establishing himself as a poet, and composed a series of poems grouped around the conflicting forces of nature and organized society. When expelled from the Venetian territory for proved adultery, he made his way to Dresden and on to Vienna where he was appointed poet to the Imperial Theatres in 1783. On his arrival in Vienna, Da Ponte had been greeted by Metastasio, but on the death of the latter the post of Caesarean poet was left vacant, and the lesser appointment of 'poet of the Imperial Theatres' was accorded to Da Ponte by his friend, Emperor Joseph II. At this stage of his career Da Ponte had not written a single theatrical work. Yet between 1786 and 1790 his librettos *Le nozze di Figaro* (1786), *Don Giovanni* (1787) and *Così fan tutte* (1790) were to render him immortal, and silence the malicious tongues of professional rivals such as Giovanni Battista Casti (1721–1803) and Giovanni Bertati (1735–1815), both of whom vied for the senior post. After the death of his patron Joseph II in 1790, Da Ponte fell from favour, and on losing his post left for Trieste. Two years later on the death of Emperor Leopold II, Da Ponte returned, but left for London in final defeat when Francis II appointed Casti to Metastasio's post. Da Ponte worked at the Drury Lane Theatre, London, from 1793 until he set out for America. He arrived there in 1805. Da Ponte is credited with having founded the Chair of Italian at Columbia University, although it has been claimed that his was a department without students! He can certainly be seen as instrumental in bringing Italian opera to the United States. Along with Manuel Garcia, the creator of Almaviva in Rossini's *Il barbiere di Siviglia*, he arranged the first American season. The repertoire included *Don Giovanni*. In 1833 he was responsible for establishing the Italian Opera House in New York.

Lorenzo Da Ponte brought all the charm and decay of the late eighteenth century to his operatic librettos. Apart from his image as an adventurer and libertine who lived for the most part on his wits, it must be remembered that his sojourn in America provided the city of New York with the first American library of Italian books, in addition to a Chair of Italian and an Italian Opera House. It was also while in the United States that he wrote his memoirs.[15] These proved to be a precious insight into the theatrical environment of his time. His topics range from the problems facing an impresario in the throes of presenting a programme, to the conflict raging between librettists, musicians and singers, all versed in a narrative of engaging satire. His principal aim in compiling an account of his varied existence was a didactic one: to provide students of Italian with a modern text. In second place was a desire to defend himself from the scandalous, and clearly not unfounded, accusations which followed him wherever he went. Finally he wished, from his place of exile, to register his love for his native Italy, to which he paid homage by virtue of his diffusion of Italian culture in America. The student of history, music and social events does indeed need to verify accounts and check information, dates and situations, often incorrect and exaggerated in the author's record of his own experiences. Yet along with the two other writers from the territory of St Mark, Goldoni and Casanova, he provides an authentic insight into the era of the powdered wig, gavotte and minuet, which successfully recaptures its grace, charm and finesse allied to corruption.

Da Ponte's *Le nozze di Figaro* has often been regarded as a mere translation and adaptation of the Beaumarchais play, carried out to provide a vehicle for the musical genius of Mozart.[16] In fact George R. Marek, in his book *Opera as Theatre*, refers to a psychological comedy consisting of condensation in adaptation. The librettist himself claims in his memoirs not to have effected

6 Lorenzo Da Ponte (1749–1838)

a translation of the French dramatist, but rather an imitation or, more precisely, an abstract. It is clear that both poet–adventurers were drawn to a topic with its essence founded on social and political abuses, the dramatic enactment of which contained elements of the classical and popular comedy. That Da Ponte's version emerges as the more subtle, graceful and amusing is in no small measure due to the fact that he succeeded in combining the best features of the Goldoni and French Enlightenment comedies. Through Beaumarchais's influence, the Italian librettist gleaned the refined qualities of the French salon comedy, the sentimental comedy and the political satire. Both comedies tell of a nobleman who wishes to seduce one of his servants, and claims the freedom to do so by virtue of his feudal rights. The efforts of the servant girl, the man she is to marry and the nobleman's wife bring his designs to nothing. Contained in the dilemma is the attitude to absolutism, rank and fortune.

Although Professor Marek provides a stimulating comparison of play and opera, illustrating clearly that Act I is indeed almost a word-for-word translation of the play, he fails to stress the manner in which Da Ponte condenses, tightens and stresses political images and symbols. In his chapter 'What happens in Figaro', he concludes that the libretto is a comedy of love: that its theme is not man's inequality, but the quality which binds man and woman. It is my belief, however, that although the nature of love is indeed a recurring theme in the work, the political dimension is strengthened by its coexistence with the love theme. At the conclusion of the opera it is the love and wit of the servants which triumphs over the lasciviousness and arrogance of their masters. By softening the satire and highlighting the humour Da Ponte succeeds in making his point without insult to either the Viennese nobility, on whose support he relied, or to his patron Joseph II. Yet if the Beaumarchais *Mariage* was regarded as revolutionary in spirit, it can be claimed that *Le nozze di Figaro* is an appraisal of the Enlightenment. It is a portrait of enlightened wit, ironically and paradoxically surfacing through the reactions of the proletariat, represented by the serving class. The palace of Count Almaviva does not merely represent the French or Viennese court but society at large, populated by aristocrats and serfs, clergymen and spies. The triumph of the young lovers over their aristocratic master is seen as a triumph of justice, spurred on by love and the inability to resist some fun at the expense of the lord of the manor. The world of the *commedia dell'arte* is very much in evidence in that the plot contains the eternal battle between the younger and older generation, while also providing the discovery of the long-lost child. Throughout, Da Ponte's extreme fluency of diction and command of colourful nouns and adjectives (this is particularly evident in the 'Aprite un po' quegli occhi' aria) provide a taste of his ability as an extemporary poet. In short, *Le nozze di Figaro* can be regarded as an expression of the intellectual and theatrical scene in eighteenth-century Italy.

The war between the classes, manifested in terms of a struggle between reason and stupidity, is projected by Da Ponte for the most part by means of symbolic objects and themes. As the opera opens, Susanna and Figaro, the comic descendants of Arlecchino and Colombina, are preparing for their marriage. Figaro is holding a measure, while Susanna admires herself in the mirror. The former's main preoccupation is whether the bed will fit into the room. Susanna's doubts are centred on the situation of the same room, and its proximity to the Count's quarters. Soon it becomes apparent that every move and situation must of necessity be *measured*. The reason? Susanna's reply makes the situation clear: '*La ragione l'ho qui [toccandosi alla fronte]*' ('I have my reason here [*touching her forehead*]' (*Le nozze di Figaro*, Act 1, Scene 1). Briefly, Susanna becomes the expression of reason contained in wit, which will conquer pride, arrogance and stupidity.[17] The 'bell duet' introduces yet another object symbol: the bell, symbol of the ruling class, to which the servants must answer:

> Così se il mattino
> Il caro Contino:
> Din, din, e ti manda
> Tre miglia lontan,
> Din din, e a mia porta
> Il diavol lo porta
> Ed ecco in tre salti. . . .
> (*Le nozze di Figaro*, Act 1, Scene 1)

(So if in the morning the dear little Count, ding ding, and he sends you three miles away. Ding ding and the devil so leads him to my door, and look, with three leaps. . . .)

Figaro's reply to the bell is introduced in the form of another symbolic object – the guitar. This instrument, associated with popular music and the popular tradition, will be the means by which Figaro will play a splendid tune, and lead the Count on a merry dance. The plot so develops in terms of a dance, in keeping with the Italian expression *portare in ballo* meaning 'to fool' or 'lead up the garden path'. At key moments in the plot the term *ballo* will appear, often alternating with references to the *marcia*, or march, alluding to the world of political combat. The term dance and the significance of the guitar are introduced in Act 1, Scene 2. The source is to be found in the Beaumarchais *Mariage*: from the two words, 'Dansez monseigneur' ('Dance, Sir'), Da Ponte has taken inspiration for the entire direction of his comedy.

>Se vuol ballare,
>Signor Contino,
>Il chitarrino
>Le suonerò.
>Se vuol venire
>Nella mia scola,
>La capriola
>Le insegnerò.
>Saprò ... ma piano
>Meglio ogni arcano
>Dissimulando
>Scoprir potrò
>L'arte schermendo,
>L'arte adoprando,
>Di qua pungendo,
>Di là scherzando,
>Tutte le macchine rovescierò.
>(*Le nozze di Figaro*, Act 1, Scene 2)

(If you wish to dance, my lord Count I will play my sweet guitar for you. If you wish to come to my school I will teach you some capers. I will know ... but quietly. I will be better able to discover every mystery by means of intrigue, by concealment, by adopting guile. Here stinging, there joking I will overturn all machines.)

The dance shall be one led by the common people, to the tune of their traditions, which shall teach its own lesson. By means of wit and intrigue, social order shall be reversed. As the plot develops and the Count's subjects, in the company of Figaro who is carrying a white wedding gown, sing in unison in praise of the Count's apparent abolition of his feudal rights, Figaro informs Susanna of the irony behind the gesture with the words: 'Eccoci in danza' ('Here we are dancing'). It is the first collective action in the libretto staged in order to embarrass the Count, and to convey to the public that the true subject of the drama is the freedom and rights of the individual. Such a dance, then, which the Count will be led, is in total contrast to the aristocratic balls to which he and his kind are accustomed. Cherubino, the amorous butterfly and *cicisbeo* in training, on taking the commission in the Count's regiment is reminded that his usual steps will be replaced by the music of combat: 'Ed invece del fandango/Una marcia per il fango' ('And instead of the fandango, a march through mud') (*Le nozze di Figaro*, Act 1, Scene 8).

Further reference is made to the dance in Act 2, Scene 10, when as prank is piled upon prank the Count exclaims: 'Che pazienza, finiamo questo ballo' ('What patience, let us be done with this dance'). As the intrigue moves towards its conclusion the fateful assignation with Susanna is set for 'L'ora del ballo' ('the hour of the ball'). Finally, as all concludes happily, those present depart 'al ballo, al gioco' ('to dance and to gamble') to the sound of 'lieta marcia' ('a merry march'). It is, however, on a note of military merriment that the libretto concludes. The day of bizarre pranks has come to a close and the merry march can be interpreted both as a reminder of the victory of Susanna and Figaro, whose marriage can now be celebrated, or as an insinuation of a military confrontation still to come.

Figaro and Susanna represent an enlightenment based on freedom and justice, looking to a brighter future. The figures of Dr Bartolo and Marcellina provide a skit on the old system, governed by codes, systems and doctrines. Bartolo (Bartholo), in the first play of the Beaumarchais triology, *Le Barbier de Séville*, sought the hand of his young ward, Rosine. The latter, with the aid of Figaro, succeeded in marrying Count Almaviva. Bartolo, by way of revenge, desires to give his old servant Marcellina to Figaro, as his wife! He calls on all the systems of the legal code to defend his cause and aid his revenge, which he defines as 'un piacer serbato ai saggi' ('a pleasure reserved for sages'):

> Se tutto il codice – dovessi volgere,
> Se tutto l'indice – dovessi leggere,
> Con un equivoco, – con un sinonimo
> Qualche garbuglio si troverà.
> (*Le nozze di Figaro*, Act 1, Scene 2)

(If I have to go through the entire Penal Code, if I have to read the entire Index, with an equivocation – with a synonym. Some loophole will be found.)

In this way the legal and judicial systems of the eighteenth century are held to ridicule. Just as Almaviva is defeated by Susanna and Figaro, so too are Bartolo and Marcellina both outclassed in astuteness by the servant Figaro. While being enlightened as regards their own social responsibilities they are forced to recognize Figaro as their long-lost child. While the rationalistic attitude to being and behaviour combined with wit leads to happiness for the serving class, the black art and contrivance of Bartolo, based on preconceptions and prejudice, can only end in final ridicule. In the face of pure reason, the arrogant pretensions of the Count carry him to a tribunal over which he presides, but from which he is forced to seek pardon. The final foil in the trick to expose the Count is the participation of his wife in the game of social pretence. Not only does she call on her servant for help, and plot on a level with her, but in masquerading as her, she is contributing threefold to the complexity of the comedy. In good old-fashioned comic tradition disguise and discovery play a part in the exposure of evil and the defence of good. In keeping with courtly customs, the couples, in disguise, can mingle as they please. This provides a gentle dig at social corruption. Finally, in changing cloaks with her servant, the Countess is agreeing to don the vest of service, if only to bring the game to an honourable conclusion. Yet the game serves to illustrate that although love is seen as a vehicle for the entertainment of the aristocracy, the lighthearted can be interpreted seriously and would-be serious attitudes can be held to ridicule. The masters have been outwitted by their servants, and in a future generation, when wit, as opposed to wealth, shall call the tune, in the words of Figaro, 'all machines shall be overturned'.

The year following the first production of Mozart's *Le nozze di Figaro* at the Teatro di Corte, Da Ponte's second libretto for the same composer received public acclaim when the opera was presented at the Teatro Nazionale, Prague. Mozart's *Don Giovanni*, described as a *dramma giocoso in due atti* (a lighthearted drama in two acts), was not, however, the first drama or opera to appear on the subject.[18] The text is based on the legend of the libertine and the stone guest who exacts retribution from him.

This has roots buried deep in folk history. The legend was dramatized in Spain, France, Britain and Italy. Before Da Ponte collaborated with Mozart, Gabriel Tellez of Madrid, a monk of the Mercedarian order, who wrote a series of plays under the name of Tirso de Molina, appears to be the first known dramatist associated with Don Juan. His drama on the notorious libertine is entitled *El burlador de Sevilla y Convidado de Pietra*, and it was first published in 1630. The protagonist is very vividly drawn, but the most outstanding feature of the drama is that it emerges as a satire on the licentiousness of the Spanish aristocracy. It therefore serves as a vehicle for social criticism, and as such must definitely have influenced Molière, whose *Don Juan, ou le festin de pierre* was first performed at the Palais-Royal, Paris, in 1665, with the author himself in the role of Sganarelle, valet to Don Juan. Molière presents his work as a moral drama, containing lectures on personal behaviour and contemplation of repentance, with the final emphasis placed on the damnation of the protagonist whose final dinner engagement takes place in hell.[19]

The first musical version of the Don Giovanni legend was by the Italian composer Alessandro Melani. His opera, *L'empio punito*, was performed in Rome in the presence of Queen Christina of Sweden in 1669. The English musician Henry Purcell provided incidental music for Thomas Shadwell's *The Libertine*, first performed in 1676. Carlo Goldoni's *Don Giovanni Tenorio, o sia il dissoluto* was one of the works performed at the carnival season at the Teatro San Samuele in 1736. By the end of the eighteenth century the Don Giovanni theme was one of the most popular subjects for dramas, operas, ballets and long poems. In 1787 alone, to quote Elizabeth Forbes,[20] there were five different musical versions. The first of these was by Giuseppe Gazzaniga, with a libretto by Giovanni Bertati. Bertati's libretto has been criticized for lacking the refinement and charm of Da Ponte's version, yet it must be admitted that it was highly influential,[21] while preserving the comic atmosphere of the improvised theatre. Da Ponte appears to have followed the framework provided by Bertati. Both dramatists provide a catalogue aria, lady-victims of the Don's lasciviousness, a dissatisfied servant, and a cemetery and supper scene. Some of the names are identical in both works: Donna Anna and Donna Elvira perform similar roles in both librettos, Maturina becomes Zerlina in Da Ponte's version, while Pasquariello, in Bertati's work rather similar to a *commedia dell'arte* Arlecchino, becomes less boisterous and more self-assertive in the form of Da Ponte's Leporello. Bertati, although less refined, brilliant and dramatically precise than Da Ponte, does present a social portrait of the eighteenth century and its uses, never ceasing to provide a skit on its more serious aspects. The catalogue aria is indeed a parody on the lists and information dear to the heart of the eighteenth-century bureaucrat.[22] What is also noteworthy is the fact that Don Giovanni, although an aristocrat, does not indulge in social distinctions: his inability to resist female charm makes him a democratic wrong-doer:

> Fra madame, cittadine,
> artigiani, contadini,
> cameriere, cuoche, e quattere,
> perchè basta che sian femmine
> per doverle amoreggiar.
> (*Don Giovanni*, Act 1, Scene 2)

(Ladies, girls from the city, working girls, and those from the provinces, maids, cooks and kitchen maids. They only need be women for him to fall in love with them.)

The libretto draws on the works of Tirso and Molière in the choice of the ladies illustrating the Don's conquests. Donna Anna exists in the Tirso drama, Donna Elvira and Maturina are both drawn from Molière. In addition he projects a new character, Donna Ximena, in the second and third scenes. Although the social dimension is not neglected by Bertati, he looks to the improvised theatre in his drawing of the servant figure. Pasquariello is presented as primarily an entertainer with little true dramatic function. His indulgence in slapstick comedy also helps to keep the pace moving. This figure of fun contrasts sharply with the ruthless seducer, conferring on the drama an element of the morality play. Retribution is the real subject of the libretto which develops in terms of a conflict between good and evil. The administration of justice is touched upon at the opening by Anna and in Scene 5 by Elvira. Finally the Commendatore states that he is the propagator of divine justice:

> Verrai tu a cena meco?
> Dammi la man per pegno.
> Eccola – ohimè, qual gelo!

OF SERVANTS AND MASTERS

> Pentiti, e temi il cielo
> che stanco è omai di te.
> (*Don Giovanni*, Act 1, Scene 5)

(Will you come to supper with me? Give me your hand as a pledge. Here it is – alas, how cold it feels! Repent and fear heaven, which has tired of you.)

When turning to an analysis of Da Ponte's libretto, it must at once be stated that the character of Don Giovanni is drawn on more heroic lines than in Bertati's work. He assumes the proportions of an anti-hero, resplendent in his decadence, which carries all the attributes of the corrupt aristocrat. Da Ponte has succeeded in drawing his characters on diverse scales. The Don towers over the other personae, who in truth are no more than symbolic abstractions, while the figure of the Commendatore is the dramatic externalization of the guilt which the liberal Don does not sense. In creating Leporello, Da Ponte provides a servant with none of the sophistication, guile or enlightened foresight of Figaro. Neither does he possess the clownish attributes of the servant-entertainer. He is one who expresses dissatisfaction with his master rather than with his social status. Although at the opening of the work he dreams of being a gentleman, such aspirations, he knows, are out of the question. At its conclusion he sets out for the tavern in order to find a new master. Our first impression of Don Giovanni is formed as a result of Leporello's words:

> Notte e giorno faticar
> per chi nulla sa gradir,
> piova o vento sopportar,
> mangiar male e mal dormir!
> Voglio fare il gentiluomo,
> e non voglio più servir.
> (*Don Giovanni*, Act 1, Scene 1)

(To toil night and day for one who does not appreciate anything. To put up with wind and rain, eat and sleep badly! I wish to live like a gentleman, I don't wish to serve any longer.)

In popular language the gentleman enjoys the lady while his servant is left out in the cold:

> Vuol star dentro con la bella
> ed io far la sentinella.
> (*Don Giovanni*, Act 1, Scene 1)

(He wishes to stay indoors with the lady, while I remain on guard.)

In fact Leporello speaks with the voice of common sense, with no pretensions towards social advancement or intellectual understanding. His is a vocabulary based on fact, as opposed to the fancy of his master:

> Caro signor padrone,
> la vita che menate è da briccone.
> (*Don Giovanni*, Act 1, Scene 4)

(My dear master, you lead the life of a rascal.)

Similarly, the ruthlessness of the protagonist is not conveyed by his own expression, which in itself would be an admission of guilt. Rather, his escapades and crimes are described and dramatized by those who witness them first-hand, namely Leporello, as already seen, and Donna Elvira and Donna Anna. Donna Elvira's tale of woe is told in the fourth scene of the first act, in the form of a confrontation with Don Giovanni:

> Cosa puoi dire
> Dopo azion sì nera? In casa mia
> entri furtivamente. A forza d'arte
> di giuramenti e di lusinghe, arrivi
> a sedurre il cor mio.
> (*Don Giovanni*, Act 1, Scene 4)

(Whatever can you say in the wake of such a dark deed? You enter my house secretly. By force of deceit, solemn promises and flattery you succeed in seducing my heart.)

Donna Anna's experience is told in more lengthy terms: the Don has combined forceful entry, disguise and seduction with murder, while fleeing for safety in the wake of his destruction. Her great scene concludes with a cry for revenge ('Or sai chi l'onore/rapire a me volse'), which is echoed collectively at the conclusion of the first act:

> Trema, trema scellerato,
> saprà tosto il mondo intero

> il misfatto orrendo e nero,
> la tua fiera crudeltà.
> Odi il tuon della vendetta
> che ti fischia intorno, intorno;
> sul tuo capo in questo giorno
> il suo fulmine cadrà.
> (*Don Giovanni*, Act 1, Scene 12)

(Tremble, tremble, evil one, soon the world at large will know of the horrid black deed, of your ferocious cruelty. Hear the thunder of revenge that whistles all around. On this very day its lightning shall strike your head.)

Justice, as is the case in *Le nozze di Figaro*, is finally seen to be done. The opera concludes with the old maxim 'as you live, so shall you die!' Da Ponte's *Don Giovanni* can be defined as a 'moral comedy' as opposed to a social one. The protagonist is an example of the Casanova-like adventurer, whose ribaldry was common among eighteenth-century aristocrats enjoying their last fling before perishing in the wake of the new established order. Don Giovanni himself is a portrait of social irresponsibility, which is manifested in one of his few expansive arias:

> Senza alcun ordine
> la danza sia:
> chi il minuetto,
> chi la follia,
> chi l'alemanna
> farai ballar.
> Ed io frattanto
> dall'altro canto
> con questa e quella
> vo'amoreggiar.
> (*Don Giovanni*, Act 1, Scene 15)

(Without further ado let there be dancing. Some the minuet, more folly and others the allemand, you will make perform. I, in the meantime, in another quarter wish to make love with this or that lady.)

Is Don Giovanni then a fully grown Cherubino? Daniela Goldin, in her study *La vera fenice*, has already posed the question,[23] alluding to various derivatives from the previous text for Mozart.

It would appear that in *Le nozze di Figaro* Da Ponte is illustrating the training, attributes and attire of the young page, the future *cavaliere servente*. In *Don Giovanni* he demonstrates the result of such a training: guilt replaces innocence, the serenade is allied to seduction, and the punishment of his superiors leads to the enactment of divine justice. It is a moral drama, which provides the fusion of serious and comic elements, and the coming together of the classes in an all-out combat against social corruption.

Da Ponte's third libretto for Mozart, *Così fan tutte*, is actually a work about the attainment of balance in society, the pursuit of moderation and the acceptance of life as it is, as opposed to as it ought to be. The title, anticipated in *Le nozze di Figaro*, in the words of Don Basilio (Act 1, Scene 7), 'Così fan tutte le belle', refers in fact to the flirtations of women. Although this is the libretto's point of departure, its true function is the relevation of a philosophy of common sense, as expounded by the servant-soubrette Despina. The projection of the doctrine of practicality is contained in the enactment of a contrived situation, stage-managed by the philosopher ex-cathedra Don Alfonso, in all matters the 'master', and performed by Despina, the servant. The result is a play within a play, cast in the same vein as Figaro's merry dance, as a school or *scola* regarding enlightened behaviour is introduced:

> Se vuol venire
> nella mia scola
> La capriola
> Le insegnerò.
> (*Le nozze di Figaro*, Act 1, Scene 2)

(If you wish to come to my school I will teach you some capers.)

> Par ch'abbian gusto – di tal dottrina;
> viva Despina – che sa servir.
> (*Così fan tutte*, Act 2, Scene 1)

(It seems that they relish such a doctrine. Long live Despina, who knows how to serve.)

In the case of both librettos, the servant assumes the role of enlightened teacher. Despina is both linguistically, dramatically and philosophically Figaro's counterpart, although the moral purpose of *Le nozze di Figaro* could be regarded as the demonstration of the infidelity of men. On the contrary, *Così fan tutte* highlights the fickleness of women which, as will be seen, serves its own social and moral purpose. Figaro is the symbol of advanced thinking and the social progress of the serving class. Despina represents the ability to convert eighteenth-century doctrines, theories and systems to the language of common sense.[24] The opera was first presented in 1790, at the K.K. National-Hof Theater, Vienna, and like *Don Giovanni* is described as a *dramma giocoso*. It was harshly criticized at its first performance for being silly and frivolous; to this day, the libretto is the subject of heated discussion. Gerhart von Westerman places it in the same category as those which 'in spite of all their beauty enjoyed no lasting success because of their poor texts'.[25] Ernst Von Possant (the first Intendant of the Prince Regent Theatre in Munich) in the wake of attempts to rewrite the text remounted the work in its original form, stressing its *buffo* characteristics. The plot is as follows: Ferrando and Guglielmo are convinced of the fidelity of their future brides, Dorabella and Fiordiligi. Don Alfonso, the sophisticated philosopher, does not believe in women's constancy and proposes a bet: the gentlemen are to disguise themselves in order to test the ladies' faithfulness. Alfonso wins over the maid Despina, and between them they undermine the girl's strict moral code. Each one then falls in love with the fiancé of the other. When the trick is revealed the ladies are forced to admit their transgressions. Don Alfonso has won his wager.

The world of the *commedia dell'arte* is projected in terms of a battle of wits, the game of pretence, the disguise of the gentlemen and later of Despina.[26] Yet this is not merely a plot of fun and games, or an example of social elegance versed in Arcadian sophistication. It is a lesson about life and living expounded from without by Don Alfonso, and from within by Despina, cast in the roles of master and servant respectively. In the end it is *finzione*, or pretence, as communicated in Despina's doctrine of common sense which wins the day. Her lesson can be absorbed in two principal sermons, the first being in her description of men, the counterpart of Figaro's opinion of women:

> Di pasta simile – son tutti quanti;
> le fronde mobili, – l'aure incostanti
> han più degli uomini – stabilità.

Mentite lagrime – fallaci sguardi,
voci ingannevoli – vezzi bugiardi
son le primarie lor qualità.
(*Così fan tutte*, Act 1, Scene 9)

(They are all tarred with the same brush! Waving branches and inconstant breezes are more stable than men. Crocodile tears, false glances, deceiving voices, lying charms are their outstanding qualities.)

It is interesting to compare Figaro's more lengthy invective against women with the above:

> Son streghe che incantano
> per farci penar.
> Sirene che cantano
> per farci affogar;
> Civette che alletano
> Per trarci le piume
> Comete che brillano
> per toglierci il lume.
> Son rose spinose,
> Son volpi vezzose
> Son orse benigne,
> Colombe maligne.
> Maestre d'inganni
> Amiche d'affanni
> Che fingono, mentono,
> Che amore non sentono.
> Non sentono pietà.
> (*Le nozze di Figaro*, Act 4, Scene 8)

(They are enchanting witches in order to make us suffer. Singing sirens, in order to suffocate us. Coquettes that ensnare, in order to humiliate us. Shining comets, in order to deprive us of light. They are prickly roses, charming wolves, benign bears, malignant doves, mistresses of deceptions, friends in time of suffering who pretend, lie, and feel no love. They feel no pity.)

Both arias reveal Da Ponte, master of extemporary composition, employing variation, contrast, colour and imagination in his descriptions of amorous activity. Despina's second lesson is an account of what women should know by the age of 15, and how they should behave.

> una donna a quindici anni – dee saper ogni gran moda,
> dee saper le maliziette – che innamorano gli amanti,
> finger riso, finger pianti – inventar i bei perché.
> Dee in un momento – dar retta a cento;
> colle pupille – parlar con mille,
> dar speme a tutti, sien belli o brutti,
> saper nascondersi – senza confondersi,
> senza arrossire – saper mentire
> e, qual regina – dall'alto soglio,
> col 'posso e voglio' – farsi ubbidir.
> (*Così fan tutte*, Act 2, Scene 1)

(A woman of fifteen years should be acquainted with every great fashion. She should know of the mischievous acts which ensnare lovers. How to feign laughs, tears and invent the most convincing excuses. She must pay attention to one hundred suitors at a time and speak a language of glances with a thousand, be they handsome or ugly, she must give them all hope. She must know how to cover up, without showing embarrassment. She must be able to lie, without blushing. And as a queen from her high throne, see that she is obeyed with the words 'I can' and 'I so wish'.)

Apart from the enchanting images of feminine guile, the libretto, in terms of distribution of arias and duets, points to the eternal social conflict between concerted accord and individualism. Da Ponte's true opinion on the subject is a matter for speculation. At the commencement of the plot we find Ferrando betrothed to Dorabella, and Guglielmo to Fiordiligi. At once one is touched by the lack of characterization adopted by Da Ponte: the gentlemen, if not singing together, merely repeat a variant on the words of the other:

> La mia Dorabella – capace non è,
> fedel quanto bella – il cielo la fè.
> (*Così fan tutte*, Act 1, Scene 1)

(My Dorabella is not capable [of infidelity], heaven made her as faithful as she is beautiful.)

> La mia Fiordiligi – tradirmi non sa,
> uguale in lei credo – costanza e beltà.
> (*Così fan tutte*, Act 1, Scene 1)

(My Fiordiligi does not know how to betray me. Both constancy and beauty to exist in her in equal measure.)

In the same way the ladies sing eulogies of their handsome gentlemen, first separately and then in unison:

> Ah guarda sorella, – se bocca più bella,
> se aspetto più nobile – si può ritrovar.
> (*Così fan tutte*, Act 1, Scene 2)

(Ah sister look – if a more pleasing mouth, a more noble appearance can be found.)

> Osserva tu un poco – osserva che fuoco,
> che fuoco ha ne' sguardi, – se fiamma
> se dardi
> non sembran scoccar.
> (*Così fan tutte*, Act 1, Scene 2)

(Look you a moment, see what fire, what fire is in his glances. Is it not true that they seem to shoot flames and darts?)

In assessing the two couples it emerges that the dominant figures are Ferrando and Fiordiligi. Each takes the initiative in praising their lover. With the introduction of the disguise and the reappearance of the gentlemen, Dorabella, originally bound to Ferrando, succumbs to the charms of Guglielmo. Eventually, with some persuasion, Fiordiligi accepts the advances of Ferrando. The result is an overturning of social balance and the laws by which opposites attract. Strong is partnered with strong, weak with weak. The ladies and gentlemen now assume more individualistic characters. Each sings alone and becomes a more convincing persona. This is the result of Despina's doctrine of common sense and Alfonso's philosophical approach to the feminine character. The final reunion of the couples indicates the restoration of order and balance, coupled with the need for acceptance of human frailty. The deception of the ladies has proved the illumination of the gentlemen.[27]

V'ingannai, ma fu l'inganno – disinganno ai vostri amanti,
che più saggi ormai saranno, – che faran quel ch'io vorrò.
(*Così fan tutte*, Act 2, Scene 18)

(I deceived you, but the same deception was a relevation to your lovers, who shall now be wiser, who will do as I wish.)

The episode has led to rational behaviour on the part of the ladies as opposed to their former irrational attitude towards life. Spontaneity and emotional reactions lead to a rationalizing of behaviour. The opera ends with all present singing in praise of common sense and the acceptance of reality, guided by reason:

Fortunato l'uomo che prende – ogni cosa pel buon verso
e tra casi e le vicende – da ragion guidar si fa
Quel che suole altrui far piangere – fia per lui cagion di riso
e del mondo in mezzo ai turbini – bella calma troverà.
(*Così fan tutte*, Act 2, Scene 18)

(Happy is the man who takes everything in his stride, and in situations and events allows himself to be guided by reason. Let that which is usually a cause for tears, for him be a source of laughter. And in the midst of the upheavals of the world, he will find precious calm.)

Così fan tutte is then not merely a frivolous situation piece in which bets and disguises contribute to the comic action. Rather, it is an illustration of enlightened attitudes at a time when the age of reason was drawing to a close. Together with *Le nozze di Figaro* it constitutes Da Ponte's humorous, whimsical view of a privileged social order in its final phase. Both comedies express a philosophy of behaviour, communicated by the serving class. *Le nozze di Figaro* points towards a change of social structures. *Così fan tutte* is about a change of social attitudes. In each libretto there emerges the undeniable fact: that servants shall soon be masters.

Part II
THE EXPRESSION OF INDIVIDUALISM

5

A CRY FOR FREEDOM: HIGH PRIESTS AND PATRIOTS

I

In Italy, during the Napoleonic regime, which coincides with the neo-classical era in art, itself an aspect of romantic idealism, the seeds of a new individualism, local patriotism and growing nationalism were sown. Following in the wake of the age of reason, which advocated adherence to a purely scientific approach to human behaviour, and heralded by the external forces of the French revolution, the Napoleonic regime was a time of reflection during which a new concept of identity was contemplated. The French brought with them a more efficient method of administration, and a more enlightened code of law than hitherto experienced. With the defeat and departure of Napoleon and the 1814–15 Restoration, the Emperor's reforms lapsed, and the aristocracy recovered their privileges and power. Yet as a direct result of the death of the old order there emerged a new agricultural and enterprising middle class. It was on a practical rather than on a patriotic level that these middle classes came to support an idea of Italian unification. To many it appeared unnecessary to have eight separate states in Italy, each with tariff barriers, individual coinage and laws. In Austrian Lombardy local patriotism flourished, and accusations of exploitation were made against the government. Above all there existed in the minds of the new industrialist class an aspiration towards centralized government which might protect economic interests. Lombardy was to become the centre of the Italian patriotic opera and of the 'new' Italian culture. While practical factors weighed as heavily as patriotic endeavours in the pursuit of Italian unity, opera, by its nature heroic, found in the political and social structures of the day a worthy cause. Ideals of nationalist idealism were cultivated by composers and librettists in order to fire public enthusiasm. This in no small way contributed to the march towards Italian unity by providing an emotional outlet for a province with a history of Spanish, French and Austrian occupations.

Following the series of reforms and counter-reforms it underwent in the eighteenth century, the Italian opera drew its inspiration from French classical drama. The *opera seria* of the close of the eighteenth century and the early years of the nineteenth was a musical enactment of classical tragedy. Two examples are Cherubini's *Médée*, with a libretto by F.B. Hoffman (1797), and Spontini's *La vestale*, with a text by Etienne de Jouy (1807). From the time of its origin Italian opera had been associated with the peninsula's principal cultural and theatrical centres, in addition to such European cities as Vienna, Prague and Paris. Notwithstanding the popularity of the art-form throughout the country, during the seventeenth century and for the greater part of the eighteenth, there was no principal operatic centre in Italy. Venice had yielded its primacy to Naples, and pride of place later went to the Court Theatre of Vienna. It was not until 1778, with the opening of the Teatro alla Scala in Milan, that a true centre of Italian opera was seen to exist. Here the diverse and contrasting genres of the art-form were produced. Soon the theatre became accepted as the principal focus of music in Italy. It was to provide a unifying force and, later in the century, the stage on which the romantic struggle between freedom and servitude, heroism and tyranny, would be played out, as the opera became the instrument of nationalistic fervour.

The nineteenth century witnessed the birth of organized nationalism in Italy. The close association between the Risorgimento and the romantic movement is the result of an orientation of all art-forms towards the goals of freedom and unity: poets, artists, dramatists and musicians directed their attention to themes and images of individual, social and national freedom, while on a theological and philosophical level the freedom of the will and the suppression of spontaneous expression were topics contained in historical novels such as Ugo Foscolo's *Le ultime lettere di Jacopo Ortis*,[1] Alessandro Manzoni's *I promessi sposi*[2] and Tommaso Grossi's *Marco Visconti*.[3]

After the final defeat of Napoleon at Waterloo, the Treaty of Vienna, concluded in 1815, reshaped the map of Europe and restored Italy to a state similar to that of 1748. The principal changes were as follows: since the congress which drafted the treaty did not favour republics the three outstanding examples were not restored. The Veneto became part of the Austrian Empire, along with Lombardy. Genoa was given to Piedmont and Lucca became a duchy. This reduced the number of political units in Italy from eleven to eight. The renewed Austrian supremacy in northern Italy effected an uneasy peace. The settlement created a number of enemies to the regime. The intellectuals resented the renewed influence of the aristocracy and the clergy. The progressive Lombards had grown to resent and decry the continued foreign domination. Venetians witnessed the autonomy of their republic vanish for all time. Since the Italians had traditionally manifested their patriotism in their love of a single town rather than of a nation, it is not surprising that nationalism began to emerge at a local level for the social, economic and intellectual reasons already referred to. Secret societies sprang up in Lombardy, Tuscany, the Papal States and Naples. The 'Sublime Perfect Masters', the 'Italian Federation' and the 'Carbonari' are the most outstanding examples. Although Italian nationalism was not originally among the declared aims of the societies, they emerged as pressure groups advocating liberal reforms. The 'Italian Federation' (1818–20) declared that its function was the liberation of Lombardy and the Veneto, which would then be linked with Piedmont in a constitutional monarchy. The most famous of the societies, the 'Carbonari', planned an armed revolution. In relation to the development of Italian political literature and opera, the most famous 'Carbonaro' Giuseppe Mazzini (1805–72) merits brief consideration, alongside his contemporary Vincenzo Gioberti. These adopted the attitudes of the early romantic writers such as Foscolo, Pellico[4] and Manzoni, who projected the national spirit as part of a structured political ideal.

Mazzini had joined the 'Carbonari' in 1827. He became disillusioned with them when they failed to respond to the July revolution of 1830 in Paris. While in prison in Savona he determined to work for the independence and unification of Italy, and set about founding his own movement, 'Young Italy'. He described his own philosophy around God, unity in humanity, and progress. He felt that the outstanding doctrine of the nineteenth century was democracy. He was convinced that his mission was to construct a revolutionary society which would teach a sense of national identity while preparing the revolution which would establish an independent, democratic Italian republic. The function of art was particularly significant in this vision. It was seen as the mouthpiece of ideal values and the revolutionary spirit. This is the role it performs in the poems of Vincenzo Monti (1754–1828), Giovanni Berchet (1783–1851) and above all in the epistolary novel *Le ultime lettere di Jacopo Ortis*.

Mazzini, it may be said, evolved a religion of patriotism, and his views concided to a considerable extent with those of Gioberti, a Piedmontese priest. But Gioberti's assessment of the needs of the masses – spiritual as well as material and social – led him to envisage the future Italy not as a republic but as a confederation of states under the pope – at the time Pius IX. His conception of brotherhood was derived from Pellico's tragedy *Francesca da Rimini*.[5] This vision of a new Italy (referred to as the 'neo-Guelf' vision) is set forth in his *Del primato morale e civile degli Italiani* (1843). Such principles gained a certain measure of popular support, and, as will be seen later, are echoed in Francesco Maria Piave's libretto for Giuseppe Verdi's opera *Ernani*.

It is clear that the patriotic literature of Foscolo, Pellico and Manzoni, containing veiled and ambiguous references to freedom, brotherhood and the individual's right to choose his or her own destiny, proved a source of inspiration to political thinkers evolving a theory of unification. But it must also be borne in mind that the religious spirit associated with patriotism in the thinking of Gioberti and Mazzini had already been given dramatic life on the operatic stage. Although Rossini's last opera, *Guglielmo Tell* (1829), with a libretto by S. de Jouy and I. Bis, has frequently been referred to as the first patriotic opera, patriotism in a serious vein had first been given expression in Gaetano Rossi's libretto for Rossini's *Tancredi* (1813), and in a satirical vein in Angelo Anelli's text *L'italiana in Algieri* (1813) for the same composer.

But the patriotic work with religious undertones that best illustrates and dramatizes the true spirit of the Risorgimento has hitherto been given little critical attention. This chapter is therefore devoted to a consideration of the librettos of Rossini's *Mosè* (1827) by an unknown librettist, Felice Romani's *Norma*,[6] written for Vincenzo Bellini, and three texts set by Giuseppe Verdi: Temistocle Solera's *Nabucco* (1842) and *I lombardi alla prima crociata* (1843),[7] and Francesco Maria Piave's *Ernani* (1848).[8]

An analysis of these works involves a consideration of the

librettist as an adaptor of French and English tragic texts. Such an approach has been adopted by Franca Cella in her most erudite studies of the French sources of the operas of Bellini and Donizetti.[9] My intention in this chapter and the next is to consider the influences of eighteenth-century cloister poetry, the tragedies of Vittorio Alfieri[10] and the lyrical light imagery of Giacomo Leopardi[11] on the poetic and dramatic expression of Romani, Solera and Piave. In addition, these chapters will underline the relationship between operatic texts and the literature of Grossi and Manzoni, illustrating and underlining the fact that there are significant analogies linking Italian romantic prose and operatic texts.

II

By way of approach to a consideration of the figure of the nun and priestess in Italian literature, it is interesting to note certain features which recur in all three of the librettos *Mosè*, *Norma* and *Nabucco*, which appeared in 1827, 1831 and 1842 respectively. Each text tells of a chosen race, the Hebrews in the case of *Mosè* and *Nabucco*, and in the case of *Norma*, the Druids. In each instance the race in question is distinguished by the nobility of its ritual and its endurance in the face of years of foreign oppression; in each, the cultural and spiritual values of the oppressed race are bound up with its steadfastness and sacrifice dictated by its leader or high priest. All the three dramas embody the cult of leadership and an association between ritual and patriot. Moses is the leader of the Hebrew people, their high priest who crosses the Red Sea with them. Norma, too, is the leader of her people, the high priestess of the Druids, daughter of Oroveso, himself a high priest. Zaccaria, who has a key role in *Nabucco*, is the high priest of the Hebrews, whose temple is desecrated by the tyrant Nabucodonosor. Each of the three operas opens with a scene in which the high priest and a chorus lament the circumstances of the people. In both *Mosè* and *Nabucco* the voices are raised in a prayer which combines religion with patriotism. In *Norma* the prayer comes slightly later, in Scene 3, when Norma beseeches the pagan goddess of the moon to grant her people peace and the postponement of an angry uprising.

The three operas are conceived with a struggle between rival races, a conflict between spirituality and barbarity and between a hero and a tyrant. In addition, there is contained the love interest, at the level of sub-plot in *Mosè* and *Nabucco*, but as part of the central conflict in *Norma*. In each opera traditional enemies fall in love, and conversion, sacrifice and divine wrath provide the final conclusions.

The role of the high priest and leader became traditionally associated with the bass voice, and was intended to be portrayed in a somewhat static manner, in order to convey dignity and wisdom, the products of age and contemplation. In addition, the success of such works led to the nineteenth-century convention of most operatic works opening with a chorus, providing a lyrical introduction to the circumstances of the action, and introducing the soloist, whose opening declamations consisted of a recitative, a *cavatina* and a *cabaletta*. The *cavatina* consisted of a slow, restrained aria usually requiring a purity of emission based on a controlled *legato*. The *cabaletta* provided an aside or change of mood, contrasting in tempo with the *cavatina*, and containing two verses. The first verse was sung 'straight', without ornamentation or decoration. The second verse, or *ritornello*, was decorated according to the taste and vocal ability of the singer. The *scena* also consisted of choral interjections, leading to a stunning climax, as in the case of the *scena* 'Sediziosi voci. ... Casta Diva. ... Ah! bello a me ritorna' in the first act of *Norma*. The romantic opera, to quote Patrick Smith in *The Tenth Muse*,[12] developed as a series of duets, arias and trios, and as a result of a fusion of French melodramatic and romantic devices and postures, became exaggeratedly human, as the *opera seria* of the seventeenth and eighteenth centuries had been exaggeratedly ideal. The patriotic themes of religion and the cult of leadership, however, brought the dignity of the earlier *opera seria* to the nineteenth century, while relying on the poetic quality of the verse and the solemnity of the plot to create the tragic effect.

The popularity of the figure of the nun and the priestess in Italian literature can in fact be traced to the early eighteenth century, and to the popularity of Alexander Pope's heroic epistle *Eloisa to Abelard*. The work tells of the suffocated passion of the protagonist, physically and emotionally imprisoned in the world of the cloister. Taking the form of the poetic juxtaposition of the active and contemplative life, it contains memories of innocence and guilt, along with a controlled longing for a sinless, happier state. It is above all a logical argument, punctuated with emotional yearning, in favour of human love. By the beginning of the nineteenth century the work had been translated four times: by Antonio Conti,[13] Giuseppe Greatti, Pietro Chiari and Gian-Vincenzo Benini. The tone and content of the work obviously impressed, and there were several imitations and derivations including Giuseppe Ceroni, *Lettere di sei donne ai lori sposi ed amanti* (1808); Francesco Gianni, *Eloisa ed Abelardo* (1827); Ippolito Pindemonte, *Lettera di una monaca a Federico IV re di Danimarca*. The most significant original work on the theme of the nun's isolation and guilty love is the *Lettera di Abelardo a Eloisa*, a poem written by Antonio Conti in reply to his own translation of Pope's epistle which was not, however, included in the poet's collection of his works in 1739 and 1756.[14] In both works Eloisa ceases to be the voice of controlled and restrained emotion in a medieval gothic setting, and becomes a romantic heroine spontaneously expressing ardour. The language closely resembles that of the melodrama and differs strongly from the tone of the *poesia di monacazione*, or social poetry of the cloister, which during the eighteenth century marked the withdrawal of a virgin from society in order to enter a religious institution. The tone of the latter, cast in the poetic tradition of Arcadia, and containing elements of Petrarchism and Neoplatonism, was for the most part restrained, and devoid of conflicting emotions. In fact *Il chiostro* ('The cloister') by Luigi Cerretti (1738–1808) and Conti's original work provide the only traces of an emotional response to the religious state.[15]

In 1807 Spontini's *La vestale* was first performed in Paris. It dramatizes the Roman vestal virgin Giulia's profane love, her punishment and subsequent pardon by Vulcan. At the time censorship did not allow for the presentation of a nun guilty of breaking her religious vows. Alessandro Manzoni's drawing of the figure of the Nun of Monza in the historical novel *I promessi sposi* was regarded as acceptable since it did not expose the predicament in the form of public entertainment. The episode in Manzoni's novel provides an example of the suppression of the emotions and their misdirection resulting in a neurotic guilt complex. The psychological portrait of the individual, and the deprivation of freedom of choice, render this nun a personification of the romantic struggle raging in the minds of all whose freedom of will, choice and activity is threatened. A political dimension is provided, in that the action of Manzoni's work takes place during the Spanish occupation of Lombardy, but was penned by Manzoni during the Austrian occupation of the province. From its title, *I promessi sposi*, it is clear that the novel develops as an exposition of the promise and its various levels of significance. Alongside betrothal, and the basic promise of marriage that the protagonists Renzo and Lucia make to one another, there is also represented the flippant bet of Don Rodrigo and the hasty commitment of the Innominato, in addition to the psychological, philosophical and theological assessment of the religious vow. In addition Manzoni takes into account all the personal, social and political attributes of personal commitment, alongside the responsibility contained in the act of freely promising. The binding force of the vow or promise is at all times stressed. Later, in 1831, another figure bound by vows, representative of a religious or social cult at a time of political conflict, appeared on the romantic literary and dramatic scene. This was the Druidic priestess Norma, a political leader and guilty mother, heroine of Felice Romani's tragedy *Norma*, with music by Vincenzo Bellini. The work was first presented at La Scala, Milan, on 26 December 1831, with Giuditta Pasta and Giulia Grisi singing the soprano roles of Norma and Adalgisa. Defined by Gerhart von Westerman as 'a work of austere grandeur',[16] which is still impressive today, its title role has been tackled by all the greatest dramatic sopranos from Pasta to Malibran, Ponselle to Callas and Tietjens to Sutherland.

Of the recent studies of the text, two lengthy essays stand out as examples of research on the sources of the libretto and its poetic quality. They are Franca Cella, 'Indagini sulle fonti francesi dei libretti di Vincenzo Bellini and Guido Paduano, 'Norma: la crisi del modello deliberativo'.[17] The former traces the sources of the work[18] and provides an interesting analysis of 'Casta Diva', Norma's first and principal aria. The latter provides a comparison with Euripides' *Medea* and treats *Norma* as a neo-classical drama. Neither stresses the fact that the work is essentially a romantic one, cast in a neo-classic framework, nor is it made clear that it is a cry for revolution and the expulsion of the Austrians from Lombardy. The Druids are, in fact, the chosen race, the Italians, threatened by the forces of a greater power, Austria. In Romani's libretto the juxtaposition of forces is subtly conceived. The censor was consequently unwilling or unable to prove a political motive for putting the forces of Rome (Austria, the Tyrant) against those of Italy. Romani's message remained clear, while the introduction

7 Felice Romani (1788–1865)

of the march, marking the arrival and departure of Norma and her priestess handmaidens, reinforced the message on a musical level.[19]

Following an overture containing the military motifs heard later in the opera, the curtain rises on ancient Gaul and the grove of the Druids, containing the stone altar to the pagan god Irminsul, and the sacred oak. To the sound of a religious march Gauls and Druids enter, followed by their high priest Oroveso. He announces that at the rise of the moon Norma shall come to cut the sacred mistletoe, so carrying out the Druidic ritual. The first scene takes the form of a prayer on the part of the Druids that the god Irminsul will fill Norma with hatred of the occupying Romans, in order that she declare war. The romantic conflicts of the entire tragedy are apparent in this opening scene: ironically the Druids pray for hatred and war, while in Scene 4 Norma prays for peace, while recalling her love for the Roman proconsul for whom she has broken her vows and borne two children. The scene develops in terms of Leopardian language of light, recapturing the limpid atmosphere of the works of Italy's greatest romantic poet. There is also established the function of light imagery and symbolism in the libretto. The moon is goddess illuminator, and a source of enlightenment.

The cry for war and destruction is launched by the chorus at the beginning of the opera:

> Dell'aura tua profetica
> Terribil Dio, l'informa,
> Sensi, O Irminsul, le ispira
> D'odio ai Romani e d'ira,
> Sensi che questa infrangano
> Pace per noi mortal.
> (*Norma*, Act 1, Scene 1)

(Oh terrible God, inspire her with your prophetic aura. Oh Irminsul, instil in her feelings of anger and hatred against the Romans, feelings that will shatter this peace, which for us is mortal.)

Following Norma's declaration of war, Oroveso foretells the defeat of the Romans by the Gauls:

> Sì: parlerà terribile
> Da queste quercie antiche,
> Sgombre farà le Gallie
> Dall'aquile nemiche;
> E del suo scudo il suono,
> Pari al fragor del tuono,
> Nella città dei Cesari
> Tremendo echeggerà.
> (*Norma*, Act 1, Scene 1)

(Yes, from these ancient oaks she will speak fearfully. She will free the Gauls from the enemy eagle. And the sound of her shield like the crashing of thunder will resound in a terrifying fashion, in the city of the Caesars.)

All those gathered associate the rising moon with the arrival of Norma: 'Luna, ti affretta a sorgere!/Norma all'altar verrà' ('O Moon, make haste, Norma shall approach the altar') (*Norma*, Act 1, Scene 1).

In Act 1, Scene 3 Norma's approach to the altar of Irminsul is marked by a prophecy of war contained in images of light:

> Norma viene: le cinge la chioma
> La verbena ai misteri sacrata;
> In sua man come luna falcata
> L'aurea falce diffonde splendor.
> Ella viene; e la stella di Roma
> Sbigottita si copre d'un velo;
> Irminsul corre i campi del cielo
> Qual cometa foriera d'orror.
> (*Norma*, Act 1, Scene 3)

(Norma approaches: her hair bound with sacred verbena. In her hand, like a crescent moon the golden sickle gives forth a brilliant light. She comes, and the star of Rome, in fright covers herself with a veil. Irminsul shoots through the fields of the sky, as a comet, the purveyor of horror.)

Norma's mission is, however, one of peace, since if she were to declare war, her lover Pollione, as Roman proconsul, would be the first to die. Thus the internal conflict of public and private matters, and the battle between duty and love, are foremost in her mind. Norma, at war with her emotions, prays for peace:

> Casta Diva, che inargenti
> Queste sacre antiche piante,
> A noi volgi il bel sembiante
> Senza nube e senza vel.
> Tempra tu de'cori ardenti,
> Tempra ancora lo zelo audace.
> Spargi in terra quella pace
> Che regnar tu fai nel ciel.
> (*Norma*, Act 1, Scene 4)

(Pure goddess, who ensilvers these ancient and sacred plants, turn your beautiful face to us, devoid of cloud or veil. You temper the burning hearts, temper once again the daring zeal. Spread that peace on earth, that you make reign in heaven.)

At this point in the opera love has been pitted against hatred, war against peace. Norma has allowed personal matters to gain priority over the public will. The priestess has been projected in an aura of light. From the moon she seeks enlightenment, associated with love. At the conclusion of the work, love does conquer, and by confessing her own guilt, Norma finally wins back the love and admiration of Pollione. Romani's drama concludes on a romantic note, avoiding the issues presented by the patriotic theme. Not, however, before Norma gives vent to hatred in her cry for war and revolution: her cry for war and the destruction of all Romans was interpreted by the public of the time as a battle-cry against Austria.

NORMA: Stragi, furore e morti.
Il cantico di guerra alzate, o forti.

Inno Guerriero
TUTTI: Guerra, guerra! Le galliche selve
Quante han quercie producon guerrier;
Qual sul gregge fameliche belve
Sui Romani van essi a cader.

II
Sangue, sangue! Le galliche scuri
Fino al trono bagnate ne son.
Sovra i flutti del Ligeri impuri
Ei gorgoglia con funebre suon.

III
Strage, strage, sterminio, vendetta,
Già comincia, si compie, s'affretta
Come biade da falci mietute
Son di Roma le schiere cadute,
Tronchi i vanni, recisi gli artigli.
Abbattuta ecco l'aquila al suol
A mirar il trionfo de' figli
Ecco il Dio sovra un raggio di sol.

(*Norma*, Act 2, Scene 7)

NORMA:	Carnage, fury and corpses, Raise your voice in battle-hymn, o mighty ones.

War hymn

ALL:	War, war! The Gallic forests produce as many warriors as they have oaks. They prepare to fall on the Romans, as ravenous beasts on a flock of sheep.

II
Blood, blood! The Gallic axes are drenched to the handle, above the impure waves of the Ligeri which gurgles with a dismal sound.

III
Carnage, carnage, extermination, revenge, already it begins, proceeds and is carried out. The Roman ranks fallen, as crops to the sickle. Wings clipped, claws cut, behold the eagle laid low. Contemplating the victory of his children, behold the god, above a ray of sun.)

The above-quoted passages demonstrate the association of war and victory with bloodshed, cruelty and gruesomeness of expression, relieved only by the 'ray of sun' (*un raggio di sol*) of the last line. Although Romani has projected justifiable frustration, ardour and desire for victory, victory and political conflict are not the sole themes or final conclusion to the tragedy. Such patriotic content renders the work expressive of popular feeling and, matched to Bellini's marches, war-cries and dignified processions, assured the opera of popular acclaim. The librettist and composer succeed in merging savagery and dignity in the dramatization of the plight of a primitive yet noble people.

However, Romani's poetry is far more complex than critics have hitherto accepted. In creating a classical drama containing popular elements, and in pitting ceremonial ritual against natural instinct and spontaneous feeling, Romani is in fact presenting both *dignified restraint* and *expression*, attributes of eighteenth- and nineteenth-century poetic form. These contrasting qualities which meet in the character of Norma are also highlighted in her encounters with the rival priestess Adalgisa. Norma represents experience, maturity and control of the situation. Adalgisa is innocence, youth and spontaneity. The language of the former differs considerably from that of the latter. Yet Norma's association with the moon, light imagery and reflections brings her close to the Leopardian world of lyrical romanticism, looking nostalgically to Enlightenment principles. She emerges finally as one who, by means of spontaneity tempered with reason, accepts her own guilt and takes responsibility for it. Adalgisa is cast in the vein of the eighteenth-century figure of the cloister. Her harmonious verses, beautifully conceived, have much in common with the poetic world of Arcadia and passages in Conti's translation of Pope's heroic epistle. Thus the romantic conflict contained in the form and content of the plot is complemented by the contrasting poetic genres contained in the poetry of the two priestesses.

The Arcadian world of the cloister is first evoked by Pollione, with his description of Adalgisa and his dream of their presence together before the altar of Venus in Rome:

> Meco all'altar di Venere
> Era Adalgisa in Roma,
> Cinta di bende candide,
> Sparsa di fior la chioma;
> Udia d'Imene i cantici,
> Vedea fumar gl'incensi.
> (*Norma*, Act 1, Scene 2)

(Adalgisa was with me at the altar of Venus in Rome, covered with white draperies, her hair strewn with flowers. I heard the sound of hyms, I saw the fumes of incense.)

White vestments, flower-bound hair, the sound of hymns, all go to constitute the idealized world of untouched beauty, reminiscent of the poetry of Eustachio Manfredi, Zaverio Bettinelli and Angelo Mazza.[20] Adalgisa's admission of her lost innocence in Act 1, Scene 6 finds its counterpart in Antonio Conti's translation of Pope's *Eloisa to Abelard*.[21]

> E tu pure, ah! tu non sai
> Quanto costi a me dolente!
> All'altare che oltraggai
> Lieta andava ed innocente ...
> Il pensier al ciel s'ergea,
> Il mio Dio vedeva in ciel ...
> Or per me spergiura e rea
> Cielo e Dio ricopre un vel.
> (*Norma*, Act 1, Scene 5)

(And you indeed! Ah you do not know the amount of sorrow you cause me. I used to go happy and innocent to the altar that I violated. I used to raise my thoughts to heaven, I saw my God in heaven. Now a veil covers heaven and God, since I am a guilty perjurer.)

Love, guilt and a rationalization of the individual's situation are here expressed. Although contained in an eighteenth-century linguistic framework, Adalgisa at this point emerges as a freethinker in search of an ideal state. In this respect she has much in common with Conti's Eloisa:

> Caro Abelardo, tu abbastanza sai
> che quando cominciaro i nostri amori
> con innocenza e santità t'ami.
> (Conti, *Eloisa ad Abelardo*, 67–9)

> Thou know'st how guiltless first I met thy flame,
> When love approach'ed me under friendship's name,
> My fancy form'd thee of angelic kind,
> Some emanation of th' all beauteous mind.
> (Pope, *Eloisa to Abelard*, 59–62)[22]

> Come stella i tuoi guardi erano ridenti,
> pien di celeste melodia il tuo canto,
> pieni di sacra autorità gli accenti.
> (Conti, *Eloisa ad Abelardo*, 73–5)

> Guiltless I gazed; Heaven listen'd while you sung;
> And truth divine came mended from that tongue.
> (Pope, *Eloisa to Abelard*, 65–6)

> Delle gioie del ciel più non mi cale,
> non cerco ne' tuoi sguardi o ne' tuoi detti
> cosa che sia celeste ed immortale.
> (Conti, *Eloisa ad Abelardo*, 82–4)

> Back through the paths of pleasing sense I ran,
> Nor wish'd an angel whom I loved a man.
> (Pope, *Eloisa to Abelard*, 69–70)

Adalgisa recalls, in the hope of bringing Pollione's promises to reality, or else in the hope of conquering her own feelings:

> Dolci qual arpa armonica
> M'erano le sue parole;

> Negli occhi suoi sorridere
> Vedea più bello un sole.
> Il fui perduta, e il sono.
> (*Norma*, Act 1, Scene 8)

(His words were for me sweet as a melodious harp: I saw in his eyes, shine most beautifully, a sun. I was, and am, ruined.)

Adalgisa, the younger priestess, is a portrait of corrupted innocence, identified with harmony of verse and visual image. The characterization of the figure cannot on any account be judged on a par with that of the protagonist Norma, which stands as a major librettistic triumph and, in the words of Patrick Smith, is 'one of the great character portraits in all of opera'.[23] The poetry of Norma herself has little in common with the more conventional melodramatic outbursts of the period. The refined Leopardian images, the light symbolism, pointing to enlightened reason, render the libretto worthy of a place beside the major poetic works of the day.

Giacomo Leopardi (1798–1836) in his *Idylls* provides a series of dialogues between Man and Nature, stressing the beauty, deceit and destructive aspect of the latter. Nature in Leopardi's world is afforded lyrical expression, but it is also rendered as a source of solace leading to the contemplation of infinity and eternity in the poem *L'infinito* (1819). It is personified as a cruel stepmother, instilling in youth a desire for happiness while withdrawing the means by which this can be attained ('A Silvia'). At times it denies even the hope of future contentment ('La sera del dì di festa'). Nature at its most perplexing is projected in the form of the moon, an example of the order and beauty of Nature, a confidant to the poet, and one to whom questions regarding being, behaviour, and the meaning and purpose of life can be addressed ('Canto notturno di un pastore errante dell' Asia'). Being immortal, it perhaps cannot comprehend the human lot, but in the poetic world of Leopardi it provides a means by which rationalization and acceptance of destiny is arrived at.

Some examples of Leopardi's addresses to the moon are:

(i)   O graziosa luna, io mi rammento
           Che, or volge l'anno, sovra questo colle
           Io venia pien d'angoscia a rimirarti:

E tu pendevi allor su quella selva
Siccome or fai, che tutta la rischiari.
('Alla luna, 1–5)[24]

(O graceful moon, I recall,
That a year has passed
Since full of anguish, I came,
To contemplate you, above this hill
And you were then suspended, over that forest
As now, illuminating all.)

(ii) O cara luna, al cui tranquillo raggio
Danzan le lepri nelle selve.
('La vita solitaria', 70–1)

(O dear moon, in whose tranquil ray
The forest hares dance.)

(iii) Salve, o benigna
Delle notti reina.
('La vita solitaria', 74–5)

(Hail, o kindly
Queen of the night.)

(iv) Or sempre loderollo, o ch'io ti miri
Veleggiar tra le nubi, o che serena
Dominatrice dell' etereo campo.
('La vita solitaria', 100–2)

(I shall always praise it, whether I see you
Sail between the clouds, or serene,
Dominator of the ethereal field.)

In the idyll 'Canto notturno di un pastore errante dell' Asia', the moon is addressed, interrogated and invoked in the following terms: 'silenziosa luna' ('silent moon'), 'vergine luna' ('virgin moon'), 'intatta luna' ('untouched moon'), 'solinga, eterna peregrina' ('solitary, eternal pilgrim'). The poem develops as a series of alternating questions and answers, the latter in the form of statements, touching on the pattern of the moon's course, man's destiny, a comparison between the life of the moon and that of the shepherd, and a final conclusion that between the mortal and immortal there may be no communication. It can be argued that Leopardi's 'Canto notturno' marks the highest point in the poet's philosophical thought, as it projects nature and reason as associated symbols, in the form of the moon. No longer does the poet accept his former juxtaposition of the rational and the natural order. Rather, he here illustrates the existence of a philosophical system within the natural order. Enlightenment and guidance can be gained from communication with a natural object. Romani's acceptance of Leopardian linguistic symbolism brings to *Norma*, wittingly or unwittingly on the part of the librettist, a philosophical dimension uniting Enlightenment and romantic principles.

Felice Romani, in the famous aria 'Casta Diva', Norma's prayer to the moon for peace, merges the lyrical and political aspects of the work. Norma prays that the goddess of the moon, by means of her light, may inspire moderation and peace. As in the poetry of Leopardi, the moon provides illumination of nature and of the mind, leading to an enlightened vision of circumstances. In addition Romani draws on Leopardian imagery, providing a continuation of the poetic world projected in the idylls of the great Italian poet:

> *Preghiera*
> Casta Diva, che inargenti
> Queste sacre antiche piante,
> A noi volgi il bel sembiante
> Senza nube e senza vel.
>
> Tempra tu de cori ardenti,
> Tempra ancora lo zelo audace,
> Spargi in terra quella pace
> Che regnar tu fai nel ciel.
> (*Norma*, Act 1, Scene 4)

> *Prayer*

(Pure goddess, who ensilvers these ancient and sacred plants, turn your beautiful face to us, devoid of cloud or veil. You temper the burning hearts. Temper once again the daring zeal. Spread that peace on earth, that you make reign in heaven.)

Norma's prayer for peace is prompted by love, as opposed to the incensed hatred of the Gauls crying out for war. Her love, however, cannot be reconciled with duty. Here is contained the basic conflict of the work: the clash between love and duty, the public and the private, the woman as opposed to the leader, and finally

A CRY FOR FREEDOM

the mother as opposed to the priestess. In the *cabaletta* following 'Casta Diva', cast in the form of an aside, Norma associates country and happiness with love:

> Ah! bello a me ritorna
> Del raggio tuo sereno,
> E vita nel tuo seno,
> E patria e cielo avrò.
> (*Norma*, Act 1, Scene 4)

(Ah beautiful to me return, you serene ray. And life in your company will be heaven on earth for me.)

In the response of the chorus, the cry for revenge is repeated.

> Sei lento, sì, sei lento,
> O giorno di vendetta,
> Ma irato il Dio t'affretta
> Che il Tebro condannò.
> (*Norma*, Act 1, Scene 4)

(Oh day of vengeance, you are slow to come, yes slow. But the angry god that condemned the Tiber hastens your coming.)

The function of the imagery of light is here threefold: on the dramatic level it brightens night, in order that the Druidic ritual may proceed; it is invoked as a source of moderation leading to peace; but above all, its function is to provide through love, a heaven on earth. In the *cabaletta* the 'fido amor primiero' ('former faithful love') is identified with 'raggio tuo sereno' ('your serene ray'). The return of Norma's former lover Pollione could in her belief lead to peace and happiness. The god Irminsul, one of cruelty, revenge and destruction, is thus juxtaposed with the goddess of the moon. In the finale love and sacrifice conquer, Pollione and Norma, Roman and Druid, are united, and together are sacrificed in order that the temple be cleansed of Norma's moral and political transgressions.

At the conclusion of the work, however, the political orientation has yielded to the human drama. Oroveso ceases to be the leader and high priest, and adopts the roles of father and grandfather, as Norma and Pollione prepare to die together:

POLLIONE: Il tuo rogo, o Norma, è il mio
Là più puro, là più santo
Incomincia eterno amor.
OROVESO: Sgorga alfin, prorompi, o pianto:
Sei permesso a un genitor.
(*Norma*, Act 2, Scene 11)

(POLLIONE: Your funeral pyre, O Norma, is mine. There, more pure and more holy, begins eternal love.
OROVESO: O sorrow, flow at last, break forth. It is permitted to a father.)

The finale of *Norma* recalls then the concept of catastrophe as employed by Metastasio. Its protagonist, like Attilio Regolo, is both tragic and triumphant. Unlike the Metastasian melodrama, however, *Norma* emerges as a harmonious and conscious fusion of opposites. Consisting of both classical and romantic elements, it also brings together the poetic diction of Arcadia and the romantic lyricism of Romani's own time. The triumph and the tragedy of the protagonist is expressed by the figure symbolizing authority, dignity and truth, the high priest Oroveso 'Ha vinto amore' (Love has conquered); 'Sgorga alfin, prorompi, o pianto' (O sorrow, flow at last, break forth). The conclusion, like the opening, represents a Druidic ritual, and fuses classical and romantic aspects of self-inflicted death – the suicidal and the sacrificial. Finally *Norma* can be judged a moral tale of crime and punishment, the conclusion of which can be afforded a political interpretation: eternal love binds political opposites while unity and peace are declared.

Historically *Norma* marks the emergence of the unchaste sacrifice, dramatized in heroic terms. The themes of religious vows and promises hitherto closeted in the poetic celebration of vocation, or part of the moral didactic of the historical novel, blazed forth on the leading Italian operatic stage. The cult of patriotism and leadership also played a part in this theatrical presentation. And whatever Romani's true intention might have been with regard to the patriotic theme, the public formed its own impression. *Norma*, then, not only occupies an important position in the history of Italian dramatic literature, but also takes its place between Rossini's *Mosè* and Verdi's *Nabucco* as a key piece of patriotic and melodramatic declamation.

III

If Solera's libretto for Verdi's *Nabucco* owes much to Felice Romani's *Norma*, the source of both is in fact the anonymous libretto for Rossini's *Mosè*,[25] presented at the Paris Opera House on 26 March 1827, and revised for La Scala in 1840. The text is an elaboration of Tottola's drama of 1818. It contains the cult of leadership and the struggle of a chosen people whose freedom is associated with religious belief and expression. The basic political conflict is between the Hebrews and Egyptians, and the action is derived from Chapters 1–15 of the book of Exodus. It is above all a historical sequence of political content, with a sub-plot containing the love theme. The aspects of the work which obviously exercised most influence on Felice Romani's libretto *Norma* are as follows: the opening chorus 'Ah dell'empio al potere feroce', Mosè's words 'No: viva il Dio di Giuda' in Act 1, Scene 7, and Mosè's prayer 'E d'Israello il Dio'.

The opening chorus takes the form of a prayer offered by the Hebrews that God release them from servitude. Freedom is seen as God's reward for sacrifice and suffering. Tyranny is represented by a fierce power:

> Ah! dell'empio al potere feroce
> Tu ci togli, gran Dio di bontà.
> Del tuo popol se pieghi alla voce,
> Alla patria tornare ei potrà.
> (*Mosè*, Act 1, Scene 1)

(O great God of goodness, release us from the ferocious power of the unholy. If you relent at the voice of your people, they will be able to return to their fatherland.)

Later, in Scene 7, Moses raises his voice in praise of the Hebrew God:

> No: viva il Dio di Giuda
> Che i figli suoi difende:
> Mira se chi l'offende
> Sia pronto a fulminar.
> (*Mosè*, Act 1, Scene 7)

(No, long live the God of Juda who defends his children. See if he is ready to strike with lightning he who offends him.)

The opera concludes with the prayer of Moses and the chorus that God protect the chosen people from the pursuing Egyptians:

MOSÈ:	E d'Israello il Dio
	Invoca sol Mosè.
	Dal tuo stellato soglio
	Signor, ti volgi a noi.
MOSÈ E CORO:	Pietà dei figli tuoi,
	Del popul tuo pietà.
	(*Mosè*, Act 4, Scene 3)
(MOSES:	And Moses alone invokes the God of Israel. From your starry firmament, oh Lord, turn to us.
MOSES AND CHORUS:	Have pity on your children, on your people have pity.)

The subject of the opera thus embraces the conflict between tyranny and freedom, the plight of the chosen people in pursuit of their promised land and God's blessing on the struggle against political absolutism and persecution. It creates the climate in which the writings of Mazzini, Balbo and Gioberti would later gain popularity, when the Hebrews would be seen as Italians, seeking the possession of the fatherland. The patriotic operatic tradition as seen in *Norma* (1831) is followed in *Nabucco* (1842) with Solera following in the Alfierian tradition and providing for the first time an operatic villainess. This also marks the emergence of the Italian dramatic soprano *par excellence*, of whom dramatic weight is demanded in addition to the ability to perform feats of vocal ornamentation. At this point in time, 1842, the prima donna assumes a new dramatic and authoritative significance which will find its culmination in the Verdian dramatic soprano roles of Elvira (*Ernani* (1844)), Odabella (*Attila* (1846)) and Lady Macbeth (*Macbeth* (1847)).

Temistocle Solera's libretto of *Nabucco* is based on Old Testament references to the Babylonian emperor Nebuchadnezzar and his subjugation of Jerusalem. Although the character of Nabucco (as it became in Italian) is historical, the other characters in the drama were invented by Solera. However, when the opera was staged in Paris it was claimed that Solera had taken his plot from *Nabuchodonsor* by Anicet-Bourgeois and Francis Cornu, first produced in 1836. The playwrights claimed a royalty. There also

8 Temistocle Solera (1815–78)

exists an Italian drama by Giovanni Battista Niccolini entitled *Nabucco*, but this has nothing in common with Solera's libretto. The Verdi/Solera *Nabucco* also introduces a new fashion in the Italian melodrama in that each act contains a title, indicating the theme of the action. Act 1 is entitled 'Gerusalemme' ('Jerusalem'), Act 2 'L'empio' ('The wicked man'), Act 3 'La profezia' ('The prophecy') and Act 4 'L'idolo infranto' ('The broken idol'). The religious and patriotic content is at once established when the Hebrews bewail their defeat by Nabucco and call upon heaven to defend their sacred temple. The chorus and prophet–high priest Zaccaria make the opening statement of belligerance and intolerance of external force. Although the framework is Rossinian, the authority of expression owes its origin to Romani's verse at the opening of *Norma*, here endowed with a greater strength of declamation as intoned by the Hebrew Virgins:

> Gran Nume, che voli sull'ale dei venti,
> Che il folgor sprigioni dai nembi frementi,
> Disperdi, distruggi d'Assiria le schiere,
> Di David la figlia ritorna al gioir.
> (*Nabucco*, Act 1, Scene 1)

(Great God, who flies on the wings of the wind, who frees the lightning from the trembling clouds, you disperse and destroy the legions of Assyria. May the daughter of David rejoice once again.)

Zaccaria's *cavatina* introduces the theme of faith and hope in God, and the *cabaletta* which follows is particularly impressive on account of Verdi's use of the chorus in unison with the soloist. In Act 2, Scene 2 Zaccaria's prayer is further reminiscent of Rossini's *Mosè*, while the use of the future tense of the verbs *risuonare* (resound), *sorgere* (arise) and *suonare* (ring) certainly find their source in Oroveso's 'Sì parlerà terribile' in Act 1, Scene 1 of *Norma*:

> OROVESO: Sì, parlerà terribile
> Da queste quercie antiche
> Sgombre farà le Gallie
> Dall'aquile nemiche.
> E del suo scudo il suono,
> Pari al fragor del tuono,
> Nella città dei Cesari

Tremendo echeggerà.
(*Norma*, Act 1, Scene 1; for translation see p. 109)

ZACCARIA: All'Assiria in forti accenti
Parla or tu col labbro mio!
E di canti a te sacrati
Ogni tempio risounerà;
Sovra gl'idoli spezzati
La tua legge sorgerà
Sovra gl'idoli spezzati,
E di canti a te sacrati,
Ogni tempio suonerà.
(*Nabucco*, Act 1, Scene 2)

(ZACCARIA: To Assyria in forceful tones, speak you now with my lips. And every temple shall resound with hymns sacred to you. Above the smashed idols your law shall rise. Above the smashed idols every temple shall resound with hymns sacred to you.)

In both arias, the victory of the persecuted is predicted. Both sections are intoned by the high priest of the people in the act of carrying out his sacred duties. The basic difference between the two situations is the fact that the Druids in *Norma* are persecuted at home. In *Nabucco*, the Hebrews are enslaved on the banks of the Euphrates river. In Act 3, Scene 2 the Jews, toiling in exile, sing of their homeland. Solera makes his effect by the simplest of means, and two lines stand out from the poetic chorus 'Va, pensiero, sull'ali dorate' ('Fly, o thought, on golden wings'). They are: 'O mia patria sì bella e perduta/O membranza sì cara e fatal' ('Oh my lost fatherland, so beautiful, oh remembrance, so dear and fatal') (*Nabucco*, Act 3, Scene 2).

The Milanese could not fail to respond to the patriotic pathos of such lines. Verdi, from 1842 until the unification of Italy nearly thirty years later, was continually plagued by the censors, who insisted on providing a political interpretation for the Alfierian-style melodramas which followed. In fact the words 'Viva Verdi' soon were assumed to replace the forbidden 'Viva l'Italia'; and later, when Victor Emmanuel had been offered the throne of a united Italy, people came to see a symbol in Verdi's name: V(ittorio) E(mmanuele) R(e) d'I(talia).

The year following the first performance of Verdi's *Nabucco*, *I lombardi alla prima crociata* had its première at La Scala, with a libretto by Temistocle Solera, after the heroic poem by the Milanese romantic writer Tommaso Grossi, a follower of Manzoni, and one who exercised no uncertain influence on the Master himself. (Grossi's *Ildegonda* is re-echoed more than once in Manzoni's tragedy *Adelchi*, which in turn provided a model for Felice Romani when he came to write the libretto of *Anna Bolena* for Donizetti, as shall be seen in the next chapter.) Grossi's *I lombardi alla prima crociata*, written between 1821 and 1824, was to some extent an imitation of Tasso's *Gerusalemme liberata*, and was considered by Manzoni to surpass it. Grossi's poem is an account of the fate of a Lombard family during the first Crusade. From its first hearing the Milanese identified the Lombards with the Italians, and the Holy Land with Italy. The Saracens became the Austrian oppressors. Of particular interest to the present argument is Act 4, Scenes 3 and 4. The chorus of Lombards has been said by the critic Charles Osborne to be 'Solera's and Verdi's cynical attempt to cash in on the success of their "Va, pensiero" in *Nabucco*.'[26] It is significant, however, in that it is yet another example of religious patriotism, which played no small part in influencing the direction of more orthodox political thought. It is yet another example of Verdi's projection of the 'prayer' which later assumes various guises (*Giovanna d'Arco*, also with a libretto by Solera; *La forza del destino*; and finally *Otello*, with the direct confrontation of evil – Iago's 'Credo' – and good – Desdemona's 'Ave Maria'). The chorus of the Lombards is a supplication to the Lord to free the Holy Land:

> O Signore, dal tetto natio
> Ci chiamasti con santa promessa,
> Noi siam corsi all'invito d'un pio
> Giubilando per l'aspro sentier.
> Ma la fronte avvilita e dimessa
> Hanno i servi già baldi e valenti!
> Deh! non far che ludibrio alle genti
> Sieno, Cristo, i tuoi fidi guerrier!
>   (*I Lombardi alla prima crociata*,
>   Act 4, Scene 3)

A CRY FOR FREEDOM

(O Lord, with a sacred promise you called us from our home; We hastened at the invitation of a pious one, rejoicing along the bitter path. But the servants, both courageous and valiant have become crestfallen and downcast. Ah! Christ do not allow that your faithful warriors be a source of derision to the people.)

In the following scene a further example of Solera's debt to Felice Romani is to be found. The 'Guerra, Guerra' chorus owes much to the war-cry already quoted from *Norma*:

> Sì ... Guerra! Guerra!
> Guerra! guerra! S'impugna la spada,
> Affrettiamoci, empiamo le schiere;
> Sulle bende il folgore cada,
> Non un capo sfuggire potrà.
> Già rifulgon le sante bandiere
> Quai comete di sangue e spavento;
> Già vittoria sull'ali del vento
> Le corone additando ci va!
> (*I lombardi alla prima crociata*,
> Act 4, Scene 4)

(Yes ... War, war, war, war. Grab your swords, let us hurry and join the legions. Let lightning fall on the drapes. Not a single head can escape. The sacred flags blaze already like comets of blood and terror. Already the crowns of victory are indicated on the wings of the wind.)

The 'comets of blood and terror' find their source in *Norma*, Act 1, Scene 3: 'Irminsul as a comet purveyor of horror/Shoots through the fields of the sky.' By 1849 Verdi was openly expressing his patriotism, having made acquaintance with many of the leaders of the nationalist and liberal movements and their literary supporters, including Giuseppe Giusti, who wished to enlist Verdi as the movements' composer. The patriotic ardour of Temistocle Solera had never been in doubt. His operatic collaboration with Verdi had followed in the wake of his father's imprisonment in the Spielberg prison, in the company of Silvio Pellico and Pietro Maroncelli, political activists whose fame has been assured by the popularity of Pellico's autobiographical novel *Le mie prigioni*. After his rupture with Verdi in 1846, during the period in which he officially occupied the post of impresario of the Teatro Reale in Madrid, he was reputed to have been, in addition to the adviser, the lover of Queen Isabella. On his return to Milan, his political commitment was employed in a new but no less fruitful activity: he became a secret agent, carrying high security information between Napoleon III and Cavour. In 1868 he was called to Egypt to reorganize the police force there. That brought an end to his political activity, and having passed through Vienna, Paris where he trafficked in antiques, and London, he finally returned to Milan, where he died destitute in 1878.

In March 1848 the Milanese had risen against their Austrian overlords. For five days there was continuous fighting in the streets, with barricades erected, fatal skirmishes and conquests. Verdi, on hearing of the fighting, wrote from Paris to the librettist Francesco Maria Piave, honouring the brave men, and all Italy.[27] He then contacted Cammarano[28] in Naples, suggesting a libretto on a subject associated with the patriotic exhortations of Giusti. Cammarano proposed a propaganda piece, depicting the defeat of Frederick Barbarossa by the Lombard League in 1176. The result was *La battaglia di Legnano*, first performed at the Teatro Argentina, Rome, in 1849. Both Mazzini and Garibaldi came for the première. After the opening chorus there were scenes of delirium and cries of 'Viva Verdi' and 'Viva l'Italia'. After several performances in other Italian towns and cities, the work was suppressed by Austrian censorship. In 1869, when the opera was performed at the Teatro Reggio, Parma, it was subtitled *La disfatta degli Austriaci* ('The defeat of the Austrians'). Verdi's and Cammarano's patriotic ardour is summed up in the opening chorus of Veronese warriors:

> Viva Italia! sacro un patto
> Tutti stringe i figli suoi:
> Esso alfin di tanti ha fatto
> Un sol popolo d'eroi! ...
>
> Viva Italia forte ed una
> Colla spada e col pensier!
> Questo suol che a noi fu cuna,
> Tomba sia dello stranier.
> (*La battaglia di Legnano*, Act 1, Scene 1)

(Long live Italy! A sacred pact binds its sons. Of so many individuals, it has created one people of heroes. Long live

Italy, strong and united with the sword and with the mind. May this land, that was a cradle for us, be the tomb of the foreigner.)

It has been illustrated that the religious hymn and the biblical prayer infused with the spirit of the Risorgimento, executed by a chorus and combined with the march (which enjoyed tremendous popularity during the first half of the nineteenth century), became one of the principal instruments of the patriotic melodrama. It must also be stressed, however, that such feeling and expression belonged not only to the world of opera. Rather, as this study attempts to illustrate, the operatic theatre is just one of the many mouthpieces of the literary and social climate of the time. In addition to its presence in the opera, the cry for freedom and unity came to the surface in historical novels and dramatic endeavours. It must also be said that political thinkers such as Mazzini, Balbo and Gioberti absorbed the religious and patriotic dimension present in the world of the melodrama from the time of Rossini's *Tancredi* and *Mosè* – long before the theoretic evolution of the religion of patriotism as demonstrated by Giuseppe Mazzini in *Le speranze d'Italia*. In other words, the operatic theatre not merely reflected taste and trends, but also proved influential in the propagation of popular and revolutionary feeling. So Gioberti's neo-Guelfism found its expression in *Ernani*,[29] when Piave's hymn of praise to Carlo Magno and Charles V, 'A Carlo Quinto sia gloria ed onor' ('To Charles the Fifth honour and glory'), was turned by Roman audiences into a hymn of praise of Pope Pius IX three years after its première. It therefore echoed popular feeling that Italy might be united in a confederation of states under the control of the papacy. Music therefore animated the spirit. Verbal puns and literary symbolism, at a time of hope and unrest, led to the acceptance of the opera as the most melodious and direct, if not always the most articulate, expression of an aspiration towards independence.

6

OF REASON AND DELIRIUM

I

It is clear that the romantic age in Italy reflected the political, social and intellectual climate leading to the final unification of the country as a political entity. Italian romanticism, taking the form of an organized movement, was for the most part politically orientated. Poets and dramatists boasted of a higher ideal than the pursuit or experience of perfect love. Rather, they cultivated the lofty ambition of freeing the fatherland from foreign occupation. The Italian province at the centre of the political struggle was Lombardy. The main sources of inspiration with regard to themes and dramatic plots were the tragedies of Alfieri.[1] Little attention, however, was given to their symbolic images pertaining to the conflict between reason and emotion.[2] Rather, the dramatic juxtaposition of tyranny and heroism was invested with nationalistic implications. Reason (as opposed to its dramatic function in the theatre and melodrama of the eighteenth century) was seen in terms of the conscience and consciousness, underlining the place of national duty. Duty, idealistic exploits and the expulsion of the foreign occupier were all regarded as both reasonable and idealistic.

In the eighteenth-century melodrama, reason was presented in both theoretic and thematic forms. Metastasio's *Attilio Regolo* is an exposition of Cartesian philosophy with the protagonist demonstrating the triumph of rationalism over emotion. The librettos of da Ponte project reason in terms of moderation. In *Così fan tutte* the attributes of practicality, common sense and philosophical doctrines are presented side by side. In other words, while in the eighteenth century, order, precision and rational behaviour dominate both character and plot, in the romantic era, passion, emotion and individualism are emphasized. Whereas Metastasio underlines the sublime rationalism of his characters, the nineteenth-century librettist emphasizes their human failings. The overloading of the emotional leads to dramatic scenes of self-expression, ambition, guilt, fear and trauma, in larger-than-life portraits of human behaviour trapped in neurosis and delusions. Scenes of delirium thus became popular. Even in operas with a patriotic theme there are examples of a momentary loss of reason, for instance in *Nabucco*, Act 3, scenes 2 and 3, and Act 4, scene 1, and in *Macbeth*, Act 1, scene 2, Act 2, scene 2, and Act 4, scene 4. In the operas devoid of a political dimension the main subject is love, with a historical, mythical or pastoral setting.

During the first part of the century Donizetti provided a series of historical operatic dramas. In addition he composed works with a historical setting while giving free power of invention to the librettist. To these groups belong *Il castello di Kenilworth* (1829, libretto by Leone Andrea Tottola), *Marin Faliero* (1835, libretto by Giovanni Emanuele Bidera) and *Roberto Devereux* (1837, libretto by Salvatore Cammarano), *Anna Bolena* (1830, libretto by Felice Romani), *Lucrezia Borgia* (1833, libretto by Felice Romani), *Lucia di Lammermoor* (1835, libretto by Salvatore Cammarano) and *Maria de Rudenz* (1838, libretto by Salvatore Cammarano). In spite of their historical settings, the main conflicts in these operas are caused by the misadventures of the protagonists, which affect their behaviour patterns and emotional stability. During the second half of the century Verdi provided dramas of love with emotional implications (*Il trovatore* (1853, libretto by Cammarano)), moral considerations (*Un ballo in maschera* (1859, libretto by Antonio Somma)) and social convention (*La traviata* (1853, libretto by Piave)). Intrigue, discovery and the death of the hero or heroine appears in opera after opera, with the result that Anna Bolena, Elisabetta d'Inghilterra, Maria Stuarda, Roberto Devereux, Count of Essex, Manrico and Riccardo are stereotypes that make their appearances time and again, performing the same function and succumbing to a similar destiny.[3] The most outstanding aspect of the romantic libretto is its central love theme, and the librettos which most concern us in this chapter are those in which the protagonists live and die at the dictates of romantic passion. Emotions are bared, and resistance is tested to such an extent that the final result is the total abandonment of reason. The outcome of such a situation finds its melodramatic expression in the operatic mad scene, which became the means by which the female protagonist displayed both her histrionic and vocal capabilities. The mad scene was developed musically as a display piece for soprano, madness becoming associated with *volate, fioriture* and *cadenzas* reaching dizzy heights, and serving to provide the artists capable of such feats with international acclaim and a place in the history of opera.

The Italian dramatization of insanity finds its sources in the works of Shakespeare. *Hamlet* and *King Lear* served as models for eighteenth-century dramatists such as Giovanni Granelli (*Sedecia, ultimo re di Giuda*), Saverio Bettinelli (*Serse re di Persia*) and Vittorio Alfieri (*Saul*). In the seventeenth century the British composer Henry Purcell had composed the lengthy aria 'Mad Bess', which provides an early vocal impression of madness. The most celebrated romantic operatic mad scenes are those from Bellini's *Il pirata* (1827, libretto by Felice Romani), Donizetti's *Anna Bolena* (1830, libretto by Felice Romani), Bellini's *I puritani* (1835, libretto by Carlo Pepolí) and Donizetti's *Lucia di Lammermoor* (1835, libretto by Salvatore Cammarano). In addition, the sleepwalking scenes in Verdi's *Macbeth* (1847, libretto by Francesco Maria Piave) and Bellini's *La sonnambula* (1831, libretto by Felice Romani) illustrate unease, guilt and psychological disturbance, which in the case of Amina, the heroine of *La sonnambula*, are banished at the public revelation of her innocence. As a result of the musical and dramatic qualities of the music expressing mental disturbance, the 'mad scene' became the rage of Europe. The French composer Ambroise Thomas (1811–96) brought operatic madness to the French stage in 1868 with his *Hamlet* in the wake of the Parisian success of *Lucia di Lammermoor*. Adolf Adam's ballet *Giselle* also contains a mad scene for its prima ballerina. Finally this conventional scene was parodied by Sir Arthur Sullivan in Mad Margaret's scene from *Ruddigore*.

The musical dramatization of insanity represents the unique fusion of ideological opposites, in addition to the combination of the lyrical and declamatory. Reason and madness are communicated in such a manner that the rational and irrational can coexist ideologically. The public is made aware of both the subjective and objective aspects of the dramatic situation. The tragedy of Lucia, the protagonist of Donizetti'sopera *Lucia di Lammermoor*, is projected in terms of its romantic illusion and horrific reality. As the delirious figure experiences an imaginary situation, or relives a moment of past happiness, it is possible to participate in the dual aspect of the dramatic presentation. For that reason, although the literary influences of the librettos can be traced to the poetry and prose of Grossi and Manzoni, historical sources and the romantic world of Sir Walter Scott, the simultaneous dramatization of reality and illustion belongs to the operatic theatre alone. The musical dimension serves to heighten the tension between the contrasting factors of the situation. In addition, the impression the singer seeks to create by means of his or her interpretation is in glaring contrast with audience reaction, since the public bears in mind not only the dramatic content of the scene, but the circumstances in which it takes place. In other words, Lucia di Lammermoor, going through an imaginary wedding ceremony with her beloved Edgardo, expresses joy and fulfilment. The public, aware of her insanity, responds to the tragedy of the situation. The impression which predominates is that of pathos. The narrow divide between illusion and reality is therefore highlighted, as the participant undergoes a psychological experience.

A further dimension to the literary and musical projection of madness is, however, worthy of consideration. This entails looking at the historical and social climate as it pertains to the individual psyche. Madness is indeed a proclamation of freedom, in the absence of which the subconscious establishes its autonomy, so denying the existence of the limits or barriers presented by time and space. Italy, in the wake of centuries of foreign occupation and frustrated cries for liberty, was socially and historically ready in the 1830s to experience histrionic escapism and freedom of expression, in the broadest sense of the word. The pathetic creatures such as Imogene, Anna, Lucia and Elvira are all victims of domestic tyranny and suppression of freedom of choice and expression. All, with the exception of Elvira whose lover is restored to her, must transcend the limitations of their enforced situations, and so pass to a state beyond the control of social, domestic or political systems.

In the analysis of the mad scenes which follows in this chapter, concepts of sorrow and despair, revenge and melancholia, wanderings and ravings will be highlighted. The literary qualities and sources will be discussed, and the contribution to dramatic storytelling will be assessed.

II

Il pirata was Bellini's second opera.[4] It marked the beginning of his successful collaboration with Felice Romani, and brought instant acclaim to composer and librettist on its production in 1827 at La Scala, Milan. It reached London in 1830, with its original cast of Méric-Lalande, Rubini and Tamburini. It was first presented in New York in 1832. The source of the work is the five-act verse tragedy by the Reverend R. C. Maturin, an Irishman and curate of Saint Peter's in Dublin. The complete title was *Bertram, or The Castle of Saint Aldebrand* (Drury Lane Theatre, London, 1816). M. A. Ruff, in his edition of the Nodlier-Taylor translation of the play (Paris, 1956) points out a possible derivation of elements in it from Scott's *Rokeby*, a French translation of which had been issued in 1820. Maturin's *Bertram* is strongly attacked by Coleridge at the end of his *Biographia Literaria*. The popularity of the work is, however, indicated by the number of editions (five in 1816 alone). It would appear that Romani was acquainted with the French translation which appeared in Paris in 1820. Hippolyte Raimond later produced an adaptation, which in 1831 was published in Milan, without a reference to Maturin, in an Italian translation.[5] That was four years after Bellini's opera was first produced.

The opera is set in thirteenth-century Sicily, in and near the castle of the Duke of Caldera, at the time of Manfred, the natural son of Frederick II of Sicily. It describes events which took place in the wake of the Angevin victory over the Swabians and the exile of the Sicilian nobility. It is a work of love, desire, lust and revenge, set against a backdrop of courtly love. Some of Felice Romani's exquisitely poetic pages reflect the heroic cult of the warrior and the symbolic perfection of the Lady. None the less, Romani's pen provides evidence of his having both studied and absorbed the poetic conventions of his own time. It contains all the ingredients of a typical nineteenth-century romance of love and despair. Imogene, married against her will in an attempt, which proves futile, to save her father's life, is accused by her husband of adultery. The latter is later killed by Imogene's lover, Gualtiero, Count of Montaldo, posing as a pirate. He is captured and condemned, and Imogene loses her reason.

The heroine's imaginative and unstable disposition is established in her aria describing her vision of Gualtiero in a dream which provides a premonition of his destiny, and in which she is dragged from her lover by her husband. The occurrence of the operatic dream, appearing in the guise of a premonition of horrors to come, and lyrically expressed in the form of an aria, marks the beginning of an operatic convention which will be later seen in *Norma* (1831, with a libretto also by Felice Romani), and *Lucia di Lammermoor* (1835, with text by Cammarano). Notwithstanding the practical advice of her confidante Adele, Imogene reacts (as does Lucia in the face of warnings from her companion Alisa) by giving herself over entirely to romantic passion. Her aria contains imagery of blood, cries, conflicts and impressions created by the already disturbed mind of the protagonist:

> Lo sognai ferito, esangue,
> In deserta, ignuda riva.
> Tutta intrisa del suo sangue,
> De' miei gridi il ciel feriva
> Nè una voce rispondea,
> L'aura istessa, il mar tacea;
> Era sorda la natura
> Al mio pianto, al mio dolor.
>
> Quando a un tratto il mio consorte
> Mi si affaccia irato e bieco.
> Io, mi grida, il trassi a morte
> E mi afferra e tragge seco,
> Muta, oppressa e sbigottita,
> Lunge, lunge io son rapita.
> E mi seguita sui venti
> Un sospir di lui che muor.
> Quel sospir io sento ancor.
> (*Il pirata*, Act 1, Scene 4)

(I dreamed of him, wounded and bloodstained on a bare, deserted shore. My cries struck heaven, nor was there a reply. The breeze itself, the sea was silent. Nature was deaf to my suffering, to my sorrow. When all of a sudden my husband, angry and sinister, stands before me. I, he shouts at me, lead him to his death. And he takes hold of me, silent, oppressed and terrified, and he drags me with him. I am carried far, far away. His dying sigh pursues me on the voice of the wind. I still hear that sigh.)

The *cavatina* 'Lo sognai ferito' is the beginning of a series of expressive melodies vocally ornamented. Just as in *Norma*, when the image of the protagonist blots out Pollione's vision of Adalgisa, so does Ernesto's image predominate and call for retribution on account of past transgressions. The conflicting images of husband and lover represent an externalization of the conflicting internal forces, symbolized by a storm at the opening of the opera, which result in the insanity and ravings of the protagonist in the final scene. The 'mad scene' is then the logical conclusion of the incidents projected at the beginning of the opera. Andrea della Corte in his work on Bellini provides a concise analysis of the scene.[6] Musically and dramatically it can be said to fall into three main sections; the recitative and *arioso* 'Ah s'io potessi' ('Ah, if I could only'), the aria 'Col sorriso d'innocenza' ('With a smile of innocence') and the final dramatic outburst 'O sole, ti vela' ('Oh sun, hide yourself'). Poetic unity is achieved with the description of a wounded warrior on a deserted shore. The bloodstained image is not, as in Act 1, that of Gualtiero, but of Ernesto, Imogene's husband. Once again, as in Act 1, Scene 4, there is the dramatic juxtaposition of figures. Yet at this moment Ernesto is presented as a father-figure, calling his child and contributing to the pathos of the piece.

IMOGENE: Gemea l'aura intorno. Ecco l'ignuda
Deserta riva, ecco giacer trafitto
Al mio fianco un guerrier. Ma non è questo,
Non è questo Gualtier. È desso Ernesto
Ei parla ... ei chiama il figlio
Il figlio è salvo.

(*Il pirata*, Act 2, Scene 10)

(IMOGENE: Around about the wind whined. See the bare deserted shore, behold a stabbed warrior lying at my feet. But this is not ... this is not Gualtiero. It is Ernesto. He speaks ... he calls his son. His son is safe.)

The fusion and juxtaposition of the figures of Gualtiero and Ernesto have the function of communicating the heroine's confusion, while providing a shock effect for the listener. The final image of death will, however, be associated with Gualtiero, as Imogene imagines she sees the scaffold on which her lover is to be hanged:

O sole! ti vela di tenebre oscure
Al guardo mi cela la barbara scure
Ma il sangue già gronda.
Ma tutta m'inonda d'angoscia
D'affanno, d'angoscia.
          (*Il pirata*, Act 2, Scene 10)

(O sun, cover yourself with dark shadows. Conceal from me the barbarous axe. But the blood already drips, but all fills me with anguish, suffering and anguish.)

The images of light and love are eclipsed by those of shadows, blood and violence. Blood is symbolic of Imogene's insanity, images of blood being a typical hallucination of the disturbed psyche.

Felice Romani, as has been seen in the case of *Norma*, and as will be illustrated later with regard to *Anna Bolena*, was a constant borrower from contemporary Italian writers. In Act 2, Scene 9 there emerge some lines of Foscolian inspiration. From the pre-romantic *poesia sepolcrale*, or poetry of the tomb, Romani draws on Foscolo's sonnet 'In morte del fratello Giovanni' ('On the death of brother Giovanni'), while reproducing the elegiac mood of the same poet's longer work *Dei sepolcri* ('On tombs'). A comparison between the lines of Romani and his more famous source of inspiration provides yet another example of the Italian literary influences on the poetry of the melodrama.

The cult of the tomb, its function as a symbol of communication between the living and the dead, and its place in pre-romantic and early romantic poetry can be related to the enthusiasm for elegiac poetry which followed the publication and translation of Gray's 'Elegy in a Country Churchyard' in the eighteenth century. Foscolo's *Dei sepolcri* (1806) was written as an outcry against the Napoleonic Edict of St Cloud, which was extended to Italy. It decreed that all should be buried in a common cemetery. Foscolo's poem upholds the religion of the ancients in honouring their dead with monuments. It establishes the tomb as not only a symbol of heroic and artistic achievement but as a link between past and present, life and death, and a source of consolation to the living. As early as 1802 Foscolo, in his sonnet on the death of his brother Giovanni, depicts his mother conversing with the ashes of the deceased. Later the romantic poet Leopardi, a strong influence on Romani, with regard to both his *Norma* and *I puritani*, follows in the heroic Foscolian tradition in his 'Canzone all'Italia' (1818, ll. 125–31) and in 'Sopra il monumento di Dante' (1818, ll. 18–34) describing the tomb as an altar.[7] He so continues the concept of a religion of heroism associated with the spot marking the place of burial.

The opening lines of Foscolo's 'In morte del fratello Giovanni' are as follows:[8]

> Un dì . . .
>   mi vedrai seduto
> Su la tua pietra, o fratel mio, gemendo
>   il fior de' tuoi gentili anni caduto.
> La madre or sol, suo dì tardo traendo,
>   parla di me col tuo cenere muto.
>
> (One day . . .
>   you will see me seated
> On your tomb, o my brother, bemoaning
> The fallen flower of your youth.
> Our mother, now alone, struggling with the
>   weight of the years,
> With your mute ashes speaks of me.)

Looking at the second verse of Romani's aria 'Tu vedrai' ('You shall see') in Act 2, Scene 9, one notes an affinity of diction and spirit with Foscolo's lines. In addition, the concept of the ability of the object (the tomb) to provide solace and information concerning the dead is entirely of Foscolian origin. Gualtiero, Romani's hero, is a propagator of heroic love, expressed in limpid terms, in keeping with the elegiac nature of the aria:

> Forse un dì, con me placata,
> Alzerà per me preghiera,
> E verrà pietosa a sera
> Sul mio sasso a lagrimar.
> Se fui spietato e fiero,
> Fui sventurato ancor.
> E parlerà la tomba
> Alle pietose genti
> De' lunghi miei tormenti,
> Del mio tradito amor.
>   (*Il pirata*, Act 1, Scene 9)

(Some day, perhaps, having made peace with me, she will raise a prayer for me. And perhaps she may come, filled with pity, to weep on my tomb. If I were cruel and proud, I was even more unfortunate. And the tomb shall speak of my lengthy torments, of my betrayed love, to those who have pity.)

The musical score concludes with Imogene's 'mad scene', providing a moving and yet highly dramatic conclusion to the opera. This is not the expression of a raving lunatic, or demented diva, but rather the lyrical outpouring of one laid low with sorrow and endurance. Love, in its every shade and level of meaning, is the subject of this romantic melodrama. The true hero of the work is, however, Gualtiero, the pirate of the title. In the original libretto, the conclusion of the opera belongs to him,[9] although Bellini did not set the final scene to music. In other words the 'mad scene' was not, in the dramatist's view, the high point of the opera, occurring as it did between Gualtiero's *scena* and the concluding scene depicting his suicide. Rather, Imogene's dementia and death from sorrow provide a lyric-dramatic interlude before the final action. Romani in *Il pirata* uses the scene, as does Cammarano in *Lucia di Lammermoor*, as a prelude to the final catastrophe and suicide of the protagonist. In Cammarano's libretto, however, the effect is slightly different, since the impression is of an anti-climax, with the disappearance of the heroine of the title, and her replacement by the tenor. *Il pirata* is essentially a tenor's opera, despite the moving and historically significant 'mad scene'. The libretto concludes with Gualtiero taking his own life, rather than be put to death by his executioners:

GUALTIERO: Scostatevi!
L'impone il vostro duce.
Un'abborita luce
Fuggo così.
(*Il pirata*, Act 2, Scene 12)

(GUALTIERO: Out of the way! Your leader orders it so.
I thus escape an abhorred light.)

As a portrait of romantic passion and despair set in a period of idealized courtly love, *Il pirata*, more than a century and a half after its first production, can still successfully hold the stage. This has been demonstrated by its many successful revivals over the last thirty years, including those in Italy, Wexford and the United States.

III

Gaetano Donizetti, spurred by the success of Vincenzo Bellini's *Il pirata* (1827) and *La straniera* (1829), concentrated his energy in the years between 1830 and 1835 on composing what were later to be regarded as his greatest tragic and comic achievements. These included *Anna Bolena* (1830), *Ugo, conte di Parigi* (1832), *L'elisir d'amore* (1832), *Parisina* and *Lucrezia Borgia* (1833), *Maria Stuarda* (1834), and *Marin Faliero* and *Lucia di Lammermoor* (1835). His collaborator for all except *Maria Stuarda*, *Marin Faliero* and *Lucia di Lammermoor* was Felice Romani. With *Lucia di Lammermoor* the composer began a highly successful association with the librettist Salvatore Cammarano, although he was also to make use of the services of Royer, Rossi and Ruffini; and in 1839 for his comic work *Gianni di Parigi* he once again availed himself of Romani's talent. Romani and Cammarano were without doubt the two greatest poets and adapters with whom he worked. *Anna Bolena* and *Lucia di Lammermoor* serve to demonstrate the felicitous artistic union. The former is a tale of betrayed innocence and repudiation. The latter tells of short-lived happiness and family pressures. Both plots conclude with the heroine giving way to madness. Anna is the absolute heroine of Romani's libretto, the work bearing her name and concluding with her delirium. Lucia, on the other hand, shares the laurels with the tenor, Edgardo, whose despair and suicide close the opera.

Romani's libretto for *Anna Bolena* provides an example of history yielding to myth, of a protagonist, the victim of personal and political ambition, driven to melancholia and despair. Romani's sources are both historical and literary. The operatic Anna Bolena bears little resemblance to England's unfortunate queen, but is based on the early romantic creations of Tommaso Grossi and Alessandro Manzoni.[10] The closest area for comparison is between Ermengarda, the heroine of Manzoni's tragedy *Adelchi*, and Romani's Anna. Both dramas have historical foundation, both tell of a queen repudiated who proclaims her innocence and dies delirious. Although Manzoni is generally regarded as Grossi's master, the protagonist of the latter's story in verse *Ildegonda* is indeed the source for Manzoni's gentle queen.[11] Death in the cloister, loss of reason, instructions for burial, reconciliation of temporal and spiritual matters are common to both dramatic personae. In addition, the two early romantic works share poetic diction and lyrical tenderness, later associated with Manzoni's lachrymose pathos.[12] Romani in 1830 was writing in the poetic tradition of the young romantic poets who became associated with the literary aspect of the Risorgimento in Lombardy.

In addition to the similarity of situation which both Ermengarda and Anna Bolena suffer, both are infused with religious sentiments associated with the early Risorgimento. Anna addresses her ladies-in-waiting with words similar in spirit to those offered by Ermengarda to the sisters keeping their final vigil over the dying queen:

ERMENGARDA: l'obblio
Sol bramo; e il mondo volentier l'accorda
Agl'infelici; oh! basta; in me finisca
La mia sventura.
(*Adelchi*, Act 1, Scene 2)

(ERMENGARDA: Oblivion is all I seek; and the world willingly bestows it on the unhappy; oh enough; may my misery end with me.)

ANNA: O mie fedeli, o sole
A me rimaste nella mia sventura
Consolatrici, ogni speranza, è vero
Posta è nel Ciel, in lui soltanto. . . . In terra
Non v'ha riparo per la mia ruina.
(*Anna Bolena*, Act 2, Scene 2)

(ANNA: O my faithful and only consolers left to me in my misfortune, it is true, every hope is placed in heaven, in Him alone. There is no shelter on earth for my disgrace.)

Both queens proclaim their innocence:

ERMENGARDA: Io stessa, io sposa tua, non rea
Pur d'un pensiero.
(*Adelchi*, Act 4, Scene 1)

(ERMENGARDA: I, I your consort, am not guilty of a single sinful thought.)

ANNA: Piegar la fronte è forza

> Al regale voler, qualunque ei sia.
> Dell'innocenza mia
> Voi testimoni siate
> Tenere amiche.
>
> (*Anna Bolena*, Act 2, Scene 2)

(ANNA: It is necessary to bow one's head to the royal will, whatever it may be. Dear friends, you are witnesses to my innocence.)

Although both protagonists are in the clutches of a depressive crisis, Anna Bolena in her final 'mad scene' totally loses contact with reality. Ermengarda, on the other hand, wishes all were a bad dream. Both protagonists beg for peace and pardon.

The overriding theme of the Romani/Donizetti *Anna Bolena* is forgiveness. Percy pardons Anna's presumed transgressions. Giovanna di Seymour asks for Anna's pardon and she concedes it. To quote Folco Portinari, pardon is the sanctifying aspect of Anna, which identifies her with Manzoni's heroine.[13] Indeed the concept of pardon is fundamental to Manzoni's *I promessi sposi*. One recalls the pardoning of Ludovico (Chapter 4) and Lucia's 'Dio perdona tante cose per un'opera di misericordia' ('God forgives so many transgressions, on account of an act of mercy'), which sums up the spirit of the entire novel (Chapter 21). Anna, then, is a helpless creature, an example of human frailty in the face of despotic absolutism.

Anna's mad scene is a penetrating image of the human psyche. From the point of view of the drama critic, the final 'tower scene' can be divided into four principal sections. The first section finds Anna in prison, imagining that she is preparing for her marriage to Enrico VIII of England. This is followed by her fear of Percy's reaction, and her relief at his smile. As the drama progresses Anna prays to heaven for relief and repose after her suffering. Finally she launches out in an invective against Enrico and Giovanna di Seymour, while declaring that she will descend into her tomb with a pardon on her lips. The alternating moods and tempi, pulsating towards a dramatically and musically triumphant finale, communicate the reactions and self-torturing feelings of doubt and ambitious aspirations, leading to Anna's triumph and fall.

As Anna relives her preparation for her wedding, conflicting emotions are displayed. In addition to her joy, her deceit of Percy is also revealed, along with a total identification with the king's will:

> È questo
> giorno di nozze. Il Re m'aspetta, è acceso,
> infiorato l'altar. Datemi tosto
> il mio candido ammanto; il crin m'ornate
> col mio serto di rose ...
> che Percy non lo sappia; il Re l'impose.
> (*Anna Bolena*, Act 2, Scene 12)

(This is my wedding day. The king is waiting for me. The altar is illuminated and covered with flowers. Quickly give me my white gown. Dress my hair with my garland of roses.... The king ordered that Percy not know of it.)

Guilt and relief follow in quick succession. The presence of the king yields to that of Percy:

> Ei viene,
> ei mi accusa ... ei mi sgrida. Ah! mi perdona.
> Infelice son io.
> (*Anna Bolena*, Act 2, Scene 12)

(He comes, he accuses me ... he upbraids me. Ah! he forgives me. I am unhappy.)

The melodramatic unhappiness introduces the first lyrical melody of the opera's final scene. It takes the form of a memory of home, and a desire for a physical return to a spot associated with love and childhood:

> Al dolce guidami
> Castel natio,
> Ai verdi platani,
> Al queto rio
> Che i nostri mormora
> Sospiri ancor.
> (*Anna Bolena*, Act 2, Scene 12)

(Guide me to my sweet native castle. To the green plane trees, to the quiet stream that still murmurs our sighs.)

The final scene in the libretto (Scenes 12, 13 and 14 are played as the 'tower scene' or 'mad scene' in theatrical productions) depicts Anna in the company of Rochefort, Percy and Smeaton, her page, on the gentlemen's exit from other prisons. Donizetti, following on Anna's aria expressing her desire to return home ('Al dolce guidami castel natio'), provides an air based on the popular tune 'Home, Sweet Home'. This is elaborated, and finally develops into an ensemble. The original is taken from the opera *Clari, the Maid of Milan* (1823) by the English composer and conductor Sir Henry Bishop.[14] Although decorated and embellished, the piece is clearly based on the English tune, and expresses a final desire to regain peace:

> Cielo, a' miei lunghi spasimi
> Concedi alfin riposo,
> E questi estremi palpiti
> Sian di speranza almen.
> (*Anna Bolena*, Act 2, Scene 14)

(Heaven, grant rest at last to my long sufferings, and may these final heart-beats at least be of hope.)

The opera closes as Anna becomes lucid, and awakens as from a dream to the sound of the pealing of bells, celebrating the marriage of Enrico and Giovanna. Her final outburst finds the music and the drama at cross-purposes. In reality 'coppia iniqua' is a statement of forgiveness in the face of death. The music on the other hand soars dramatically, as Anna's voice rises over the heavy orchestration, in a series of long trills rising from B flat to F sharp, and reaching their climax on 'pietà' ('pity') as the prisoners are led to execution:

> Nel sepolcro che aperto m'aspetta,
> Col perdono sul labbro si scenda.
> Ei m'acquisti clemenza e favore
> Al cospetto d'un Dio di pietà.
> (*Anna Bolena*, Act 2, Scene 14)

(I descend into the open tomb that awaits me with [words of] pardon on my lips. May it win me clemency and favour in the presence of a God of pity.)

In June 1834 the Neapolitan librettist Salvatore Cammarano (1801–52) was responsible for the staging of *Anna Bolena* at the San Carlo Theatre, Naples.[15] In addition to overseeing the entire production, he also wrote a few additional lines to the libretto.

This proved to be the initial and preparatory stage for a collaboration with Donizetti which began with *Lucia di Lammermoor* (1835) and continued with *Belisario* (1836), *L'assedio di Calais* (1836), *Pia de' Tolomei* (1837), *Roberto Devereux* (1837) and *Maria di Rudenz* (1838). To quote Gary Schmidgall, the story of the *Bride of Lammermoor* 'is far more compelling as an opera than in its original narrative form'.[16] This he believes to be so on account of Cammarano's extensive cuts from the extraneous material of the original. The Italian librettist refused to become swamped in detailed descriptions of the dress or appearance of the protagonists at highly dramatic moments in the story. Rather, he preferred to highlight action and reactions, in the pursuit of a human drama with a tragically horrific outcome. Cammarano's was not the first adaptation of Scott's *The Bride of Lammermoor*, which was published in London and Edinburgh in 1819. There were in fact three prior operatic dramatizations of the work: *Le nozze di Lammermoor* by Carafa di Colobrano (1832), *Bruden frä Lammermoor* by H. Ch. Anderson and I. F. Breda (1832) and *La fidanzata di Lammermoor* by P. Beltrame and A. Mazzucato (1834). In addition, an Italian translation of the novel by G. Barbieri had appeared in Milan in 1824.[17] Scott's world of lugubrious melancholy touched by northern mists and mythology made it ideal material for operatic adaptation. Almost all of the writer's heroes and heroines have in some guise or form trodden the Italian operatic boards. None has managed to inspire the same interest and loyalty as 'poor Miss Lucy', whose misadventures, almost 160 years after her first appearance, are seldom out of the repertoire of the principal theatres. The following list provides some indication of the Italian popularity of Scott, and the operatic versions of his works produced during the nineteenth century.

1819   *La donna del lago* (A. L. Tottola-Rossini)
1820   *Vallace o L'eroe scozzese* (F. Romani-G. Pacini)
1829   *Il talismano* (G. Barbieri-G. Pacini)
1829   *I fidanzati* (D. Gilardoni-G. Pacini)
1829   *I contestabili di Chester* (F. Strepponi)
1829   *Elisabetta al castello di Kenilworth* (A. L. Tottala-G. Donizetti)
1830   *La dama bianca d'Avenello* (G. Rossi-S. Pavesi)
1835   *I puritani (e i cavalieri) di Scozia* (C. Pepoli-V. Bellini)
1838   *Le prigioni di Edimburgo* (G. Rossi-F. Ricci)

19 – 1801.
Salv. Cammarano
poeta melodrammatico
nasce a Napoli.

9   Salvatore Cammarano (1801–52)

1839	*Il castello di Woodstock* (F. Romani-T. Tonasso e P. Collavo)
1840	*Il templario* (G. B. Marini-O. E. Nicolai)
1848	*Allen Cameron* (F. M. Piave-G. Pacini)
1848	*Kenilworth* (F. V. Schira)
1852	*Matilde di Scozia* (F. Romani-G. Winter)
1856	*I fidanzati* (F. M. Piave-A. Peri)
1865	*Rebecca* (F. M. Piave-B. Pisani)
1865	*Carlo il temerario* (G. F. Piazzano)
1877	*La bella fanciulla di Perth* (D. Lucilla)

The original 'bride of Lammermoor' who fired Scott's imagination was Miss Janet Dalrymple, the daughter of the first Lord Stair. Against the wishes of her parents, she became engaged to Lord Rutherford. Shortly afterwards her family insisted that she marry David Dunbar of Baldoon. On the wedding night, completely insane, she stabbed her bridegroom, and died two weeks later. Her remains lie in the family vault of the Viscounts of Stair, in the parish church of Kirkliston, just outside Edinburgh.

Cammarano, in his adaptation of the novel for Donizetti's music, condenses the plot in such a way as to focus on a series of major transformations. Of particular significance is the abolition of the roles of Lord and Lady Stair (Ashton), the parents of the bride. Instead of yielding to duty as laid down by her parents, Lucia gives way to the tyranny of her brother Enrico Ashton. Also eliminated are the witches, who proclaim prophecies of doom on the evening of the wedding. Premonitions are conveyed in the opera by Lucia's description of the bloodstained ghost in the *cavatina* 'Regnava nel silenzio'. In the novel, Lucia's bridegroom miraculously survives the assault by his bride, and her betrothed loses his life in the quicksands of Kilpy. Cammarano, wishing his protagonists to conform more closely to the social ethic of the world of the melodrama, allows the hapless Sir Arturo Bucklaw to die at Lucia's hand, while the distraught Edgardo takes his own life, surrounded by the tombs of his ancestors. A final and striking difference between Cammarano's text and his source is the fact that in Scott there is no 'mad scene'. Lucy's insanity is conveyed by the words 'Tak up your bonny bridegroom', uttered when her family broke down the door of the bridal chamber on hearing wild piercing screams and hideous shrieks.

On consideration of the changes and omissions effected by Cammarano, it becomes clear that the struggle between freedom and tyranny, as a preliminary to psychological imbalance, is played out between the baritone and the soprano (Lucia's brother Enrico and the protagonist herself). The deaths of both Edgardo and Lucia further accentuate the pursuit of total freedom beyond the limits of society and mortal life, while the 'mad scene' proves the dramatic and psychological culmination of the entire sequence of events.

Just as Romani in *Il pirata* introduces his female protagonist in a scene of dramatic storytelling, identified with horrors past and premonitions of more to come, so too does Cammarano present Lucia haunted by visions of bloodstained spectres. The essential information regarding the history of the Ravenswood family and Lucia's own neurotic disposition is contained in the recitative to the *cavatina* 'Regnava nel silenzio':

LUCIA: Quella fonte mai,
Senza tremar, non veggio ... Ah tuo lo sai,
Un Ravenswood, ardendo
Di geloso furor, l'amata donna
Celà trafisse; l'infelice cadde
Nell'onda, ed ivi rimanea sepolta ...
M'apparve l'ombra sua.
(*Lucia di Lammermoor*, Act 1, Scene 4)

(LUCIA: Never do I behold that fountain without
trembling. Ah, you know that a Ravenswood,
burning with jealous fury, there stabbed his

beloved. The unfortunate girl fell into the water, and there was buried. Her ghost appeared to me.)

As Lucia goes on to describe the circumstances of the apparition, it becomes clear that she is subconsciously accepting identification with the murdered woman. Also, while performing the role of unhappy lover, Lucia is used by Cammarano as the instrument of family revenge; indirectly she is the cause of the suicide of a Ravenswood, while the murder of her bridegroom brings a chapter of blood and fury to its conclusion. The opera *Lucia di Lammermoor* is therefore not merely a facile adaptation by an Italian librettist of the work of a more celebrated English novelist. Rather, it develops as a psychological drama, the subject of which is in reality the disturbed mind of its protagonist. Therefore it can be argued that the histories of the rival families, and the lurid happenings which took place before the rise of the curtain, are of essential importance to the plot. Added to Lucia's pursuit of absolute freedom is her romantic self-identification with a hapless lover, which, in her fragile mental condition, sparks off a tragedy of revenge. This is played out within her own psyche, the dramatic externalization of which is the 'mad scene'. Lucia's colourful narrative, which can indeed be said to capture some of Scott's original gloomy quality, is as follows:

> Regnava nel silenzio
> Alta la notte e bruna ...
> Colpia la fronte un pallido[18]
> Raggio di tetra luna.
> Quando sommesso gemito
> Fra l'aure udir si fè;
> Ed ecco su quel margine
> L'ombra mostrarsi a me!
> Qual di chi parla, muoversi
> Il labbro suo vedea,
> E con la mano esanime
> Chiamarmi a sè parea.
> Stette un momento immobile,
> Poi ratto dileguò ...
> E l'onda pria si limpida
> Di sangue rosseggiò.[19]
> (*Lucia di Lammermoor*, Act 1, Scene 4)

(The full night reigned in the dark silence. A pale ray of light from the gloomy moon touched my brow, when a stifled groan was heard on the breeze. And look, right at that spot the ghost appeared. I saw it move its lips as one speaking, and with its lifeless hand it seemed to beckon me. For a moment it stood motionless, then suddenly disappeared. And the water, previously so clear, ran red with blood.)

The harp obbligato, written as a prelude to the scene, provides an idyllic quality, and echoes Scott's description of 'the silvery voice of Lucy Ashton'. This is, however, superseded by the foreboding nature of the introductory orchestral passage to the *cavatina* 'Regnava nel silenzio'. The appearance of the bloodstained ghost, and its beckoning to Lucia, seals the heroine's fate in Act 1, Scene 4 of the opera. The opening of the Edgardo/Lucia love duet contains a renewal of the former's vow of revenge against Lucia's house, which despite his love for her, he feels he could still fulfil:

EDGARDO: Sulla tomba che rinserra
Il tradito genitore,
Al tuo sangue eterna guerra
Io giurai nel mio furore
Pur quel voto non è infranto
Io potrei compirlo ancor.
   (*Lucia di Lammermoor*, Act 1, Scene 4)

(EDGARDO: On the tomb that imprisons my betrayed father, in my fury I swore eternal war on your family. That vow is not yet broken. I could still carry it out.)

Lucia's 'mad scene' falls into two principal sections. The first contains impressions of an imaginary wedding ceremony to Edgardo. The second part of the scene reveals her realization that she has married another, and is close to death. Cammarano's stage directions demand her appearance 'as a ghost, rather than a living creature, convulsive in movements, and with a smiling face, manifesting dementia and closeness to death'. Her opening lines are affected by the sound of Edgardo's voice:

Il dolce suono,

> Mi colpì di sua voce! Ah quella voce
> M'è qui nel cor discesa!
> (*Lucia di Lammermoor*, Act 2, Scene 5)

(The sweet sound of his voice impressed me. Ah, that voice has entered my heart.)

Instantly, however, she is filled with memories of the ghostly apparition revealed in the 'Regnava' *cavatina*. They manifest themselves in physical symptoms:

> Un gelo
> Mi serpeggia nel sen ... trema ogni fibra! ...
> Vacilla il piè! ... presso la fonte meco
> T'assidi alquanto ... ahimè ... sorge il tremendo
> Fantasma e ne separa.
> (*Lucia di Lammermoor*, Act 2, Scene 5)

(An icy chill tightens in my breast ... every fibre trembles. My foot falters ... you often sit with me by the fountain. Alas! The terrible ghost rises and separates us.)

The memory of the ghost is central to the conclusion of the opera, and the musical line rises dramatically as Lucia pronounces 'il fantasma' three times. The scene then develops in terms of impressions of what one hears, feels and sees, but does not express. The music rises to a climax at the conclusion of the imaginary wedding, in a highly elaborate cadenza for soprano and flute. The soprano's technical agility and vocal acrobatics demonstrate not only the ideological escape from imposed limits, but also a freedom of musical expression. Here the scale, deprived of a melodic order, communicates in its logical form the departure of the heroine from all preconceived order. Lucia, married to her Edgardo, insanely and idealistically describes her own vision of the scene:

> Ardon gl'incensi ... splendon
> Le sacre faci intorno!
> Ecco il ministro! ... Porgimi
> La destra... Oh lieto giorno!
> Alfin son tua, alfin sei mio.
> A me ti dona un Dio.
> (*Lucia di Lammermoor*, Act 2, Scene 5)

(The incense burns ... the sacred tapers flicker all around. Here is the minister! ... Give me your right hand. Oh! happy day. At last I am yours. At last you are mine. A god has given you to me.

The second part of the 'mad scene' is Scene 6 in the libretto. Lucia appears to understand clearly the circumstances and consequences of her signing of the marriage register. In a passage frequently omitted from modern performances of the opera she sings:

> Non mi guarda sì fiero
> Segnai quel foglio, è vero ...
> Nell'ira sua terribile
> Calpesta, oh Dio, l'anello!
> Mi maledice! ... Ah! vittima
> Fui d'un crudel fratello;
> Ma ognor t'amai ... lo giuro.
> (*Lucia di Lammermoor*, Act 2, Scene 6)

(Do not look on me so angrily. It is true that I signed the document. In his terrible anger, oh God, he tramples on the ring. He curses me! Ah, I was victim of a cruel brother, but I always loved you. I swear it.)

The memory of losing Edgardo for ever leads to the final resignation to fate. Her last words are of religious resignation:

> Spargi d'amaro pianto
> Il mio terrestre velo,
> Mentre lassù nel cielo
> Io pregherò per te.
> (*Lucia di Lammermoor*, Act 2, Scene 6)

(Bestow bitter tears on my earthly remains, while up there in heaven I will pray for you.)

This 'mad scene' is one of the most tragically dramatic scenes in all romantic opera. It can be argued that it stems from the inability or unwillingness of the heroine to exercise her own will, and so to avoid the final catastrophe. However, Cammarano's libretto serves to illustrate, as does Manzoni's portrait of the tormented Gertrude in the novel *I promessi sposi*, that the violent attempt to suffocate or suppress the emotions merely leads to their misdirection. The question remains whether Lucia is merely a spineless creature with an overactive imagination, or a psychological portrait of a battle with fate, concluding inevitably in the breakdown of the psyche, demonstrated in the course of a horror story. I am inclined to believe the latter, which places *Lucia di Lammermoor* in the genre of psychological drama, as opposed to mere stylized melodrama.

Bellini's final opera *I puritani di Scozia*, with a libretto by Count Carlo Pepoli, friend and adviser of the poet Giacomo Leopardi, was first produced at the Théâtre National du Vaudeville, in Paris, 1833. It is an example of glorious melodies, contrived dramatic situations and moments of effective and touching lyrical poetry. One such moment is contained in Elvira's 'mad scene' where Leopardian influence is apparent. Although Pepoli is clearly no Romani, Elvira is an example of a heroine driven to despair by the loss of her beloved, who manages to regain her sanity on his reappearance. The lengthy 'mad scene', in reality a bravura piece for soprano, opens, as does Lucia's *scena*, with reference to the sound of the voice of the beloved:

> Qui la voce sua soave
> Mi chiamava . . . e poi sparì.
> Qui giurava esser fedele
> Poi crudele – mi fuggì!
> Ah! mai più qui assorti insieme
> Nella gioia de' sospir,
> Ah rendetemi la speme,
> O lasciatemi morir.
> (*I puritani*, Act 2, Scene 2)

(Here his sweet voice was calling me . . . and then it faded. Here he swore to me to be faithful, then cruelly he abandoned me. Ah! never to be here together again sighing joyfully. Ah give me back hope – or let me die.)

Unlike Lucia's scene, however, there is little ground for psychological probing. The second section of the scene finds lunacy identified with love in an idyllic setting:

> Vien diletto, è in ciel la luna!
> Tutto tace intorno, intorno;

> Fin che spunti in ciel il giorno,
> Vieni, ti posa sul mio cor.
> (*I puritani*, Act 2, Scene 1)

(Come, beloved, there is a moon. All about is silent. Come, rest on my heart until day breaks.)

In *I puritani* the heroine's constant alternating between lucidity and delirium renders the opera a dated expression of nineteenth-century style and taste. Historically speaking, the work is never the less significant. From the point of view of the diffusion of English literature in nineteenth-century Italy, *Il pirata* and *Lucia di Lammermoor* are worthy of note, while *Anna Bolena* reveals Romani as a poet following in the true Italian romantic tradition.[20] Only *Lucia di Lammermoor*, however, stands as a pathological dramatization of madness, while providing the prima donna with the definitive 'mad scene' against which all other such scenes are measured.

7

JESTER, TROUBADOUR AND COURTESAN

I

Verdi's early period of operatic composition had been devoted to historical and political drama. It had inspired patriotic feeling, while it brought to life biblical figures, medieval conflicts and literary personae. In collaboration with the outstanding poet–librettists Solera, Cammarano and Piave, Verdi carried opera from the innocence and introspection which characterized the works of Donizetti and Bellini to a spectacular and grandiose art-form. Between 1842 and 1850 his plots included adaptations of works by Hugo (*Ernani*), Byron (*I due Foscari*), Schiller (*Giovanna d'Arco*, *I masnadieri* and *Luisa Miller*), Voltaire (*Alzira*) and Shakespeare (*Macbeth*). In these operas the ensemble marked the high point of the proceedings. The dramatic took precedence over the lyrical, and the plots for the most part dealt with heroic exploits. The librettist so provided figures of larger-than-life proportions in an effort to fire and capture the imagination of the public. By 1850, however, Verdi's creative genius was being employed in a new direction. Historically the period of the early Risorgimento and high romanticism was over. A more subtle, if somewhat cynical, approach was employed as regards life in general and its artistic representation. There grew a desire for the particular in place of the general, for the scene in place of the spectacle. A new intimacy, bringing with it a more precise psychological projection of being, was pursued by poets and musicians. Verdi, like all great innovators, was not, in his compositions, consciously following any preconceived pattern. Rather, after having distanced himself from the everyday life and emotions of his operatic characters in his early period, he later set about providing pointed characterizations and realistic portraits of happiness and misery.

Rigoletto (1851), *Il trovatore* (1853) and *La traviata* (1853) are regarded as the masterpieces of Verdi's middle period. Viewed collectively they illustrate Verdi's choice of three significant figures: a court jester, a troubadour and a courtesan, drawn from three diverse historical periods and settings – Renaissance, medieval and contemporary. Each contains a subtle *mise-en-scène* of human relations. In *Rigoletto* one witnesses a tender enactment of the father-daughter relationship, *Il trovatore* highlights the bond between mother and son, while in *La traviata* Verdi musically demonstrates a father's protectiveness towards his son. The subject of all three operas is love. *Rigoletto* shows the contrast between the libertinism of the Duke of Mantua, the girlish innocence of Gilda and the marketable charms of Maddalena. *Il trovatore* is set in an atmosphere of courtly love in northern Spain, while *La traviata* tells the story of the *demi-mondaine* Violetta Valéry who sacrifices all for love.

When one considers that the three operas were written in the short space of three years, one cannot but marvel at the composer's creative energy and versatility. Each of the three works is extremely different from the others. The protagonist in each case reveals to the full the dramatic possibilities of its class of voice. Rigoletto, the tormented jester, is brought to life as a lyric-dramatic baritone. Manrico, the troubadour of the title, is a heroic tenor. Violetta, 'la traviata' ('the led astray'), conveys the reckless gaiety and despair of her situation by means of lyric coloratura. At this point in his career Verdi sought to provide dramatic colour and atmosphere by carefully choosing the voice register and quality. With *Rigoletto* Italian opera had taken the first step away from traditional melodrama,[1] in order to prepare for the later 'music drama' of Wagner, and the ideal fusion of words and music in Verdi's *Otello* and *Falstaff*.

It is clear that Verdi, from the time he wrote the conclusion of *Luisa Miller* (1849) (which reveals a new, more intimate style of vocal writing, and an attempt to dramatize bourgeois values), was seeking to capture musically the dramatic possibilities of a text. It is therefore not surprising that *Rigoletto*, *Il trovatore* and *La traviata* are adapted from dramas which were controversial, if not actually successful. Verdi regarded Hugo's *Le Roi s'amuse* as 'one of the greatest subjects, and perhaps the greatest drama of modern times'.² He was struck by the boldness and novelty of Antonio García Gutiérrez's drama *El trovador*. Having seen a performance of the younger Dumas's *La Dame aux camélias* in Paris in 1852, he resolved to make it the subject of one of his future operas. In composing his three 'middle masterpieces', he engaged Francesco Maria Piave for *Rigoletto* and *La traviata*, and Salvatore Cammarano for *Il trovatore*. Cammarano died in July 1852 leaving part of the third and all of the fourth acts of the libretto unwritten. Verdi commissioned the young Neapolitan poet, Leone Emmanuele Bardare, to complete the text from Cammarano's notes. The three operas contain a strong individual flavour. As Charles Osborne points out, 'there is no mistaking pages of *Rigoletto*, *La traviata* or *Il trovatore* for one another. Each has its distinctive range of orchestral colour, its melodic shape and its overall dramatic form.'³ It is with the latter aspect of the works that this chapter is concerned.

Early in 1850 Verdi had been asked to write a new opera for the Fenice Theatre, Venice. Having attained success with his previous Venetian premières of *Ernani* and *Attila*, he set about looking for a suitable subject. With a view to the presentation of an opera for the carnival season of 1851, he contacted his librettist Francesco Maria Piave with whom he had successfully collaborated on *Ernani* (1844), *I due Foscari* (1844) and *Stiffelio* (1850). Eventually they settled on Victor Hugo's *Le Roi s'amuse*. This drama had been produced at the Théâtre-Français, Paris, on 22 November 1832. It tells of the adventures of the lascivious King Francis I of France, and the role played by his hunchback court jester Triboulet in the abduction of the wives and daughters of courtiers and noblemen. Verdi was extremely enthusiastic about the subject, as can be seen in his correspondence with Piave: 'Oh *Le Roi s'amuse* è il più gran soggetto e forse il più gran dramma dei tempi moderni. Tribolet è creazione degna di Shakespeare' (Oh *Le Roi s'amuse* is the greatest subject and perhaps the greatest drama of modern times. Tribolet is a creation worthy of Shakespeare!').⁴ Piave assured Verdi that the Austrian censors would not object to the subject, and the librettist set about his work.

It is indeed surprising that neither Verdi nor Piave foresaw censorship difficulties when one considers the circumstances surrounding the first, and only, performance of Hugo's drama in 1832, and its disastrous consequences. The day following the production Hugo received the following communication from

M. Jouslin de la Salle, artistic director of the Théâtre-Français: 'Il est dix heures et demie, et je reçois à l'instant *l'ordre* de suspendre les représentations du *Roi s'amuse*. C'est M. Taylor qui me communique cet ordre de la part du ministre. 23 novembre.' ('It is half-past ten and I receive at this moment *the order* to suspend the performances of *Le Roi s'amuse*. It is M. Taylor who communicates this order on behalf of the Minister. 23 November.')[5] The dramatist's first reaction was one of incredulity since the freedom of the theatre was implicitly written into the Constitution. As the Comédie-Française appealed for the decision to be revoked, what was on 23 November merely the order of a Minister became the order of the Ministry on 24 November. What was initially a 'suspension' became a 'prohibition'. Hugo determined to vindicate his freedom of expression by acting through the courts[6] and by appealing to public opinion. It was a case he could not possibly have won, despite his insistence that the plot of *Le Roi s'amuse* was highly moral. His argument was as follows:

> Why is the piece considered immoral? Is it because of the plot? The plot is as follows: Triboulet is deformed, Triboulet is ill, Triboulet is the court jester ... Triboulet hates the king because he is the king, the gentry because they are the gentry, ordinary men because they are not hunchbacks. His pastime is relentlessly to incite the gentry to opposition to the king. He corrupts the king, and pushes him towards tyranny and vice. In Triboulet's hands, the king is nothing more than a puppet. ... M. de Saint-Vallier forces his way into the king's presence and rebukes him on account of the dishonouring of Diane de Poitiers. Triboulet insults him, and M. de Saint-Vallier raises his arms and curses Triboulet. ... The true subject of the drama is the curse of M. de Saint-Vallier. On whom does this curse fall? On Triboulet, the king's clown? No. On Triboulet the man, the father, who has a heart, who has a daughter ... the old man's curse touches Triboulet in the sole person in the world whom he loves, his daughter. This same king, whom Triboulet encourages to indulge in fornication, seduces Triboulet's daughter. The clown is struck by Destiny in the same manner as M. de Saint-Vallier ... the curse of Diane's father is effected on Blanche's father. Without doubt it does not

rest with us to decide if that is a dramatic idea, but it certainly is a moral one.[7]

The government of Louis Philippe prohibited the piece, which continued to be banned during the Second Empire, not surprisingly since at that time Hugo himself was in political exile. In 1873 under the Third Republic, it was banned once again. When it was finally given a hearing in 1882, fifty years after the initial fiasco, the silence which greeted its staging was, to quote Ubersfeld, 'a hundred times more cruel than the fury and whistles of 1832'.[8]

Verdi and Piave experienced no fewer difficulties in their attempt to bring *Le Roi s'amuse* to the operatic stage. Just three months before the projected first performance, the management of the Fenice Theatre received a communication stating that the Military Governor Chevalier Gorzkowski had directed that the performance should not take place on account of the 'revolting immorality and obscene triviality of the libretto'[9] which Verdi had intended calling 'La maledizione' ('The curse'). The censors had reacted against a libretto which showed a reigning monarch as corrupt and licentious, and which offended church teaching by showing the effects of a curse. Verdi defended his choice and eventually a compromise was arrived at. The dramatic situations in Hugo's play were unaltered. The setting and the names of the characters were changed.[10] Francis I became the Duke of Mantua.[11] The jester's name was changed from Triboletto, an Italianized version of Hugo's Triboulet, to Rigoletto, deriving from *rigoler*, the French for 'guffaw', and this also became the title of the opera. The work was an outstanding success, but in order to pass the various censors, it was performed under a variety of titles including *Lionello*, *Clara di Perth* and *Viscardello*. It is said that Hugo resented the popularity of the opera until he heard its music; he was then prepared to admit its greatness.

Rigoletto marks Verdi's preoccupation with psychological drama. It reveals a search beyond the surface of social behaviour, in order to probe the secrets of the human heart. In doing so it demonstrates cause and effect, combining black comedy and pathetic tragedy. If one concludes that *La traviata* is primarily a social tragedy, one can state that *Rigoletto* is tragicomedy. Piave and Verdi, in bringing Hugo's work to the nineteenth-century opera-goer, were not merely diffusing French culture, but providing both the straight and operatic theatre with a fusion of genres. In doing so they succeeded in giving musical and dramatic life to a series of opposites, while introducing a discourse on evil and its operation, which prepares the way for the poetry and drama of Arrigo Boito.

The Italian adaptation of *Le Roi s'amuse* has a protagonist who enacts the roles of jester and father. In doing so he participates in black comedy and tragedy. The comic concerns his amusing tricks and acrobatic feats, which he performs in order to amuse his king and the courtiers whom he despises. As a father he witnesses the dishonour and murder of his daughter. Laughter and tears so form the daily anguish of Piave's protagonist; he weeps at the memory of his dead wife who took pity on a deformed jester:

> Deh non parlare al misero
> Del suo perduto bene ...
> Ella sentia, quell'angelo,
> Pietà delle mie pene.
> Solo, difforme, povero,
> Per compassion m'amò.
> Morrìa. ...
> (*Rigoletto*, Act 1, Scene 9)

(Ah do not speak to the unfortunate one of his lost love. That angel, she felt pity on account of my sorrow. Alone, deformed, poor, she loved me out of compassion. She died....)

The complexity of the hunchback jester's life and experience is here revealed. Both jester and lover are seen in a confession of sorrow. In addition, reference is made to his deformity. This points to another dimension that the drama embraces. Rigoletto, symbolizing ugliness, is juxtaposed with beauty, represented by his daughter Gilda. The constrast can be carried further, in that Gilda also stands for youth, innocence and virginity. Throughout the text she is described as an angel. Her father, as aged, ugly and experienced, is nothing short of a devilish figure. Together, father and daughter can be seen as personifications of good and evil. The symbolism does not, however, end just there. Their relationship is a dramatized projection of the closeness of the forces of light and darkness, and of the difficulty of defining their limits. While the angelic quality of Gilda is unsoiled by her dishonour and the evil with which she comes in contact, Rigoletto the father's tragic loss, and his adoration of his daughter, save him from appearing merely a grotesque parody on human existence.

Rigoletto heralds a new and moral theme which will appear again and again in Verdi's work, and will culminate in his masterpiece *Otello*. There is a new preoccupation with evil, and an attempt to come to terms with man's control over it. Only with his collaboration with Boito will he succeed in projecting a clear and uncontradictory vision of its operation in the human mind and will. Hugo's claim that *Le Roi s'amuse* was a moral work was apparently accepted by Verdi and Piave. What both failed to consider, however, was the ecclesiastical reaction to what amounted to a negation of free will.[12] A similar attitude is revealed in *La forza del destino* (1862), also with a libretto by Piave.

Rigoletto blames others for his misfortune:

> O uomini, o natura
> Vil scellerato mi faceste voi! ...
>   O dannazione!
> Odio a voi, cortigiani schernitori!
> Quanta in mordervi ho gioia!
> Se iniquo son, per cagion vostro è solo.
>   (*Rigoletto*, Act 1, Scene 8)

(Oh men, oh nature. It was you who made me a vile, wicked one. Oh! Damnation. Hatred to you, oh scoffing courtiers. How I rejoice in wounding you. If I am evil, it is on account of you.)

Destiny, it seems, has made Rigoletto evil. The physical and the moral are seen to complement each other. Monterone's curse is an attempt to effect justice by means of vice. Rigoletto's tragic error is his willingness to allow such forces to govern his being. His philosophy of revenge, in addition to provoking an upheaval of the elements, carries in its wake the human tragedy of a bereft father. The true cry of the opera is contained in the lines: 'Egli è Delitto, Punizion son io' ('He is Crime, I am Punishment') (*Rigoletto*, Act 3, Scene 4).

As Rigoletto exercises judgement and vengeance the allegorical nature of the work is made clear at its conclusion. It is a drama of libertinism, betrayal, envy and hatred. It tells of a being, the centre of a tragedy of revenge and counter-revenge, who does not do unto others as he would have them do unto himself, and who, in a final desperate cry of revenge, destroys the one remaining light in his life.

Rigoletto illustrates the working of evil, and the destruction of good through evil. Piave here demonstrates the frailty and futility of human judgement when imprisoned in a world of parody and pretence, symbolized by the court of Mantua. In the libretto *La forza del destino*, the individual will be presented, devoid of all ability to control the events governing his own life. Finally in *Otello*, Verdi, in collaboration with Arrigo Boito, traces more subtly the source and nature of evil, and the futility of the pursuit of virtue through vice.

Is *Le Roi s'amuse* a morality play or an immoral drama? Is *Rigoletto* a romantic tragedy or a theological dilemma? These are some of the questions which present themselves to the reader of today, engaged in the study of the Italian opera as an interdisciplinary exercise, and a watershed in the history of European ideas.

II

Salvatore Cammarano acquired a copy of Antonio García Gutiérrez's *drama cabbaleresco El Trovador* in January 1851. The work had achieved extraordinary success when first presented in Madrid in August 1836. Soon the young writer's name had spread throughout Europe, bringing him fame on a par with that of Victor Hugo and Lord Byron, authors whose works had already inspired some of Verdi's finest operatic writing. Gutiérrez's original drama, one of unbridled emotion, is written partly in prose and partly in verse, and set against the backdrop of a Spanish civil war in the fifteenth century. When Cammarano presented Verdi with his first draft of the libretto, the composer replied with a long letter, in which he suggested that the librettist had perhaps not found the work congenial.[13] He suggested that they might find an alternative text to adapt.[14] Although already suffering from the illness which would prove fatal in July 1852, Cammarano did not wish to renounce work on *Il trovatore*. After agreeing to submit to all the maestro's demands, he managed to complete almost three acts before his untimely death.

Verdi's main criticism of Cammarano's first draft was that it did not convey the strength and novelty of the original, and that

Azucena did not maintain her 'strange and novel' disposition. Her devotion to both her mother and son were not, he felt, communicated in forceful enough a manner. Verdi had always regarded the gypsy Azucena as the true heroine of the work, and insisted on the significance of her role throughout the opera, in all his correspondence on the subject. On Cammarano's demise Leone Emmanuele Bardare was entrusted with the task of completing the work. Born in Naples in 1820, he had already written *Le nozze di Pulcinella*, set by a group of composers in 1851. Later he would provide about a dozen librettos, for composers whose works today are forgotten. As soon as Verdi entered into negotiations with Bardare he set out a number of changes and additions which he required. First, he insisted on a long set-piece for Azucena in Act 2. 'Stride la vampa' as it stands today is Bardare's composition. The second change which Verdi effected was to have the Count Di Luna's *Romanza* omitted from Act 3, and an aria added for him in Act 2. Bardare did as he was told, and wrote the now famous 'Il balen' for the Count Di Luna. The omission of the Count's *Romanza* from Act 3 left an unfortunate gap in the poetry and music, so in its place Bardare wrote Leonora's 'D'amor sull'ali rosee'. Indeed it can be said that Bardare wrote some of the most attractive lines of the libretto. In addition, Verdi's own claim to the title of librettist should not be understated.[15] Just five weeks before the opening night of *Il trovatore*, Verdi made two further changes. At the conclusion of Act 2 he removed a sixteen-line passage, reduced four of Cammarano's lines to two, and rewrote the last lines of the opera. *Il trovatore* is truly then a drama in four acts, after Gutiérrez, with text by Cammarano, Bardare and Verdi, and music by Verdi.

Of the five sections into which Gutiérrez divided his drama ('El duello', 'El convento', 'La gitana', 'La revelacíon' and 'El suplicio'), Cammarano retained four, so providing each act with a title of its own. *Il trovatore* represents a return to the world of romance, of courtly love, duty, honour and loyalty, as the titles of its acts convey: 'Il duello ('The duel'), 'La gitana' ('The gipsy'), 'Il figlio della Zingara' ('The gipsy's son') and 'Il supplizio' ('The execution'). It can be said that the plot of *Il trovatore* shows two highly coloured and contrasting worlds to lyric and dramatic advantage. The first is the world of courtly love, symbolized by the wandering minstrel of the title. The second is one of popular cults and local traditions, the highly imaginative world of the gypsies, curses, spells and screech owls, conceived at a time before Mérimée or Verga had created their ideal vehicles for operatic realism. The protagonist Manrico belongs to both traditions, and the unity of plot is arrived at through him. A gypsy by upbringing, in reality the brother of the Count Di Luna, to whom he is the rival for the hand of Lady Leonora of Aragon, Manrico by virtue of his serenades, military prowess and noble birth belongs to the tradition of the courtly romance. The conflicting element of the plot is further highlighted by the rivalry of Leonora's two suitors, Di Luna and Manrico, count and minstrel, baritone and tenor, and in reality brothers. In poetic terms the contrasts are expressed in terms of light imagery, with chivalric society projected through limpid images of moonlight encounters. The world of popular storytelling and fairy-tale superstition is seen through the impassioned outbursts of Manrico and Azucena, in which love, hatred and ardour are communicated through images of fire, blood and blackness, associated with smoke, ashes and death.

The folkloristic aspect of the libretto, and the place of storytelling in the plot, are established in Act 1, Scene 1 ('Il duello'/'The duel') as Ferrando, captain of the Count Di Luna's guard, relates the gloomy history of the Count's family:

> Abbietta zingara, fosca vegliarda!
> Cingeva i simboli di maliarda!
> E sul fanciullo, con viso arcigno,
> L'occhio affiggeva, torvo, sanguigno! ...
>
> La fattucchiera perseguitata
> Fu presa, e al rogo fu condannata;
> Ma rimaneva la maledetta
> Figlia, ministra di ria vendetta.
> (*Il trovatore*, Act 1, Scene 1)

(Vile gypsy, dark old woman. She wore the trappings of a wizard! She fixed her dark, passionate glance, with sullen expression, on the child.

The sorceress was pursued, captured and condemned to the pyre. But there yet remained her cursed daughter, the minister of guilty revenge.)

Images of darkness predominate, as they also do in the following passage which transforms the tale into a horror story. The episode is related by the bass Ferrando, who vocally provides the necessary atmosphere. Scenically a similar impression is created, with the narrative related at midnight:

> È credenza che dimori
> Ancor nel mondo l'anima perduta
> Dell'empia strega, e quando il ciel è nero
> In varie forme altrui si mostri.
> (*Il trovatore*, Act 1, Scene 1)

(Belief has it that the damned soul of the evil witch still dwells in this world, and when the sky is black she shows herself in various forms.)

In addition to its function as a popular tale of charms, spells and the power of the 'evil eye', the atmosphere of the fairy-tale has been established, so providing an easy introduction to the world of the courtly romance in the following scenes. Azucena's account of the same incident is dramatically charged with movement and physical reactions. The only light present is that of the flames which quickly consume the condemned – her mother.

AZUCENA: Stride la vampa! – la folla indomita
Corre a quel fuoco – lieta in sembianza;
Urli di gioia – intorno echeggiano:
Cinta di sgherri – donna s'avanza!
Sinistra splende – sui volti orribili
La tetra fiamma – che s'alza al ciel.
Stride la vampa! giunge la vittima
Nero vestita, – discinta e scalza!
Grido feroce – di morte levasi;
L'eco il ripete – di balza in balza.
(*Il trovatore*, Act 2, Scene 1)

(AZUCENA: The flame roars! The mob, joyful in appearance, runs to that fire. Shouts of joy resound. Flanked by guards, a woman advances. The dark flame, which rises towards heaven, blazes grimly on the horrible faces. The flame roars! The victim arrives clad in black, in disarray, and barefooted. A horrifying cry of death rises, the echo of which resounds from cliff to cliff.)

Azucena continues to relate that in a moment of confusion and desire for revenge at her mother's being burned at the stake, she kidnapped the child of Count Di Luna, and flung it into the flames. When she recovered her composure, the Count's child was still by her side. She had burned her own son! Smouldering emotions, burning hatreds and heated rivalry is the stuff of which *Il trovatore* is made. The introduction to the lyrical and courtly aspect of the opera is also accompanied by dark foreboding reminiscent of Cammarano's Act 1, Scene 2 of *Lucia di Lammermoor*, when Alisa attempts to deter Lucia from her disastrous romantic involvement. In *Il trovatore* the words are uttered by Ines, Leonora's confidante. As is apparent, the chivalric and popular themes are linked by the imagery of flames:

INES: Perigliosa fiamma
Tu nutri! ... Oh come, dove
La premiera favilla
In te s'appresse? ...

Dubbio ma triste presentimento
In me risveglia quest'uomo arcano.
(*Il trovatore*, Act 1, Scene 2)

(INES: You nurture a dangerous flame! How and where was the first spark ignited in you? ... I have doubts. This mysterious man awakens a sad foreboding in me.)

Leonora's reply refers to the time of their meeting 'when civil war was *burning*'. Her narrative follows the conventional form and content of the chivalric tradition. Tommaso Grossi's *Ildegonda* is the Italian work which contains lines which most closely resemble Leonora's words.[16]

The troubadour's serenade is cast in an atmosphere of idyllic beauty and delicacy of expression:

LEONORA: Tacea la notte placida
E bella in ciel sereno
La luna il viso argenteo
Mostrava lieto e pieno.
Quando suonar per l'aere,
Infin allor sì muto,
Dolci s'udiro e flebili
Gli accordi di un liuto,

> E versi melancolici
> Un Trovator cantò.
> 			(*Il trovatore*, Act 1, Scene 2)

(LEONORA: The peaceful night was silent, and the moon, beautiful in the clear sky, showed her silvery face full and happy. When through the air up to then so quiet there was heard the sweet and plaintive harmony of a lute. And a troubadour sang melancholy verses.)

The same light imagery predominates in the lines of Count Di Luna:

> Oh! Leonora,
> Tu desta sei; mel dice
> Da quel verone, tremolante un raggio
> Della notturna lampa. ...
> Ah! l'amorosa fiamma.
> 			(*Il trovatore*, Act 1, Scene 2)

(O Leonora, you are awake; the trembling ray of the night light from that balcony tells me so. Ah! the amorous flame!)

The Count's aria in Act 2, Scene 3 is dedicated to the light of Leonora's smile:

> Il balen del suo sorriso
> D'una stella vince il raggio!
> Il fulgor del suo bel viso
> Novo infonde in me coraggio! ...
> Ah l'amor, l'amore ond'ardo
> Le favelli in mio favore!

(The light of her smile is more radiant than a star! The splendour of her beautiful face instils in me new courage. Ah, love, the love with which I burn may it speak on my behalf.)

Manrico, it has been stated, is the unifying force between the two diverse poetic worlds and societies depicted in the opera. If he belongs to both, however, he is finally forced to make a choice between being a son or a lover (Act 3, Scene 6). His first expression of the life of the troubadour is in Act 1, Scene 3.

> Deserto sulla terra,
> Col rio destino in guerra,
> È sola speme un cor
> Al Trovator!
> Ma s'ei quel cor possiede,
> Bello di casta fede,
> È d'ogni re maggior
> Il Trovator.

(Alone in the world, with adverse destiny in war, a heart is the troubadour's only hope. But if he possesses that heart, beautiful in its pure fidelity, the troubadour is greater than every king.)

His choice is expressed in the highly dramatic 'Di quella pira'. Although preparing for his marriage to Leonora who remarks that their nuptials are overshadowed by a gloomy light, when confronted with the news of his mother's arrest and impending execution, he makes no apologies for his departure. The language and imagery return to that of Act 2. Manrico's attempt to save Azucena is communicated through images of the extinction of fire. The aria also contains his statement of loyalty to his mother and the popular folk world of the gypsies:

> Di quella pira l'orrendo foco
> Tutte le fibre m'arse, avvampò! ...
> Empi, spegnetela, o ch'io fra poco
> Col sangue vostro la spegnerò ...
> Era già figlio prima d'amarti,
> Non può frenarmi il tuo martir,
> Madre infelice, corro a salvarti,
> O teco almeno corro a morir.
> (*Il trovatore*, Act 3, Scene 6)

(The horrible fire of the funeral pile burned all my nerves. It smouldered. Evil ones, put it out, or I shall extinguish it with your blood. Before I fell in love with you, I was already a son, and your suffering cannot hold me back. Unhappy mother, I rush to save you or else I rush, at least, to die with you.)

Verdi, in stressing the filial and maternal love in the libretto, was pointing indirectly to the fundamental theme of the opera. The conflict between two contrasting societies, the differences between birth and upbringing, and the meeting of the two forces in the person of Manrico: this is indeed the subject of the opera. A final reunion of personae occurs in the last scene of the work. Manrico and Azucena, in prison, are joined by Leonora and Di Luna. Leonora, having taken poison to avoid marriage with the Count exclaims, touching her breast, 'Ma qui, qui foco orribile arde' ('But here, here a horrible fire burns').[17]

The final victory belongs to fire, its memory and prospect. The ultimate triumph belongs to Azucena who, on Manrico's execution exclaims. 'Egli era tuo fratello! Sei vendicata, o madre!' ('He was your brother! You are avenged, o mother!')

Here the gypsy finally reveals the complexity of her own character, and the conflicting emotions which make up her relationship with Manrico. *Il trovatore* is thus one of the most colourful and individual tragedies of revenge of nineteenth-century melodrama. Despite its heroic theme and Verdi's use of chorus and ensemble, the opera, with its subtle analysis and dramatic projection of Azucena, points towards the character drawing on a grand scale of *Un ballo in maschera* and *Otello*.

III

Verdi's desire for innovation and his aim to come to grips with the literary climate of his day became manifest in the early 1850s. In *Rigoletto*, apart from experimenting with a fusion of theatrical genres, and providing both a hearing and free publicity for the banned *Le Roi s'amuse*, he gave the public the first of his pieces that could truly be regarded as modern. In *Il trovatore*, while returning to the *romanzesco*, he provided a subtle exploration of human relations, in addition to musing on family loyalties. *La traviata* represents, however, a complete departure from tradition. As well as abandoning history, and providing a plot set in modern times, Verdi's opera also examines a topic which had become something of an issue not only in his own day but also as regards his personal life: namely the social standing of a 'kept woman', a fallen woman or, as he preferred to define her, 'la traviata' ('the led astray'). Piave's libretto is a social document which departs little from the younger Dumas's tragedy *La Dame aux camélias*. Violetta is portrayed as representative of a class which falls victim to the morals of bourgeois society. Yet the tragedy of Violetta, paradoxically, points to the permanence of the social ethic to which Verdi himself eventually bowed. *La traviata* is not merely, as has often been stated, 'a portrait of a woman', but a portrait of Parisian society, and the conflict between the *demi-monde* and the *petit monde* of moral scruples. However, Verdi's refined and delicate melodies, calling for vocal purity and elegance of emission, render Violetta a romantic victim *par excellence*, caught in a vulgar and realistically contrived setting in which her fragile beauty cannot possibly survive.

La Dame aux camélias by Alexandre Dumas the younger was first published in novel form in 1848. Verdi may well have read, or at least been acquainted with, the book, since he and Giuseppina Strepponi spent some time in Paris that year. However, it was not until 1852 that he saw the dramatized form of the work, and at once asked his French editor to send him a copy. Having read it he commissioned Piave to provide him with a libretto. It is obvious that Verdi was drawn to the subject – that of a courtesan who attains happiness through love, only to sacrifice all as a result of social pressure – on account of the state of his own private affairs.[18] Since 1849 he had been living with the soprano Giuseppina Strepponi (1815–97), who had helped him to get his first opera *Oberto* produced, and had created the role of Abigaille in *Nabucco* (1842). Their cohabitation scandalized Busseto, and Strepponi was ostracized by the locals. Verdi also succeeded in incurring the wrath of his benefactor and ex-father-in-law Antonio Barezzi, who accused him of scandalous behaviour in not legalizing his union with Strepponi. It would appear that Dumas's projection of the dignity and independence of Marguerite Gautier,[19] his heroine, touched Verdi deeply. Piave, in *La traviata*, Act 2, scene 5, reproduces exactly the original French of *La Dame aux camélias*, Act 3, scene 4:

MARGUERITE: Pardonnez-moi, monsieur; mais je suis femme et je suis chez moi. . . . Je vous prie de permettre que je me retire, encore plus pour vous que pour moi-même.
(*La Dame aux camélias*, Act 3, Scene 4)[20]

VIOLETTA [*alzandosi risentita*].
Donna son io, signore, ed in mia casa;

> Ch'io vi lasci assentite,
> Più per voi che per me.
>   (*La traviata*, Act 2, Scene 5)

(Sir, I am a lady, and in my own house. Allow me to leave you, more for your sake than for my own.)[21]

Giuseppina's independence and right to courtesy from all who visited Verdi had been spelled out by him in a letter to his ex-father-in-law in the autumn of 1851, some months before the première of *La Dame aux camélias*. The spirit of the letter reflects his sympathy for creatures such as Marguerite, and his social commitment to their defence:

> There lives in my house a lady, free and independent, who like myself, prefers a solitary life, and in possession of a fortune that caters for all her needs. Neither I nor she is obliged to account to anyone for our actions. But who knows what our relations are? What affairs? What ties? What rights I have over her or she over me? Who knows whether she is my wife or not? And if she is, who knows what the reasons may be for not publicly announcing the fact? Who knows whether that is a good or a bad thing? Might it not be a good thing? And even if it is a bad thing, who has the right to ostracize us? I will say this, however: in my house she is entitled to as much respect as myself, more even. And no one is allowed to forget that for any reason. And finally she has every right, both because of her conduct and her character, to that consideration she habitually shows to others.[22]

Never the less Verdi eventually conformed to the social dictates of the day. He and Giuseppina were married in 1859 and by all accounts 'lived happily ever after'.[23]

Although Piave's libretto follows the play extremely closely, and at times provides a literal translation of it, the character of Marguerite is essentially different from that of Piave's creation, Violetta Valéry. The latter is essentially a romantic figure, incorporating all the requisites of romantic tragedy: youth, beauty, illness, an unhappy love affair and finally death from that romantic illness *par excellence*, consumption. In spite of the garishness of the circle in which she moves, Violetta conserves a degree of innocence denied by Dumas to his protagonist. In addition, Violetta is seen

10 Francesco Maria Piave (1810–76)

to act on instinct, at the dictates of her emotion. Marguerite, on the contrary, before deciding to dedicate some time to her relationship with Armand, cynically and objectively assesses the attributes and nature of love. In fact the speech beginning 'Pourquoi? Tu veux le savoir', the source for the aria 'Ah fors'è lui' is a case in point. The French text reveals a clear-cut analysis of her situation and that of her kind. Violetta's aria is a piece of romantic idealism.

As part of a consideration of the similarities and differences between the two heroines, it is useful to bear in mind the European literary climate of the early 1850s. By those years the initial impetus and originality of the romantic movement had given way to a more objective assessment of the times and the state of organized society. As early as the 1830s in France, Stendhal had employed realistic symbolism in *Le Rouge et le noir* (1830) and *La Chartreuse de Parme* (1839). Balzac, in his novels, sought to reproduce the everyday humdrum existence of the masses, and in doing demonstrated the effect of environment on the individual's behaviour. In other words, a scientific approach to being and behaviour was adopted. The study of an individual was based on the study of the society in which he or she moved. Realism reached Italy as a result of the success of writers such as Dumas the younger, Balzac and Zola. Unlike the form it took in France, centred as it was for the most part on urban settings, the world of courtesans and of the back-street tavern, Italian realism reached its high point in depicting provincialism, peasant existence, and the lives of miners, olive pickers and fisherfolk, complete with local colour. The first significant expression of this social vision was the Sicilian writer Giovanni Verga's *Vita dei campi* (1880), which appeared some twenty-seven years after the first performance of *La traviata*. Verga's works were enthusiastically received. They established logic and objectivity as the foremost tools of the storyteller, and projected clearly what was and was not, as opposed to what ought to have been.

Dumas's *La Dame aux camélias* can be regarded as a realistic work. Its subject had already been touched upon by Prevost in *Manon Lescaut* (1731) and by Hugo in *Marion de Lorme* (1829). In dramatized form, however, it forced audiences to face up to the social issues it presents. Dumas's work depicts a world of coarse gaiety, and reveals Marguerite as a product of such society:

MARGUERITE: Ou que j'y croie, alors vous aurez une triste société, celle d'une femme nerveuse, malade, triste, ou gaie d'une gaieté plus triste que le chagrin. Une femme qui dépense cent mille francs par an, c'est bon pour un vieux richard comme le duc, mais c'est bien ennuyeux pour un jeune homme comme vous.

(*La Dame aux camélias*, Act 1, Scene 10)

(MARGUERITE: Or rather, were I to believe in it, then you would be subject to a sad companionship. To that of an excitable, ill and sad women, or one of a cheerfulness more wretched than sorrow.

A woman who spends 100,000 francs a year, that is all right for a rich old fellow like the duke, but it is very boring for a young man like yourself.)

Marguerite's realistic (as opposed to idealistic) review of her position is revealed in Act 2, Scene 5. The second act of the play has no counterpart in Verdi's opera. In it Marguerite considers the possibility of going to live with Armand, and its implications. Although the central ideas expressed in Scene 5 would appear to be Piave's source of inspiration for the recitative 'È strano, è strano!', Dumas reveals a far more calculating character than his adapter, who has condensed the piece and softened the edges in order to produce a more gentle persona:

Qui m'eût dit, il y a huit jours, que cet homme, dont je ne soupçonnais pas l'existance, occuperait à ce point, et si vite, mon coeur et ma pensée? M'aime-t-il d'ailleurs? Sais-je seulement si je l'aime, moi qui n'ai jamais aimé? Mais pourquoi sacrifier une joie? Pourquoi ne pas se laisser aller aux caprices de son coeur? – Que suis-je? Une créature du hasard! Laissons donc le hasard faire de moi ce qu'il voudra. – C'est égal, il me semble que je suis plus heureuse que je ne l'ai encore été.

(*La Dame aux camélias*, Act 2, Scene 5)

(Who would have told me, a week ago, that this man, whose existence I did not even suspect, would occupy my heart and my thoughts so fully and so quickly? Does he love me, moreover? Do I know if I love him, I who have never loved? But why sacrifice a pleasure? Why not let oneself follow the caprices of one's heart? What am I? A creature of fortune! Then let fortune do with me as it will – it makes no difference. It seems to me that I am happier than I have ever been.)

È strano! ... è strano! ... in core
Scolpiti ho quegli accenti!
Saria per me sventura un serio amore?
Che risolvi, o turbata anima mia?
Null'uomo ancora t'accendeva. ... O gioia
Ch'io non conobbi, essere amata amando!
E sdegnarla, poss'io
Per l'aride follie del viver mio?
  (*La traviata*, Act 1, Scene 5)

(It is strange ... it is strange. ... These words are engraved on my heart! Would a serious love be a disaster for me? What do you think, o my troubled soul? No man has yet conquered you. Oh joy unknown, to be loved, while loving. And can I forgo it, on account of the fruitless madness of my lifestyle?)

In Dumas's tragedy Marguerite reveals a certain disdain for her lovers, while expressing the hope of finding one who might make no demands upon her. Piave uses only the second section of Marguerite's 'confession' of her life and impressions. The first part reveals a knowing, shrewd and egocentric woman, an aspect of the character which both Piave and Verdi were anxious to ignore:

MARGUERITE: Nous paraissons heureuses, et l'on nous envie. En effet, nous avons des amants qui se ruinent, non pas pour nous, comme ils le disent, mais pour leur vanité; nous sommes les premières dans leur amour-propre, les dernières dans leur estime. ...

Je rêvais donc, par moments, sans oser le dire à personne, de recontrer un homme assez élevé pour ne me demander compte de rien, et pour vouloir bien être l'amant de mes impressions. Cet homme, je l'avais trouvé dans le duc; mais la vieillesse ne protège ni ne console.
  (*La Dame aux camélias*, Act 2, Scene 13)

(MARGUERITE: We appear happy, and are envied. In reality, we have lovers who ruin themselves, not for us, as they say, but on account of their vanity. We are the highest creatures in their self-respect, the lowest in their esteem. ...

At certain moments, then, I used to dream, without daring to tell anyone about it, of meeting a man sufficiently noble of heart not to ask me to account for anything but to be willing to be the lover of my imagination. I had found that man in the duke; but old age neither protects nor consoles.)

Part of the conclusion of Marguerite's speech is contained in the second part of the first act aria 'Ah fors'è lui' which is usually cut in theatrical performances:

MARGUERITE: En une minute, comme une folle, j'ai bâti tout un avenir sur ton amour, j'ai rêvé campagne, pureté; je me suis souvenue de mon enfance.
(*La Dame aux camélias*, Act 2, Scene 13)

(MARGUERITE: In a moment, like one crazed, I built a whole future on your love. I dreamed of the countryside, pureness, I remembered my childhood.)

VIOLETTA: A me fanciulla, un candido
E trepido desire
Quest'effigiò dolcissimo
Signor dell'avvenire,
Quando ne' ciel il raggio
Di sua beltà vedea,
E tutta me pascea
Di quel divino error. . . .
Follie! . . . follie . . . delirio vano è questo!
(*La traviata*, Act 1, Scene 5)

(VIOLETTA: As a young girl, a trepid and innocent desire fashioned this gentleman of the future. And when I saw in heaven the ray of his beauty, I fed my entire being on that divine invention. Folly, folly. This is vain delirium.)

A final example of Piave's softening of the contours of his heroine is to be seen in an exchange between Marguerite and Père Duval, which was excluded from the opera:

M. DUVAL: On me l'avait bien dit, que vous étiez une dangereuse personne.
MARGUERITE: Oui, monsieur, dangereuse, mais pour moi et non pour les autres.
(*La Dame aux camélias*, Act 3, Scene 4)

(M. DUVAL: I have been rightly informed that you are a dangerous woman.
MARGUERITE: Yes, sir, dangerous, but for myself, not for others.)

Piave's libretto is a portrait of Parisian night-life and the drinking, gambling and total dedication to frenetic pleasure of the *demi-monde*. It brings to life a society which admits of no limitations, imposed by either god or man. Paradoxically Violetta represents the rapid passing of the flower of youth. She is a romantic creature who must of necessity perish in a world of all-consuming pleasure, betrayals and orgies. While Piave's social milieu is in no way as stark as that of Dumas, there is nevertheless the frequent reference to frenetic pleasure, and a total disregard for marital fidelity. The true nature of Violetta's 'profession' is brought home by means of the supporting characters of Flora, Gaston, Baron Douphol and the chorus. Act 1 is a masterpiece of fast-moving dialogue, with the recurrence of terms such as 'gioie' ('jewels'), 'brillare' ('shine'), 'diletto' ('delight') and 'piacere' ('pleasure'). Violetta's first words are as follows:

> Flora, amici, la notte che resta
> D'altre gioie qui fate brillare.
> Fra le tazze è più viva la festa.
> (*La traviata*, Act 1, Scene 1)

(Flora, friends, let what remains of the night glitter with new jewels. The party is more lively in the company of wine glasses.)

The fact that the heroine's life is totally dedicated to pleasure in order to make her forget her illness is communicated in her next lines. These stress her *willingness* to live as she does:

> Lo voglio;
> Al piacer m'affido, ed io soglio
> Con tal farmaco i mali sopir.
> (*La traviata*, Act 1, Scene 1)

(It is my wish; I entrust myself to pleasure, and I am accustomed to drown my sorrow in such medicine.)

There then follow further words in praise of liquor. The first verse of the drinking song celebrates wine as the purveyor of love.

Sung by Alfredo (Armand), it is a linguistic device to reveal to Violetta that he has identified with her earlier vocabulary: 'lieti calici' ('merry glasses'), 'dolci fremiti' ('sweet tremors'), 'caldi baci' ('hot kisses'). Violetta's second verse is a confirmation of what is already clear. Her life is dedicated to reckless gaiety:

> Tra voi saprò dividere
> Il tempo mio giocondo;
> Tutto è follia nel mondo
> Ciò che non è piacer.
> Godiamo, fugace e rapido
> È il gaudio dell'amore;
> È un fior che nasce e muore,
> Ne più si può goder.
> Godiamo, c'invita un fervido
> Accento lusinghier.
> (*La traviata*, Act 1, Scene 2)

(With you I shall share my happy times. All in the world which is not given over to pleasure is folly. Let us enjoy ourselves, swift and fleeting is the sensation of love. It is a flower which is born and dies, and soon can be no longer tasted. Let us make merry. A fervent and flattering voice bids us do so.)

If further proof were needed of Violetta's hunger for enjoyment, Piave provides it in the conclusion to Act 1. Yet he also reveals a woman helplessly trapped in a world of corrupt gaiety, from which she cannot realistically hope to escape. As a result, she throws herself into it more feverishly than her companions:

> Povera donna, sola,
> Abbandonata in questo
> Popoloso deserto
> Che appellano Parigi;
> Che spero or più? ... Che far degg'io ... Gioire,
> Di voluttà nei vortici perire.
> Sempre libera degg'io
> Folleggiar di gioia in gioia,
> Vo' che scorra il viver mio
> Pei sentieri del piacer.
> Nasca il giorno, o il giorno muoia,
> Sempre lieta ne' ritrovi

> A diletti sempre nuovi
> Dee volare il mio pensier.
> (*La traviata*, Act 1, Scene 5)

(Unfortunate woman, alone, abandoned in this populated desert called Paris. What more can I hope for? ... What must I do? ... Make merry, and die in a whirlpool of pleasure. Always freely, I must frolic from delight to delight. I wish my life to flit along the paths of enjoyment, be it daybreak or nightfall always happy at gatherings, my thoughts must always pursue new delights.)

George R. Marek in his essay '*La traviata* – a chamber opera' states that 'there is only one central protagonist, lovingly delineated; there is no hero and, strictly speaking, no villain.'[24] If indeed a villain can be found, it is the social circle in which Violetta resides, which both creates and destroys her. The *demi-monde* is frequented by dukes, barons, viscounts and other scions of the aristocracy. Paris, that 'popoloso deserto', is seen in contrast to a world of pure emotions, represented by Provence and symbolized by Alfredo. The latter merely enters Violetta's world in pursuit of her. By and large, he is a stranger in such circles. The opera's Act 2 serves as an illustration of the peace and harmony of that 'other world' dreamed of by Violetta, but which is durable from neither a practical nor a financial viewpoint. As Annina says, 'Lo spendio è grande a viver qui solinghi' ('The expense of living here alone is great') (*La traviata*, Act 2, Scene 1).

The romantic idyll is shattered by both economic necessity and bourgeois respectability. The reality of Violetta's situation provides her with no option other than to return to the only world she knows. In Act 1 Piave shows the courtesan's salon, her guests, lovers and pretenders, dominated by the beauty and elegance of the heroine. The realistic effects are created by the banquet, toast and ball. All seems possible when love is about to conquer. Act 2, Scene 9 brings to sight another salon, in the home of another *demi-monde*. The recklessness of life is brought to mind by the pre-eminence of the gambling table. In this society life is seen merely as a gamble, in which the most reckless player wins. Violetta is at this point broken and defeated. She is no longer mistress of the dramatic situation, as was the case in Act 1. For that reason the environment appears all the more decadent, the 'gentlemen' all the more vulgar and her plight all the more hapless.

A veil is dropped on the past, as masked matadors and gypsies enter, and all look to the future. From the viewpoint of dramatic spectacle the chorus and ballet of the gypsies and matadors add a further dimension to the performance of the opera. Seen within the context of the tragedy, however, they demonstrate the escapism of a gathering whose major preoccupation is the celebration of the 'bue grasso' ('fattened ox'), the symbol of marital infidelity. In Act 3, Scene 4, as Violetta lies on her deathbed, and the revellers outside her window celebrate carnival, the world to which she belonged is seen in all its shallowness and depravity. The two verses in praise of the 'bue grasso' precede the arrival of Alfredo, and are Piave's final example of a world which a repentant Violetta cannot totally embrace, and outside which she has no place:

> Largo al quadrupede
> Sir della festa,
> Di fiori e pampini
> Cinto la testa. ...
> Largo al più docile
> D'ogni cornuto
> Di corni e pifferi
> Abbia il saluto.
> Parigini, date passo
> Al trionfo del Bue grasso.
> L'Asia nè l'Africa
> Vide il più bello
> Vanto ed orgoglio
> d'ogni macello. ...
> Allegre maschere,
> Pazzi garzoni,
> Tutti plauditelo
> Con canti e suoni!
> Parigini, date passo
> Al trionfo del Bue grasso.
> (*La traviata*, Act 3, Scene 4)

(Make way for the four-footed Lord of the festival, with its head bound with flowers and vine-leaves. Make way for the most docile of horned creatures.[25] May he be greeted by horns and drums. Parisians, give way for the triumph of the fattened ox. Neither Asia nor Africa has seen a greater beauty, the boast and pride of every slaughterhouse. Merry masks, crazy young boys, all applaud it, with songs and sounds! Parisians, give way to the triumph of the fattened ox.)

Can one regard *La traviata* as a cynical projection of a shabby society? While one of the reasons for the opera's failure to please at its first performance was probably, in addition to its being performed in contemporary dress, its somewhat daring theme, the unpardoning hypocrisy of polite society was without doubt a contributory factor to its later success. The opera is in reality about the impossibility of erasing past failings, although all personae at one time or another wish to cancel former activities. Germont père, expressing his admiration of Violetta, cries:

GERMONT: Ah, il passato perchè, perchè v'accusa?
VIOLETTA: Più non esiste ... or amo Alfredo, e Dio
Lo cancellò col pentimento, mio.
(*La traviata*, Act 2, Scene 5)

(GERMONT: Ah, why, oh why must the past accuse you?
VIOLETTA: It no longer exists, now I love Alfredo, and God wiped it out, on account of my repentance.)

Yet ironically Germont states that Violetta's past is putting Alfredo's future into jeopardy. She must put her affair with him behind her. Her return to the company of Flora and her friends is an attempt to do just this:

TUTTI: Su via, si stenda un velo
Sui fatti del passato;
Già quel ch'è stato è stato,
Badate all'avvenir.
(*La traviata*, Act 2, Scene 10)

(ALL: Go, and spread a veil over past happenings. Already that which has happened cannot be changed. Take care of the future.)

Violetta's famous last act aria 'addio del passato bei sogni ridenti' ('Goodbye to the beautiful happy dreams of the past') is a final farewell to her past as a courtesan: 'Ah, della traviata sorridi al desio/a lei, deh, perdona; tu accoglila, O Dio' ('Ah, as a strayed one, I laughed in the face of desire. Ah forgive her, you receive her, O God') (*La traviata*, Act 3, Scene 4).

What is most dramatically effective in the libretto is Piave's juxtaposition of past and present, and his subtle stressing of the permanence of the social view that the past can seldom be disregarded. The time sequence in *La traviata* has always held a fascination for producers and directors. Zeffirelli, in his production of the opera for the Dallas Civic Opera in 1958 with Maria Callas in the title role, presented the work as a series of flashbacks. In the opening, Violetta was displayed in full view on her sickbed, to the poignant strains of the prelude. This is based on two musical themes. Both are associated with Violetta: the first with the illness, resignation and death of the heroine, the second with her separation from Alfredo in Act 2. In *La traviata* the passing of time is not always effectively communicated. This is largely on account of Piave's dispensing with Act 2 of the play. At the end of the opera's first act Violetta has proclaimed her intention of continuing her dangerous life-style. Act 2 finds her in the country with Alfredo, having renounced her past, as she believes, for ever.

La traviata, from a theatrical and literary viewpoint, has made an important contribution to the Italian history of ideas. With it social realism was introduced into the Italian theatre. As a realistic sociological document it demonstrates the life of, and the options open to, the *demi-mondaine*. The death of Violetta carries its own symbolism. Having changed her life she can no longer in conscience live as a courtesan, yet 'polite' society bans one with her past. The work ends without a satisfactory solution.

Musically, *La traviata* is one of Verdi's most successful works. In it he achieved both an intensity and intimacy in the drawing of his protagonist which render her tragically innocent, despite her profession. Perhaps the librettist's and composer's greatest accomplishment is to have set this most tragic of romantic heroines in a realistic and shabby framework, which has never succeeded in soiling her or depriving her of the public's sympathy and love.

8

THE DEVIL'S ADVOCATE: EVIL IN THE WORKS OF ARRIGO BOITO

I

Although it is generally accepted that Italian realism reached its high point in Verga's portraits of provincial deprivation, in a society both geographically and intellectually isolated from material progress, the origins and sources of inspiration of such a literature have been largely ignored. Apart from the widely held opinion that all that is realistic in Italian literature found its antecedent in France, little research has been directed towards establishing the existence of a realistic tradition in the Italian theatre before the advent of Verga, which can be directly related to the climate in which D'Annunzio's tragedies and the bourgeois comedies of Giacosa prospered. It is my belief that the true birth of realism took place on the operatic stage. Librettists such as Piave and Boito, alongside giants like Verdi and Ponchielli, had carried public taste from the idealistic upholding of patriotic principles to an outright protest against high society, and a rejection of the conventional. The establishment of the anti-romantic as the order of the day found some support from traditionalists as well as from other quarters. The formal statement of a desire and need to turn away from the hitherto accepted formulas was made by a group of artists, who, in the 1860s and 1870s, assumed responsibility for reforming the arts and, in doing so, shocking society into attention. This was the *Scapigliatura milanese*,[1] which was to prove of social, historical and ideological significance. Its most famous member, Arrigo Boito,[2] was to outgrow it, and achieve his greatest success in collaboration with Giuseppe Verdi, whose work he had denounced and rejected during his period as a *scapigliato*.[3] Yet it cannot be denied that the germs of his own *Mefistofele* and of his adaptation of Shakespeare's *Othello* for Verdi are to be found in his *Libro dei versi* and *Re orso*, the fruits of his early bohemian existence.

As has already been stated in the previous chapter, Piave's libretto for *La traviata* marked the introduction of social realism into the Italian theatre. It marked the operatic establishment of the social barriers and limitations imposed by a world of bourgeois affluence. Two years earlier, however, Piave and Verdi, in adapting *Le Roi s'amuse* by Hugo, had projected an ideological realism which contained all of the opposites and conflicting forces brought together in Boito's 'Dualismo' ('Duality'). *Rigoletto* also proved to be the first of a series of operatic compositions in which the forces of evil and their operation in society are dramatically probed. Others include *Simon Boccanegra* (Verdi/Piave, revised by Boito), *La forza del destino* (Verdi/Piave), *Don Carlo* (Verdi/-Schiller, translated by de Lauzières and Zanardini), *Mefistofele* (Boito), *La Gioconda* (Ponchielli/Tobia Gorrio (Arrigo Boito)) and *Otello* (Verdi/Boito). Boito, in his opera *Mefistofele* which in 1868 proved a spectacular failure but in a revised form in 1875 managed to convince audiences of its worth, sought to provide a philosophical reality, embracing the entire universe and arriving at a universality of expression. Although public and critics were, and still are, aware of what he was trying to achieve,[4] the abstract treatment of a subject already familiar to theatre-goers failed to win it true popularity. It was not until Boito collaborated with Verdi for *Otello* that he can be said to have perfected his techniques as a poet, adapter and philosophical dramatist. In doing so he contributed to the creation of the greatest music-drama of the Italian repertoire, and a masterpiece of psychological realism. It can be argued therefore that social, ideological, philosophical and psychological realism existed in the operatic theatre in Italy before realistic literary schools or movements became established or recognized in the peninsula.

The *Scapigliatura* can be defined as an association of writers, artists and musicians, active in Lombardy in the 1860s and 1870s. Of the extremely versatile group of young men, Emilio Praga (1839–75), Ugo Tarchetti (1841–69), Arrigo Boito (1842–1918) and Giovanni Camerana (1845–1905) stand out as the most distinguished. The poet, dramatist and baritone Antonio Ghislanzoni, who was immortalized by his libretto for Verdi's *Aida*, was also associated with the group, which set itself a task of innovation and reform.⁵ Its principal aim was, in breaking with all conventional forms, to associate poetry and music with the figurative arts. In rejecting the romantic, and taking note of what romantic idealism had *not* achieved, they sought to embrace the realistic, not, however, by stressing objectivity, but rather by taking the human psyche into account, and advocating psychological realism. This they felt was best communicated by means of a poetry of symbols and sensations. In this respect the *Scapigliatura* can be regarded not only as the precursor of realism, but also of modern Italian poetry as a whole, and in particular the dimmed imagery of the 'Crepuscolari'.

Arrigo Boito studied the violin, pianoforte and composition at the Milan Conservatorio. After travels in France, Germany and his mother's native Poland, he returned to Milan where he became acquainted with the composer/conductor Franco Faccio and Emilio Praga. In collaboration with the latter he wrote *Le madri galanti* (1863), which was a failure at its première. Boito felt the need of a newspaper to diffuse the theories on art and its rebirth which he believed could change the face of Italian culture. Together with Praga he founded the *Figaro*. This was a weekly publication, financed by the painter Carlo Mancini and the musician and composer Marco Sala. The first number appeared on 1 January 1864 and within three months, after the thirteenth issue, *Figaro* went out of circulation. It was intended to herald the triumphant arrival of a new and revolutionary operatic form. Its pages abounded with criticisms of current taste and in particular the low level of operatic composition represented by Giuseppe Verdi. With the failure of their mouthpiece to inspire or to convince musicians of the shortcomings of Italy's leading composer, Boito, Praga and Faccio went in search of pastures new. When the war against Austria broke out all three enrolled in the ranks of Garibaldi. Their departure was announced on 17 June 1866.

The unavoidable antithesis which governed Boito's life and art sprang from an uncontrollable ideal which, until his later life, he was unable to restrain or contain. He saw himself, as did later D'Annunzio, as something of a *super-artist* with a mission to revive and to reform.⁶ In the pursuit of an artistic ideal, he attempted to fuse various artistic disciplines, in an effort to transcend all that had already been expressed. As a result one finds that particularly in *Mefistofele* what can be more easily defined as a 'confusion' of sounds and images emerges. Statements and

11 Antonio Ghislanzoni (1824–93)

interpretations are moulded in an attempt to bring together facts and opinions, while a scientific literary approach is applied to the expression of the ideal, in spiritual, philosophical and bourgeois terms. It is my belief that his enormous task might have arrived at a greater degree of success had it not in itself been of such a contradictory nature: the rejection of the conventional in order to provide an ideal, which necessitated expression in realistic terms. Beauty, Truth, Order and Harmony juxtaposed and fused with their opposites emerge as realism toying with the abstract. The result, to quote Scarsi, is a 'tendency to reveal the unfinished, developing its potential, and resulting in suggestion rather than statement'.[7] From a philosophical viewpoint Boito's dramatic works are a projection of Good as static and Evil as active and progressive. Life, creativity and enterprise are facets of Evil. Good is merely cultivated in its essence. Boito, at this point, would appear to see himself as the man in the middle – Faust, tormented by his ambitions and artistic pursuits. But unable to stand personification as a mere man, he aspires to being a god, one, however, that rejects tradition and destroys, in order to recreate, civilization. The result is the self-identification of Boito with Mefistofele (*Mefistofele*), Alvise and Barnaba (*La Gioconda*) and Jago (*Otello*). Boito's god is, then, one of evil omnipotence. At the conclusion of *Mefistofele*, however, when Faust has tasted the Real, Ideal and Absolute Ideal, and has relegated all to the area of experience, his final realization is that the Reality was sorrow, and the Ideal a mere dream ('Ma il Real fu dolore / E l'Ideal fu sogno'). In a final search for infinity he identifies his dream with heavenly poetry ('la sacra poesia'), the final desire of his being.

The story, then, of Boito's struggle with destiny is one of an individual without all of the intellectual qualities necessary to carry out the demands of his imagination; of one who chooses a sinful man, in order to express experiences beyond human perception, and finally of a poet philosopher, directed by his own material, towards an artistic acceptance of evil, not of his initial or ultimate choice, but which he is unable to dominate intellectually. The most significant movements in this symphony of rationalization are the poetic inspirations of his *Scapigliatura* days, collected and published in the *Re orso* (Milan, 1865) and *Il libro dei versi – Re orso* (Turin, 1877); the almighty failure of *Mefistofele* (1868) and its relative success in its newly pruned form (1875); the libretto *La Gioconda* for Ponchielli (1876) written under the pseudonym Tobia Gorrio and his masterpiece of adaptation, *Otello* (1887) for Verdi.

DEVIL'S ADVOCATE

12 Arrigo Boito (1842–1918)

II

The antithesis contained in all of Boito's artistic creations, which often deprives his art of any overall or overriding quality, is expressed in the poem 'Dualismo'. In it the poet claims to be all things: light and shade, butterfly or worm, angel or devil. Never still, however, he is in constant pursuit of an ideal state, or an extension of his present one, which fails to satisfy. In an attempt to be all, the poet loses sight of the particular nature of his goal and remains in a state of balance and transition, perceived as active contemplation:

> Son luce ed ombra: angelica
> Farfalla o verme immondo,
> Sono un caduto chèrubo
> Dannato a errar sul mondo,
> O un demone che sale,
> Affaticando l'ale,
> Verso un lontano ciel.
> (Boito, 'Dualismo')[8]

(I am light and shade; an angelic butterfly or a filthy worm. I am a fallen cherub damned to wander on earth, or a devil rising winging wearily towards a far distant sky.)

Even the seven above-quoted lines are loaded with polemic, since his statement of effect ('luce ed ombra') is tempered by insecurity of being ('farfalla o verme'), symbolic of absolutes of good and evil, perceived beyond mortal existence ('chèrubo o demone'). The only absolute reality of the poem is contained in the active verb to dream. The subject of the dream is without certainty of abode. Besides, the poet is unable to reach his hypothetical destination and remains in a state of intellectual pursuit:

> E sogno un'Arte eterea
> Che forse in cielo ha norma,
> Franca dai rudi vincoli
> Del metro e della forma,
> Piena dell'Ideale
> Che mi fa batter l'ale
> E che seguir non so.
> (Boito, 'Dualismo')

(And I dream of an ethereal Art that perhaps in heaven has an order free of the coarse chains of metre and form; free of the ideal that makes my wings beat, and which I cannot follow.)

The poet pursues a superior order without the discipline and limitations of the ideal brought to realization. The personification of the ideal, realistically assessed, is the mutilated corpse in 'Lezione d'anatomia'. At one time blonde and beautiful, she no longer constitutes a source of poetic inspiration based on beauty, but a subject of physiological analysis leading to a finer comprehension of human activity:

> Delitto! e sanguina
> Per piaga immonda
> Il petto a quella! ...
> Ed era giovane!
> Ed era bionda!
> Ed era bella!
> (Boito, 'Lezione d'anatomia')

(O crime! and bloodstained from a filthy wound is her breast! ... And she was young! And she was blonde! And she was beautiful!)

The anatomy lesson proceeds and the poetic language alternates between the technical and the idyllic, marking the conflict between ideal and reality:

> Io penso ai teneri
> Casi passati
> Su quella testa,
> Ai sogni estatici
> Invan sognati
> Da quella mesta.

(I think of the tender thoughts which passed through that head, of the ecstatic dreams, dreamed in vain by that unfortunate one.)

The squalid image of a violent death, decay and decomposition is accorded yet another function: it becomes symbolic of poetic creativity: nurtured in the imagination, beautiful on contemplation, yet pale and languishing when realistically assessed.

> Perdona o pallida
> Adolescente!
> Fanciulla pia,
> Dolce, purissima,

Fiore languente
Di poesia.

Pardon, o pallid adolescent, pious young girl, sweet and most pure, languishing flower of poetry.

Boito has managed to contain his artistic horizons in a symbol of youth, violence, life and death. In 'Lezione d'anatomia' the scale adopted is minute and the society pointed to of the lowest order. In his reformed vision of the melodrama he set himself instead a gigantic, unbounded scale, with Faust symbolizing Everyman, in a universe dissolving into intellectual abstractions. What was, however, intended to inaugurate a new era in artistic expression, resulted in one of the most spectacular failures in the history of the theatre.

There were many contributing reasons for *Mefistofele*'s failure at its first performance at La Scala, Milan, in 1868. Apart from Boito's youthful arrogance, his open criticism of Verdi and his negative approach to all artistic endeavours excepting his own, the real problem with the original *Mefistofele* was its length. When Boito decided to refashion the work, he destroyed all traces of the original music, except for two pieces which were published separately. The entire libretto of the original remains, and many portions of it were incorporated into the final version with little or no revision. All critics who heard the 1868 and 1875 versions of the opera agree that the duet 'Lontano, lontano, lontano', Margherita's 'Sputa l'aurora pallida' and the fugue which concludes Act 2 exist in the 1875 version only. There is no doubt that the libretto of 1868 was a successful attempt to reduce Parts I and II of *Faust* to the requirements of the operatic stage. Neither can one disregard the originality of the music. At a time 'when Verdi was patiently tinkering with the traditional structures of Italian romantic opera, Boito simply discarded them.'[9] Yet the work is not stylistically of great significance. His dispensing with the aria as the centre of operatic activity, and his over-use of the chorus without the heroic trappings still retained by Verdi in *Don Carlo* and *Aida* is in no way influential. Realistic opera in the hands of Catalani and Puccini developed in a totally different direction. It is Boito the librettist who moulded operatic ideology, and it is in this respect that his work must be assessed.

The libretto of *Mefistofele* falls into a prologue, four acts and an epilogue. It can be called a philosophical exposition on the battle between light and shade, with dramatic illustrations from the real and the ideal worlds. The character of Mefistofele towers above the world, which is projected in terms of a tiny glass ball, from which Faust is accorded crystalline images of beauty. The prologue, by means of a series of prayers, highlights the conflict between light and darkness, philosophy and theology. Mefistofele, in contrast to the liturgical chants of the chorus of celestial bodies, mystical beings, cherubim and penitents, begins his address in words loaded with Leopardian irony, contained in a language verging on informal slang. The scene serves to illustrate Mefistofele's intention to trap Faust, and to convey in terms of infinity and universality the confines of knowledge.

The first words of the opera are in praise of God:

PRIMA FALANGE: 'Ave' Signor degli angeli e dei santi
E delle sfere erranti
E dei volanti – cherubini d'ôr.
(*Mefistofele*, Prologue)

(FIRST TROOP: Hail, Lord of the angels and saints and of the moving spheres and of the flying golden cherubim.)

There follows Mefistofele's ironic vision of the world, and his interpretation of human reason as mere illusion. In a Leopardian device[10] he reduces man to a chirping cricket, with its sight upon the stars and its song in the grass:

MEFISTOFELE: Il Dio piccin della piccina terra
Ognor traligna ed erra
E, al par di grillo saltellante, a caso
Spinge fra gli astri il naso.
Poi con tenace fatuità superba
Fa il suo trillo nell'erba.
Boriosa polve, tracotato atòmo!
Fantasima dell'uomo!
E tale il fa quell'ebra illusione
Ch'egli chiama Ragione.
(*Mefistofele*, Prologue)

(The tiny God of the tiny earth loses his direction all the time, and gets lost. And like a jumping cricket, he by chance pushes his nose among the stars. Then with unyielding proud conceit he chirps in the grass. Arrogant dust, haughty atom! Spectre of man! And that intoxicated illusion which he calls Reason renders him so.)

The chorus of penitents alternates the 'Ave Maria' with the 'Salve Regina', while the celestial bodies intone the 'Sanctus'. The cherubim, in the form of clouds, perform a continual, circular dance. 'La danza in angelica spira/Si gira, si gira, si gira' ('The dance, in an angelic whirl, revolves around and around and around') (*Mefistofele*, Prologue).

Act 1 of the opera reveals Faust's dream brought to reality. Paradoxically, it is the realization of a dream populated by all social groups – the masses, the crowd, the bourgeoisie and the peasants. In such a society in miniature Faust has both the leisure and stimulation for further philosophical contemplation ('Dai campi, dai prati' ('From the fields and meadows'). Mefistofele, who has changed his disguise from that of a monk to a knight, and Faust indulge in philosophical exchange:

FAUST:	Come ti chiami?
MEFISTOFELE:	La domanda è inezia
	Puerile per tal che gli argomenti
	Sdegna del Verbo e crede solo agli Enti.
FAUST:	In voi, messeri, il nome ha tale virtù
	Che rivela l'Essenza. Dimmi or su
	Chi sei tu dunque?
MEFISTOFELE:	Una parte vivente
	Di quella forza che perpetuamente
	Pensa il Male e fa il Bene. . . .
	Voglio il Nulla e del Creato
	La ruina universal.
	È atmosfera mia vital
	Ciò che chiamasi peccato,
	Morte e Mal.

(*Mefistofele*, Act 1, Scene 2)

(FAUST:	What is your name?
MEFISTOFELE:	That is a childishly inane question for one who disdains the arguments of the Word, and believes only in Being.
FAUST:	In your case, sir, the name contains such

	virtue as to reveal the Essence. Tell me anyway who you are.
MEFISTOFELE:	A living part of that force that perpetually thinks Evil and does Good. ... I desire Nothingness, and the universal ruin of Creation. The atmosphere essential to me is that which is called Sin, Death and Evil!)

The second act brings Faust into contact with the actual realization of his dreams: the ideal takes the form of his idyllic relationship with Margherita. The rustic maiden emerges as perfection in miniature. However, her words of simplistic purity are interpreted by Faust in terms of superhuman voluptuousness:

MARGHERITA:	Cavaliero illustre e saggio, Come mai vi può allettar La fanciulla del villaggio Col suo rustico parlar?
FAUST:	Dalle labbra imporporate Spandi accento sovruman[11] Parla, parla.

(Mefistofele, Act 2, Scene 1)

(MARGHERITA:	Illustrious and wise knight, however can the rustic speech of the village maiden make you happy?
FAUST:	From your reddened lips you outpour superhuman words, speak, speak.)

Here, and in the scene of Margherita's delirium, Boito indulges in an exaggeration and misinterpretation of impressions. The rustic maiden *in effect* becomes a torrid seductress. At a later point in the mad ravings of the unfortunate heroine Boito infuses a beauty and simplicity of expression which belie the reality of her situation. When she eventually recovers her reason, and is clearly aware of her true situation, her language resembles melodramatic declamation, devoid of lyricism, and reminiscent of the chilling realism of the poetry of the *Scapigliatura*. In other words, the illusion is contained in the lyrical expression. It is afforded a form of poetic escapism denied to reality:

MARGHERITA:	L'altra notte in fondo al mare Il mio bimbo hanno gittato;

>   Or per farmi delirare
>   Voglion ch'io l'abbia affogato.
>   L'aura è fredda, il carcer fosco,
>   E la mesta anima mia.
>   Come il passero del bosco
>   Vola via.
>
>   (*Mefistofele*, Act 3, Scene 1)

(MARGHERITA: Last night they threw my baby to the bottom of the sea; and in order to drive me insane they wish to make out that I drowned it. The air is cold, the prison dark, and my sad soul flies away like the sparrow in the wood.)

>   ho avvelenato
>   La mia povera madre ed ho affogato
>   Il fantolino mio. . . . Qua, la tua mano
>   Vien, vo' narrarti il tetro ordin di tombe
>   Che doman scaverai . . . là fra le zolle
>   Più verdeggianti . . . stenderai mia madre
>   Nel più bel sito del cimiter . . . discosto . . .
>   Ma pur vicino . . . scaverai la mia . . .
>   La mia povera fossa . . . il mio bambino
>   Poserà sul mio sen.
>
>   (*Mefistofele*, Act 3, Scene 1)

(I poisoned my unfortunate mother and I drowned my baby . . . give me your hand – come. I wish to relate to you the dismal series of graves that you will dig tomorrow. There among the greenest sods you will lay my mother. In the most beautiful location of the cemetery you will dig mine . . . my poor resting place. My child will be placed on my breast.)

In the figure of Margherita is contained the fusion of illusion and reality, the romantic and realistic. In addition she is the symbol of the transient in life, as opposed to the absolute ideal represented by Elena:

>   La tranquilla immagine – della fanciulla blanda
>   Ch'amai là fra le nebbie – d'una perduta landa
>   Già svanì, conquiso – m'ha un più sublime sguardo

> Più fulgurato viso – e adora e tremo ed ardo.
> (*Mefistofele*, Act 4, Scene 1)

(The serene image of the gentle girl that I loved, there in the mist of a lost plain, soon vanished. A more sublime glance, a more splendid countenance conquered me. And she adores, I tremble and burn.)

Elena, 'Forma ideal! purissima – della bellezza eterna' ('Ideal – most pure form of eternal beauty!'), is not destroyed or made to vanish by any shortcomings in her own being, but as a result of the inability of the human mind to permanently maintain its image. In the epilogue, which provides the opera with a poetic unity, in that the praises of God, absolute order and the supreme harmony of the universe are repeated by the heavenly troops, Faust is seen as still in pursuit of an ideal beyond the intellectual perception of the human mind. It is finally externalized as heavenly poetry – an example of the intellectual fusion of the human and the sublime: 'Voglio che questo sogno sia la santa poesia/E l'ultimo bisogno – dell'esistenza mia' ('I wish this dream to be heavenly poetry, and the last need of my existence') (*Mefistofele*, Epilogue).

The conclusion of the work finds Faust again in search of the unattainable, having proved that the means by which he sought to transcend human limitations were both illusionary and transient. This philosophic treatise on art, scientifically and intellectually conceived, can at its conclusion be reduced to the following equations: for Faust illusion proves to be a reality rejected by the mind in favour of an attainable, but non-retainable, absolute illusion. Mefistofele proves that human reason is an illusion. Although the devil fails to win Faust's soul, it would appear that he wins the argument: the final achievement is the contemplation of the abstract—'il Nulla' ('Nothingness') and the destruction of Faust's earlier sequence of creative thoughts. Yet Mefistofele, along with his created illusions, passes into the realm of sorrowful experience, while the higher order of creation remains untasted. The ideal is triumphant, but the means by which it can be attained remains a mystery.

In his collected poems dating from his association with the *Scapigliatura milanese*, Boito uses a series of juxtaposed images, in order to sustain a negative social comment, as well as to illustrate the perilous position of man, constantly wavering between the idealistic and the realistic. In *Mefistofele*, which proved to be the poet's greatest artistic effort, if not achievement, the linguistic antitheses project a philosophical exposition of good and evil. The subject of the opera is man's quest for superhuman ideals in a world contained in human limitations. The crucial factor of the individual's choice between good and evil is highlighted. The operatic libretto which appeared in 1876, a year after the successful re-staging of *Mefistofele*, also contains an example of evil at work in society.[12] In *La Gioconda* (music by Ponchielli), adapted from Victor Hugo's *Angelo, tyran de Padoue* (1835), Boito, with the introduction of the character La Cieca, not part of the French drama, allows for the projection of the macabre as an integral part of the action. Boito avoids creating visual images as symbols of evil, but rather communicates the diversity of expressions through the concept of song. Barnaba, a spy of the Venetian Inquisition, is a ballad singer, like Gioconda, the protagonist. His song is directed towards the possession of Gioconda, the destruction of Laura, her rival for the hand of Enzo, prince of Santafior, and the annihilation of her blind mother. His guitar assumes sinister proportions as it prepares the tune of betrayal and accusation:

> E cantan su lor tombe!
> E la morte li guata!
> E mentre s'erge il ceppo o la cuccagna,
> Fra due colonne tesse la sua ragna
> Barnaba, il cantastorie; e le sue file
> [*Guarda e tocca la sua chitarra*]
> Sono le corde di questo apparecchio.
> (*La Gioconda*, Act 1, Scene 2)

(And they sing on their tombs! And death gazes on them! And while either the block or good fortune manifests itself, Barnaba, the ballad singer, wove his web between two columns. [*Observes and touches his guitar*] And his threads are the strings of this instrument.)

Beauty and truth are likewise communicated in terms of song raised as prayer. For example, La Cieca: 'Tu canti agli uomini – le tue canzoni,/Io canto agli angeli – le mie orazioni' ('You sing your songs to men, I sing my orations to the angels') (*La Gioconda*, Act 1, Scene 3). The subtle Boitian fusion of opposites is contained in the persona of La Cieca. Barnaba's diabolical reversal of values is communicated by means of his accusation of

Gioconda's blind mother. What formally was a symbol of divine grace, paradoxically deprived of physical sight, is accused of witchcraft. Her prayers are interpreted as evil incantations and her blindness is denied:

> BARNABA: Suo covo è un tugurio laggiù alla Giudeca,
> Tien sempre quell'orrido zendado, ed è cieca,
> Ha vuote le occhiaie, ma pure (chi il crede?!)
> La Cieca ci guarda, la Cieca ci vede.
> (*La Gioconda*, Act 1, Scene 4)

> (BARNABA: Her den is a hovel down there on the Giudecca, she permanently wears that horrible shawl, and she is blind. Her eye-sockets are empty, and (who indeed will believe it?!) the Blind One watches us, the Blind One sees us.)

Boito provides the visual antithesis of good and allows a symbolic interpretation of the image to to take precedence over the truth of the situation. La Cieca is finally rescued from the mob, and in recognition bestows a rosary on her benefactor. This symbolic object functions as a foil to Barnaba's guitar for the remainder of the opera. The final victory, however, belongs to the powers of darkness: Barnaba drowns La Cieca, and Gioconda stabs herself to death rather than succumb to his embraces.

III

After the first Milanese production of *Aida* in February 1872 Verdi believed that his career as an operatic composer was over. In this work, for the inauguration of the Suez Canal, he had combined all the features which had contributed to his successes over the previous thirty years: a patriotic theme of divided loyalties, magnificence and splendour of presentation, and the pre-eminence of the chorus. In addition, the exotic setting was reflected in the musical line, while the dramatic reflections of the personae made for melodic and dramatic continuity, carrying Verdi closer than at any time before to 'music drama', as revealed in the Italian productions of early Wagnerian operas. The maestro, by 'modernizing' and perfecting in the light of his own evolution all features of his technique, was prepared to settle for retirement.

The young editor Giulio Ricordi, backed by the conductor-composer Faccio, in an effort to bring Verdi back to the theatre, sought a reconcilation between him and his critic and enemy Arrigo Boito. The latter, however, in the years since the appearance and dimise of *Figaro* (1864) and the failure and subsequent success of *Mefistofele*, had matured as both an artist and an individual, and had even become an ardent admirer of Verdi. In June 1879 Verdi dined with Ricordi and Faccio at the Grand Hotel near La Scala. The subject of *Otello* was approached, and Boito's name was put forward as a possible librettist.[13] Boito and Verdi were reconciled on the following day, according to the critic Charles Osborne,[14] and three days later he provided Verdi with a scenario for the opera. The most famous and illustrious collaboration in operatic history was about to begin.

The plot of Shakespeare's *Othello* derives from Giraldi Cinthio's seventh *novella*, in the third decade of his *Hecartommihi* (Venice, 1566). Boito's most important primary source was Victor Hugo's French translation of Shakespeare,[15] of which Boito possessed at least three copies. James A. Hepokoski makes the point that a large number of the pages marked in the edition in the Scala museum, many of them the work of the summer of 1879, correspond with the eventual *Otello* libretto.[16] Although Boito's work on *Otello* was extensive, Verdi does not appear to have committed himself totally to the venture until he had the opportunity of working closely with Boito. This came about in 1880, when Verdi wrote to his future librettist from Genoa, asking him to provide some revisions to the libretto of *Simon Boccanegra* (1857). The most substantial additions provided by Boito are the Grand Council scene of Act 1 and Paolo's monologue, Act 2, Scene 2. He also rewrote in full the first two scenes of the third act.[17]

It is not surprising that Boito found himself drawn to Verdi's later works. The preoccupation with evil and the supernatural, apparent in Verdi's *Rigoletto*, *Simon Boccanegra*, *La forza del destino* and *Don Carlo*, which constituted the subject-matter of *Mefistofele* and *La Gioconda*, are finally resolved in Boito's adaptation of Shakespeare. In Verdi's operatic masterpiece the subject-matter is accorded a treatment in which supernatural and subconscious are identified, and a realistic and psychologically convincing portrait of human behaviour is achieved.

Boito's *Otello* is a concentrated, condensed and simplified account of Shakespeare's *Othello*. In telling the tale of the Moor of Venice the Italian librettist reflects the essential elements of the English tragedian's plot. He refines the action, dispensing with unnecessary scenes and characters, until a psychologically charged presentation of human reactions is attained. Yet it is true to say that 'Otello is Othello'. Boito has laboured to render the tragedy of the Moor more heart-rending and more inevitable. By eliminating Shakespeare's Act 1 he provides unity of place, allowing the entire action to evolve in Cyprus.[18] He also deprives the drama, to some degree at least, of its racist nature by dispensing with the character of Desdemona's father. This allows both Otello and Desdemona to exist dramatically on an equal footing. It also alters the Shakespearian dimension of the drama as a conflict between two civilizations. Instead, Boito's drama develops as a conflict between good and evil, based on malice. The essential battle is between Jago and Otello, and finds its origin in a political issue. The juxtaposition of 'black and white', instead of being established as in Shakespeare's Act 1 between Otello and his wife, is more subtly effected. It surfaces in Boito's Act 2 in Jago's 'Credo' and in his subsequent conversation with Cassio. Desdemona, symbolic of good, is merely a pawn in the Machiavellian game, in which good is seen as no more than the means by which evil can be effected.

Otello, then, like the majority of Boito's earlier works, incorporates a struggle between good and evil. In further pursuit of this dimension Boito provides Otello with an entry in which he defies the powers of nature and emerges as a victorious warrior proclaiming victory. The opening cries of the chorus are contained in a prayer for Otello's salvation as his ship is tossed between heaven and the bottom of the sea:

MONTANO:	Or s'affonda,
	Or s'inciela....
METÀ DEL CORO:	Nelle nubi si cela e nel mar.
	E alla luce dei lampi ne appar....
TUTTI:	Dio, fulgor della bufera!
	Dio, sorriso della duna!
	Salva l'arca e la bandiera
	Della veneta fortuna!
	Tu, che reggi gli astri e il Fato!
	Tu, che imperi al mondo e al ciel!
	Fa che in fondo al mar placato

	Posi l'ancora fedel.
	(*Otello*, Act 1, Scene 1)
(MONTANO:	Now it sinks, now it rises towards the sky.
HALF OF THE CHORUS:	It is concealed in the clouds and in the sea. And in the light, flashes of it appear.
ALL:	Oh God, splendour of the blizzard! Oh God, smile of the dune! Save the ship and the flag of Venetian fortune, you who control the stars and Fate, you who reign over land and sea, make him drop the faithful anchor in the depths of a calm sea.)

Otello emerges victorious from a physical battle which is in sharp contrast to the psychological one which he is about to lose. There is no equivalent in Shakespeare to the 'Esultate' created by Boito to highlight the victory of Otello the warrior, in preparation for the defeat of Otello the man:

OTELLO:	Esultate! L'orgoglio musulmano
	Sepolto è nel mar, nostra e del ciel è gloria!
	Dopo l'armi lo vinse l'uragano.
	(*Otello*, Act 1, Scene 1)
(OTELLO:	Rejoice! The Moslem pride is buried in the sea. Ours and heaven's is the glory. After the armed victory, the hurricane laid it low.)

Jago's initial step towards destroying Otello is, as in Shakespeare, centred on the disgrace of Cassio. The linguistic juxtaposition of light and darkness is achieved by the contrasting descriptions of Otello ('i foschi baci / Di quel selvaggio dalle gonfie labbra' ('the dark kisses of that swollen-lipped savage')) and the beautiful Desdemona. Love, hate, appearances and reality are contained in Jago's confession: 'Bench'io finga d'amarlo, odio quel Moro' ('Although I pretend to love him, I hate that Moor!') (*Otello*, Act 1, Scene 1).

In Act 2 Jago emerges as the villain-hero of the work. His 'Credo' raises him above the other character of the play over whom, by dint of his evil, he has gained control. Otello, on the other hand, materializes as his psychological victim, and his own physical victim. Jago's manipulation of Otello's reactions is contained in his ability to allow him to alternate between certainty and doubt, reality and illusion, until he is unable to distinguish one from the other. The battle, then, between good and evil is between 'black' Otello and 'white' Jago, a battle in which Boito overturns the symbolism of the antithesis, in providing a black angel and a white devil.

In his 'Credo', a denial of the doctrine of free will, the essence of Christianity and the immortality of the soul, Jago cries out that he is evil because he is man:

> Credo in un Dio crudel che m'ha creato
> Simile a sè, e che nell'ira io nomo.
> Dalla viltà d'un germe o d'un atòmo
> Vile son nato,
> Sono scellerato
> Perchè sono uomo. . . .
> Vien dopo tanta irrisïon la morte.
> - E poi? – La Morte è il Nulla.
> E vecchia fola il ciel.
> > (*Otello*, Act 2, Scene 2)

(I believe in a God of cruelty, who has created me in his image, and that in anger I name. From the baseness of an embryo or of an atom, vile, I was born. I am a scoundrel because I am a man. . . . After all that mockery comes Death. – And then? – Death is Nothingness, and heaven is an old wives' tale.)

In Shakespeare Iago's 'Creed' is only partially expounded. In Boito it becomes an anti-doctrine in which, by means of four principal negations, Jago destroys the concept of divine mercy and justice and reinforces the theory of predestination. In the following scene sailors, children and ladies offer prayers and venerate Desdemona as a sacred image:

MARINAI: Vogliam Desdemona
            Coi doni nostri
            Come un'immagine
            Sacra adornar.
> > (*Otello*, Act 2, Scene 3)

(SAILORS: With our gifts we wish to adorn Desdemona as a sacred image.)

The final lines of the scene, uttered by Jago, offer a further foil to the series of prayers contained in the libretto ('Esultate', 'Ti offriamo il giglio', 'Ave Maria'): 'Beltà e amor in dolce inno concordi,/I vostri infrangerò soavi accordi' ('Beauty and love concordant in sweet hymn, I will shatter your delightful union') (*Otello*, Act 2, Scene 3).

The battle between the forces of light and darkness is waged within the mind of Otello, based on the tangible and intangible: Desdemona's handkerchief and Cassio's dream. The latter is conjured in an atmosphere of mystery, insinuatingly effective, and expressed in onomatopoeia leading to the crucial 'Il rio destino impreco che al Moro ti donò' ('I curse the cruel fate that gave thee to the Moor'). The description of the tangible, symbolic image of the handkerchief belies its sinister function in the plot:

> Miracolo vago
> Dell'aspo e dell'ago
> Che in raggi tramuta
> Le fila d'un vel,
> Più bianco, più lieve
> Che fiocco di neve,
> Che nube tessuta
> Dall'aure del ciel.
> (*Otello*, Act 3, Scene 5)

(Beauteous miracle of weaver and needle, that transforms to rays the threads of a gauze. Lighter and whiter than a snowflake, than a cloud woven by the breeze of heaven.)

In Boito's *Otello* the protagonists Desdemona and Otello are both victims of the psychological violence exercised on Otello by Jago. Although evil conquers, the poetic image of death incorporates the concept of beauty in the face of misfortune. Unlike the subject of Boito's 'Lezione d'anatomia', Desdemona retains the image of beauty and piety that her death serves to reinforce. With the fleeing of the personification of evil (Jago), the stage is cleared for the lyrical reminiscence of the 'love duet':

E tu, . . . come sei pallida! e stanca, e muta, e bella,
Pia creatura nata sotto maligna stella.

DEVIL'S ADVOCATE

Fredda come la casta tua vita, e in cielo assorta.
Desdemona! Desdemona! ... Ah! ... morta! ... morta! ... morta!

(Otello, Act 4, Scene 3)

(And you, how pale you are! And wan, and silent and beautiful. A pious creature, born under an evil star. Cold, as your chaste life, and risen to heaven. Desdemona! Desdemona! ... Ah! ... dead! ... dead! ... dead!

It is as though, in his greatest work, Boito had reconciled his philosophical and theological difficulties by projecting the triumph of beauty and the endurance of purity in death. His final work *Nerone*, abandoned in order to work with Verdi, then resumed and elaborated after their second collaboration on *Falstaff*, was unfinished at the time of his death in 1918. It was completed by Tommasini and Toscanini and produced at La Scala, Milan, in 1924. It reveals a dying pagan world giving way to the new era of Christianity. Boito's attempts to embrace the entire universe and the destiny of humankind met with much less success than his adaptations, which minutely explored human failings. In *Otello*, he was still playing the devil's advocate – a devil whose manipulations of human situations served to highlight details and aspects of the human psyche. Boito's Jago helped to carry the melodrama across the threshold of psychological realism. Writing of Boito in 1887 Verdi stated, 'he has much talent, aspires to originality, but his results are for the most part strange. He lacks spontaneity and stimulation; he possesses many fine musical qualities.'[19]

Arrigo Boito personified the artistic unrest directed against romanticism after the mid-nineteenth century. He represented a cry for reform, a turning towards realism and a rejection and negation of all beauty and idealism. In collaboration with Giuseppe Verdi he demonstrated his talents to their greatest advantage. In *Otello* both light and shade are shown as affected by evil, destiny and violence.

NOTES

1 ARISTOCRATIC BEGINNINGS IN FLORENCE, MANTUA AND ROME

1 Jacopo da Lentini (documents available refer to 1233–40): notary at the court of Frederick II of Swabia, at Palermo, where there developed a school of lyric poetry based on the Provençal idiom, but expressed in the Sicilian vernacular, with infiltrations of other dialects as well as Latin and Provençal. This poetry also contains symbols of feudalism, with the adoration of the troubadour for his lady, analogous to the service paid by the vassal to the feudal lord. It is the first serious poetry to appear in what can be called the 'Italian language'.
2 Francesco Petrarca (1304–74), the Italian poet who is credited with bringing the traditional Italian lyric to perfection. In Italian and other literatures 'Petrarchism' has been a source of influence and inspiration. The image of the laurel is widely used by Petrarch to recall the myth of the sun god Apollo and his love for the nymph Daphne, who was transformed into a laurel before he could embrace her. See Aldo S. Bernardo, *Petrarch, Laura and the Triumphs* (New York, 1974); Morris Bishop, *Petrarch and his World* (Bloomington, 1963); Jennifer Petrie, *Petrarch, the Augustan Poets, the Italian Tradition and the 'Canzoniere'* (Dublin, 1983).
3 See Claude V. Palisca, 'The Alterati of Florence', in William Austin (ed.) *New Looks at Italian Opera* (New York, 1968), pp. 9–37. This article was first delivered in the form of a paper read at a meeting of the Greater New York Chapter of the American Musicological Society at the New York Public Library on 28 April 1962. See also C.V. Palisca (ed.) *Girolamo Mei: Letters on Ancient and Modern Music to Vincenzo Galilei and Giovanni Bardi* (New York, 1960); Nino Pirrotta, 'Temperaments and tendencies in the Florentine Camerata', *Musical Quarterly* XL (1954), pp. 169–89.
4 Palisca, op. cit., p. 9.
5 Dante Alighieri, *La divina commedia: Inferno*, Canto XXXIII. The episode tells of the starvation of Count Ugolino della Gherardesca

NOTES

and his family, in a tower in Pisa, as a result of the treachery of Archbishop Ruggieri degli Ubaldini, in July 1288.

6 See Nino Pirrotta, 'Early opera and aria', in Austin, op. cit., pp. 39–107.
7 For a description of the court festivities see Grace O'Brien, *The Golden Age of Italian Music* (London, n.d.), pp. 106–9; Angelo Solerti, *Gli albori del melodramma*, 2nd edn (Bologna, 1976), pp. 73–117.
8 Mario Apollonio, *Storia della letteratura italiana*, 3rd edn (Brescia, 1963), p. 179.
9 Nino Pirrota, *Li due Orfei: da Poliziano a Monteverdi*, 2nd edn (Turin, 1981), p. 8.
10 ibid., p. 5.
11 Angelo Solerti, *Opere minori in versi di T. Tasso, vol. 3: Teatro* (Bologna, 1895), p. cxvii. See also Anna Amalie, 'Tasso, Guarini e l'opera', *Nuova Rivista Musicale Italiana* 4 (1970), pp. 827–40.
12 For details of events surrounding the first production of *Dafne*, see William V. Porter, 'Peri and Corsi's *Dafne*: some new discoveries and observations', *Journal of the American Musicological Society* 17 (1965), pp. 170–96.
13 Marco da Gagliano (b. Florence, 1582, d. Florence, 1643), Italian composer. *Maestro da cappella* at Medici Court and at the cathedral in Florence.
14 For accounts of the life and achievement of Ottavio Rinuccini, see F. Meda, *Ottavio Rinuccini* (Milan, 1894); G. Mazzoni, 'Cenni su Ottavio Rinuccini', in *Commemorazione della riforma melodrammatica* (Florence, 1894); A. Civita, *Ottavio Rinuccini e il sorgere del melodramma in Italia* (Mantua, 1900); C. Calcaterra, *Poesie e canto, studi sulla poesia melica italiana e sulla favola per musica* (Bologna, 1951); Barbara R. Hanning, 'Apologia pro Ottavio Rinuccini', *Journal of the American Musicological Society*, 26 (1973), pp. 24–62; A. Tomlinson, 'Ancora su Ottavio Rinuccini', *Journal of the American Musicological Society* 28 (1975); F.W. Sternfield, 'The first printed opera libretto' in *Musica lirica* 59 (1978).
15 Ulderico Rolandi, *Il libretto per musica attraverso i tempi* (Rome, 1951), pp. 28–32, discusses the libretto of Rinuccini's *Dafne*.
16 Nino Pirrotta in fact regards *Euridice* as the first successful operatic libretto by Rinuccini and provides little information on the earlier attempt with *Dafne*, 1981, op. cit.
17 In Solerti, 1976, op. cit., vol. 1.
18 See dedication in ibid.
19 In ibid.
20 For details on the life and works of the composer, see S. Davari, *Claudio Monteverdi, notizie biografiche* (Mantua, 1885); Henry Prunières, *Claudio Monteverdi* (Paris, 1924); L. Schneider, *Claudio Monteverdi* (Paris, 1921). More recent critical studies include: Leo Schrade, *Monteverdi, Creator of Modern Music* (New York, 1950); Nino Pirrotta, 'Monteverdi e i problemi dell'opera', in *Studi sul*

teatro veneto tra Rinascimento e età barocca (Florence, 1971) pp. 321–43, and 'Teatro, scene, e musica nelle opere di Monteverdi', in R. Monterosso (ed.) *Claudio Monteverdi e il suo tempo* (Venice, Mantua, Cremona, 1963), p. 51. For an account of Monteverdi in Mantua, see O'Brien, op. cit., pp. 108–10.

21 Patrick Smith, *The Tenth Muse* (London, 1971), p. 7.
22 Alessandro Striggio (b. Mantua, 1573, d. Venice, 1630) wrote, in addition to *La favola d'Orfeo*, *Tirsi e Clori* (1615) and the lost *Lamento d'Apollo*. Bibliography: L. Mazzoldi, R. Giusti and R. Salvadori, *Mantova Storia*, vol. 3 (Mantua, 1963); B.R. Hamming, *The Influence of the Human Thought and Italian Renaissance Poetry on the Formation of Opera* (Yale, 1963), chapters 3, 4; Pirrotta, 1971, op. cit.
23 In Solerti, 1976, op. cit., vol. 3.
24 Each cantica of Dante's *La divina commedia* (*The Divine Comedy*) concludes with the word *stelle* (stars). The final line of *Inferno* reads 'E quindi uscimmo a riveder le stelle' (And hence we out did go, to see the stars once more).
25 The address to Hope is clearly based on the lines from Dante:

>   Or va, ch'un sol volere è d'ambedue:
>   Tu duca, tu signore e tu maestro,
>   Così li dissi; e poi che mosso fue,
>   Intrai per lo cammino alto e silvestro.
>   (Dante, *Inferno*, Canto II, lines 139–42)

>   (Now go, you leader, lord and master,
>   since we are of but a single will.
>   So thus to him I spoke. As soon as he
>   set out
>   I entered on the deep and leafy track.)

26

>   Per me si va ne la città dolente,
>   Per me si va ne l' etterno dolore,
>   Per me si va tra la perduta gente.
>   Giustizia mosse il mio alto fattore;
>   Fecemi la divina potestate,
>   La somma sapienza e 'l primo amore.
>   Dinanzi a me non fuor cose create
>   Se non etterne, ed io etterno duro.
>   Lasciate ogne speranza, voi ch'entrate.
>   (Dante, *Inferno*, Canto III, lines 1–9)

>   (Through me one enters the city of sorrow.
>   Through me one witnesses eternal misery,
>   Through me one encounters the damned.
>   Justice moved by my maker on High.
>   Divine Power, Supreme Wisdom and
>   Primal Love made me.

NOTES

> Before me, nothing but eternal things were
> created, and I eternal am
> Abandon hope all ye that enter.)

27 In Solerti, op. cit., vol. 1, p. 145; translated by the author.
28 In ibid.
29 See ibid., pp. 191–2.
30 For a detailed account of Roman opera during the seventeenth century, see A. Ademollo, *I teatri di Roma nel secolo XVII* (Rome, 1888; reprint Bologna, 1969); A. della Corte, *Drammi per musica dal Rinuccini allo Zeno* (Turin, 1958); Margaret Murata, *Operas for the Papal Court 1631–1668* (Michigan, 1981). The last work studies the history of the operas, in addition to aspects of style in the librettos, and the evolution of an operatic style.
31 For details on the Barberini palace, see Anthony Blunt, 'The Palazzo Barberini', *Journal of the Warburg and Courtauld Institutes* 21 (1958), pp. 256–87; For an account of the Barberini family, see the following: Maria Grazia Iodice, 'Il Cardinal Francesco Barberini', unpublished thesis, University of Rome, 1965; Marilyn Aronberg Lavin, *Seventeenth-century Barberini Documents and Inventories of Art* (New York, 1975).
32 For a consideration of the texts of operas derived from Tasso, see A. Einstein, *Orlando furioso* and *La Gerusalemme liberata* as set to music during the sixteenth and seventeenth centuries', *Notes* 8 (1950–1), pp. 623–30; Murata, op. cit., pp. 22–7.
33 Alessandro Ademollo, 'Il melodramma italiano e Clemente IX', *Opinione* 279 (1879); Giovanni Canevazzi, *Papa Clemente IX poeta* (Modena, 1900); Margaret Murata, 'Rospigliosiana ovvero gli equivoci innocenti', in *Studi musicali* 4 (1975), pp. 131–43; Murata, 1981, op. cit., pp. 1–11; Abd-el-Kader, 'Drammi inediti di Giulio Rospigliosi', in *Rivista musicale italiana* 14 (1975), pp. 473–508.
34 See P. Bjurstrom, *Feast and Theatre in Queen Christina's Rome* (Stockholm, 1966); Alberto Cametti, *Cristina di Svezia, l'arte musicale e gli spettacoli teatrali in Rome* (Rome, 1931).

2 POPULAR SUCCESS AND MATURITY IN VENICE: BUSENELLO, BADOARO AND CICOGNINI

1 Claudio Merulo of Correggio: real name Merlotti (1533–1604), organist at St Mark's, Venice, composer of organ music.
2 Andrea Gabrieli (b. Venice, c. 1520, d. Venice, 1586): little is known about his early life; he may have been a singer at St Mark's but was certainly organist at the Church of San Geremia in 1558. Later he went to Munich. On returning to Venice in 1566, he became organist at St Mark's. His greatest music was not published until after his death in 1586.
    Giovanni Gabrieli (b. Venice, 1557, d. Venice, 1612): nephew of Andrea Gabrieli. Like his uncle, he went to Munich to work with Lassus. He served as a musician at the Bavarian court for several

years. In 1584 his uncle arranged for him to replace Merulo at St Mark's. He also became part-time organist to the School of San Rocco. His greatest achievements are in the field of church music, where he developed his uncle's techniques. Much of his music is published in *Sacrae Symphoniae* (1597).

3   San Cassiano Theatre: founded by the librettist Benedetto Ferrari in 1637, it was the first Italian opera house opened for public performances. See Giovanni Morelli and Thomas Walker, 'Tre controversie intorno al San Cassiano', in Maria Teresa Muraro (ed.) *Venezia e il melodramma nel Seicento* (Florence, 1976), pp. 97–120.
4   Benedetto Ferrari (b. Reggio Emilia, 1603, d. Modena, 1681) established with Francesco Manelli public opera performances in Venice. A librettist, his works include *Andromeda*, which inaugurated the San Cassiano Theatre in 1637; *La maga fulminata* (1638); *Il pastor regio* (1640); *La ninfa avara* and *Proserpina rapita* (1642). He was active in Venice between 1637 and 1644, and in 1653 he was appointed court choirmaster at Modena.
5   See J. Merrill Knapp, *The Magic of Opera* (London, 1975), pp. 22–34; Patrick Smith, *The Tenth Muse* (London, 1971).
6   Bruno Brizi, 'G.F. Busenello e *L'incoronazione di Poppea*', in Muraro, op. cit., p. 52.
7   Wolfgang Osthoff, 'Antonio Cesti's *Alessandro vincitor di se stesso*', *Studien zur Musikwissenschaft* 24 (1960), pp. 13–43.
8   Simon Townley-Worsthorne, *Venetian Opera in the Seventeenth Century* (London, 1954).
9   Nino Pirrotta, 'Le prime opere di Antonio Cesti', in Pietro Castiglia (ed.) *L'orchestra* (Florence, 1954), pp. 153–81, and 'Tre capitoli su Cesti', in *La scuola romana* (Siena, 1953), pp. 27–79.
10 Brizi, op. cit., pp. 51–68.
11 Thomas Walker, 'Gli errori di *Minerva al tavolino*', in Muraro, op. cit., pp. 7–16.
12 Gianfranco Folena, 'Introduction', in Muraro, op. cit., p. 8, points out that in the Faculty of Letters at the University of Padua research activity is flourishing in the field of metre in the Italian operatic libretto, from the origins to the time of Metastasio. During the academic session 1966–7, L. Cervaro completed the thesis, 'Il linguaggio melodrammatico di Ottavio Rinuccini', under Professor Folena's direction.
13 See Cristoforo Ivanovich, *La Minerva al tavolino* (Venice, 1681). It contains twenty chapters on musical and theatrical life in Venice in the seventeenth century. See also Milos Velimirovic, 'Cristoforo Ivanovich from Budva, the first historian of the Venetian opera', in *The Yugoslav Music Review* (ZVUK) (1967), pp. 77–8, 135–45.
14 Walker, op. cit.
15 ibid., p. 12.
16 Wolfgang Osthoff, 'Zur Bologneser Aufführuna von Monteverdi's *Ritorno di Ulisse* im Jahre 1640', in *Anzeiger der philosophisch-historischen Klasse der Österr Akademie der Wissenschaften* (1958),

NOTES

pp. 155–60, and 'Zu den Quellen von Monteverdi's *Ritorno di Ulisse in patria*', *Studien zur Musikwissenschaft* 23 (1956), pp. 67–78.

17 Gian Francesco Busenello (b. Venice, 1598, d. Legnaro-Padua, 1659): in addition to Ivanovich, op. cit., see G. Spini, *Ricerca di libertini* (Rome, 1950); F. de Grada, 'G.F. Busenello e il libretto dell'*Incoronazione di Poppea*' in R. Monterosso (ed.) *Claudio Monteverdi e il suo tempo* (Venice, Mantua, Cremona, 1963), pp. 81–102; Bruno Brizi, 'Teoria e prassi melodrammatica di G.F. Busenello e *L'Incoronazione di Poppea*', in Muraro, op. cit., pp. 51–68; A. Chiarelli, '*L'incoronazione di Poppea o Il Nerone* – problemi di filologia', in *Rivista italiana di musicoligia* 9 (1974), pp. 117–51.

18 See 'Lucrezia degli Obizzi' in *Racconto storico* (Milan, 1936); A. Benacchio, 'Pio Enea II degli Obizzi', *Bollettino del Museo Civico di Padova* (1911), p. 70; Biblioteca Correr, Venice, cod.3052, doc. 18, p. 75.

19 Giovanni Battista Marino (b. Naples, 1569, d. Naples, 1625): came of a family of lawyers, but soon abandoned the law for the pursuit of letters. Collections of poems include: *La lira* (1614), *La galleria* (1619), *La sampogna* (1620) and finally *Adone* (1623) which achieved outstanding success. He spent from 1615 to 1623 in France, and was fêted in all cities and towns through which he passed. He is regarded the 'capo-scuola' of baroque literature.

20 Giacomo Badoaro (b. Venice, 1602, d. Venice, 1654): an aristocrat and man of letters, his operatic libretti include *Il ritorno di Ulisse in patria* (1640, music by Monteverdi), *Ulisse errante* (1644, music by Sacrati), *L'Helena rapita da Theseo* (1653, music by Cavalli). A member of the Accademia degli Incogniti, he was financially involved in the Teatro Novissimo, Venice, at the time of its closure in 1645. See C. Ivanovich, op. cit.; Walker, op. cit.; A. Livingston, *La vita veneziana nelle opere di Gian Francesco Busenello* (Venice, 1913); L. Bianconi and Thomas Walker, 'Dalla Finta pazza alla Veremonda, storie di Febiarmonici', *RIM* 10 (1975), pp. 379–454.

21 De Grada, op. cit.

22 See Ellen Rosand, 'Aria as drama in the early operas of Francesco Cavalli', in Muraro, op. cit., pp. 81–4. Rosand approaches the arias from a musical rather than a literary viewpoint. Nevertheless, it remains an interesting contribution to the study of the text of some of Cavalli's operas.

23 Angelo Solerti, *Gli albori del melodramma*, vol. 1 (Bologna, 1976), p. 88.

24 Rosand, op. cit., p. 81.

25 ibid., p. 90.

26 ibid., p. 74.

27 William C. Holmes, 'Giacinto Andrea Cicognini's and Antonio Cesti's *Orontea* (1649)', in William W. Austin (ed.) *New Looks at Italian Opera* (Westport, Conn., 1968), pp. 108–32.

28 ibid., p. 111.

29 See introductory remarks to *Giasone* (Venice, 1649).
30 Holmes, op. cit., p. 121.
31 See Solerti, op. cit., vol. 4, p. 333.

3 INNOVATION AND REFORM: ZENO, METASTASIO AND CALZABIGI

1 For detailed information concerning the Neapolitan opera, see B. Croce, 'I teatri di Napoli', *Archivio storico per le province napoletane* (Naples, 1889); C. Sartori, 'Gli Scarlatti a Napoli', *Rivista di musicologia italiana* 46 (1942), pp. 380–3; M. Scherillo, *L'opera buffa napoletana* (Naples, 1916); Giampiero Tintori, *L'opera napolitana* (Milan, 1958); Michael F. Robinson, *Naples and Neapolitan Opera* (Oxford, 1972); Paolo Gallarati, *Musica e maschera* (Turin, 1984), pp. 107–24.
2 See Robinson, op. cit., pp. 36–71, for an account of serious or heroic texts; and pp. 178–204, for the development of comic material.
3 See D. O'Grady, *Alexander Pope and Eighteenth-Century Italian Poetry* (Berne/New York, 1986).
4 For an account of the Accademia dell'Arcadia, see W. Binni, *L'Arcadia e il Metastasio* (Florence, 1963), pp. 3–46.
5 See *Della perfetta poesia italiana*, Books 3, 4, 5, 6 (Venice, 1730), in which Ludovico Antonio Muratori accuses the melodrama of having corrupted public taste and morality, but states that it can yet become a school of good customs and a seat of moral wisdom.
6 Gian-Vincenzo Gravina, *Della tragedia* (Naples, 1715), and *Della ragion poetica* (1708). For a critical approach to Gravina as a tragic writer, see G. Natali, Introduction, *Della ragion poetica* (Lanciano, 1920–33), and G. Bàrberi-Squarotti, 'Appunti per il Gravina', in *Metodo, stile, storia* (Milan, 1962), pp. 419–40.
7 Robinson, op. cit., p. 43.
8 F. Negri, *La vita di A. Zeno* (Venice, 1816); L. Pistorelli, *I melodrammi di A. Zeno* (Padua, 1894); R. Freeman, 'Apostolo Zeno's reform of the libretto', *Journal of the American Musicological Society* 21 (1968), n. 3, pp. 321–41; D.J. Grant, 'La Griselda di Zeno e il libretto dell'opera di Scarlatti', *Nuova Rivista Musicale Italiana* 2 (1968), n. 2, pp. 207–25.
9 See Gallarati's analysis of Zeno's technique with particular reference to *Griselda* (op. cit., pp. 7–18).
10 A. Zeno, *Drammi scelti*, ed M. Fehr (Bari, 1929).
11 See F. Petrarca, sonnet 311, 'Quel rosignuol, che si soave piagne', in *Rime e Trionfi* (Turin, 1968), p. 428.
12 *Griselda, Drama per Musica, da Rappresentarsi nel Teatro di S. Cassiano, L'Anno MDCCI*.
13 'In una Tragedia si possono osservar religiosamente sì fatte regole, anzi si debbono. In un Dramma bisogna dare qualche cosa all'abuso del secolo, alla decorazione, alla musica.' ('In a Tragedy one can observe precise rules. Indeed one must observe them. In a Drama one must concede something to the abuses of the time, to

ornamentation and to the music.') (Letter to Pier Caterino Zeno, Vienna, 6 January 1720)

14 See C. Levi, 'La critica metastasiana in Italia', *Rivista teatrale italiana* 12–14 (1913–15); B. Brunelli, *Tutte le opere di P. Metastasio* (Milan, 1943–54), pp. 825–37; F. Gavazzeni, *Opere scelte di P. Metastasio* (Turin, 1968), pp. 67–83. For an analysis of Metastasio's contribution to the melodrama, see A. della Corte, 'L'estetica musicale di P. Metastasio', in *Settecento italiano: Paisiello, l'estetica musicale di P. Metastasio* (Turin, 1922); A. Bonaventura, 'P. Metastasio musicista', *Musica Oggi* (January 1932); Patrick Smith, *The Tenth Muse* (London, 1971); Elena Sala di Felice, 'Il desiderio della parola e il piacere delle lagrime nel melodramma metastasiana', in *Metastasio e il mondo musicale* (Venice, 1982), *Metastasio, ideologia, drammaturgia, spettacolo* (Milan, 1983), pp. 166–8, and *Metastasio e il melodramma* (Padua, 1985); Gallarati, op. cit., pp. 19–51.
15 See Guido Nicastro, *Metastasio e il teatro del primo Settecento* (Bari, 1973), pp. 69–74.
16 F. De Sanctis, *Storia della letteratura italiana* (Turin, 1958), vol. 2, p. 862.
17 The influence of Descartes's *Des passions de l'âme* (1649) is the subject of E. Raimondi's essay 'Il teatro allo specchio' in his *Il concerto interrotto* (Pisa, 1979).
18 *Tutte le opere di P. Metastasio*, ed B. Brunelli (Milan, 1943–54), vol. 1.
19 Maria Grazia Accorsi, 'Metastasio e l'idea dell'amore', *Italianistica* 13, n. 1–2 (January–August 1984), pp. 71–123. Of particular interest is the section 'Un amore ragionevole', pp. 109–23.
20 See F. Gavazzeni, 'Le disuguaglianze stilistiche della *Didone*', in *Studi metastasiani* (Padua, 1964).
21 Smith, op. cit., pp. 92–8, provides an analysis of *Attilio Regolo*.
22 *Tutte le opere di P. Metastasio*, vol. 1.
23 For details of Calzabigi's 'reform', see Gallarati, op. cit., pp. 70–87, especially the section referring exclusively to Gluck's music, 'La musica di Gluck e la liricizzazione del testo', pp. 77–82.
24 M. Donà, 'Dagli archivi milanesi: lettere di Ranieri de' Calzabigi e di Antonia Bernasconi', *Analecta musicologica* 14 (1974), pp. 268–300.
25 See Gallerati, 'Isolamento della riforma gluckiana', op. cit., pp. 85–7; Gerhart von Westerman, *Opera Guide* (London, 1964), pp. 71–80.

4 OF SERVANTS AND MASTERS: FEDERICO, GOLDONI AND DA PONTE

1. The following provide an account of the Italian intermezzo: C.E. Troy, *The Comic Intermezzo* (Michigan, 1979); P. Gallarati, *Musica e maschera* (Turin, 1984), pp. 97–106.
2. For a basic background to the improvised comic theatre, see M. Apollonio, *Storia del teatro* (Florence, 1950), vol. 3; F. Taviani, *La commedia dell'Arte e la Società barocca* (Rome, 1976); S. Ferrone, *La commedia dell'arte* (Milan, 1985).
3. For a consideration of the mask and of the affinity between Shakespearian comedy and the *commedia dell'arte*, see Allardyce Nicoll, *The World of Harlequin* (Cambridge, 1963).
4. For the diverse levels of interpretation of Goldoni's *Mirandolina*, see Mario Baratto's most searching article 'Nota sulla *Locandiera*' in the posthumously published *La letteratura teatrale del Settecento in Italia* (Vicenza, 1985), pp. 125–35.
5. See Gianfranco Folena, 'Il linguaggio della *Serva padrona*', in *L'italiano in Europa: esperienze linguistiche del Settecento* (Turin, 1983), pp. 282–301; Gallarati, op. cit., pp. 282–301.
6. Folena, op. cit., p. 291.
7. See C. Goldoni, *Memorie* (Milan, 1985), pp. 44–6.
8. In his study *Goldoni and the Venice of his Time* (New York, 1921), J.S. Kennard provides an account of the social and literary ambience into which the writer was born. See also F. Fido, *Guida a Goldoni: teatro e società nel Settecento* (Turin, 1977).
9. Andrea della Corte, in *L'opera comica italiana nel Settecento* (Bari, 1923), p. 50, calls Goldoni the most influential comic librettist of the eighteenth century.
10. For an outline of Goldoni's career, see E. Steele, *Goldoni, Life, Work and Times* (Ravenna, 1981).
11. These three periods are considered and assessed by Gianfranco Folena in his article 'Goldoni librettista comico', in Maria Teresa Muraro (ed.) *Venezia e il melodramma nel Settecento*, vol. 2 (Florence, 1978), pp. 21–32.
12. Little detailed research has been carried out on the influence of the *commedia dell'arte* on the operatic theatre. For this reason Nino Pirrotta's essay, '*Commedia dell'arte* and opera', *Musical Quarterly*, July 1955, is particularly valuable.
13. For an account of the career and escapades of Caron de Beaumarchais, see Cynthia Cox, *The Real Figaro* (London, 1962). Critical studies of the dramatist and his work include: L. de Loménie, *Beaumarchais et son temps* (Paris, 1856; reprint Geneva, 1970); J. Scherer, *La Dramaturgie de Beaumarchais* (Paris, 1980); J.B. Ratermanis and W.R. Irwin, *The Comic Style of Beaumarchais* (Seattle, 1961).
14. Studies of Lorenzo Da Ponte's life include: April Fitzlyon, *The Libertine Librettist* (London, 1955); Sheila Hodges, *Lorenzo da Ponte: the Life and Times of Mozart's Librettist* (London, 1985).

NOTES

See also Daniela Goldin, *La vera fenice* (Turin, 1985), pp. 77–148. In the chapter entitled 'Mozart, Da Ponte e il linguaggio dell'opera buffa', the author analyses the linguistic features of the three librettos written for Mozart. A further chapter, pp. 149–63, is devoted to *Don Giovanni*. Also of much interest is the section 'Da Ponte e Mozart' in Gallarati, op. cit., pp. 162–202, which also includes a short assessment of the operatic scene following on the footsteps of Da Ponte, before the birth of the 'new' Italian opera.

15 See G. Pagnini (ed.) *Memorie ed altri scritti di Lorenzo Da Ponte* (Milan, 1971).
16 Two close readings of *Le nozze di Figaro* provide a detailed account of the plot and dramatic action: George R. Marek's 'What happens in Figaro', in *Opera as Theatre* (2nd edn, Westport, Conn., 1972), pp. 2–38, traces the differences and similarities between the Beaumarchais and Da Ponte texts. Massimo Mila, *Letture delle 'Nozze di Figaro'* (Turin, 1979), takes a more detailed approach to the musical form and the division of the drama into solos, duets and ensembles.
17 This is an interpretation accepted by Riccardo Bacchelli and carried over in his own satirical comedy, *La famiglia di Figaro*. See R. Bacchelli, *Teatro*, vol. 2 (Milan, 1964), pp. 276–367. See also D. O'Grady, 'Bacchelli e il teatro del Settecento', in *Riccardo Bacchelli uomo e scrittore* (Modena, 1990), pp. 123–8. See G. Macchia, *Vita, avventure e morte di Don Giovanni* (Bari, 1966/Turin, 1978).
18 An interesting review of the sources of Da Ponte's *Don Giovanni* is contained in Elizabeth Forbes's article 'The libertine and the statue', *Wexford Festival Opera* (1988), pp. 45–8.
19 See F. Orlando, in his essay 'L'ultima festa dell'ancien regime: Mozart e le commedie di Beaumarchais e Molière', in *La letteratura e le arti, Scritti in onore di Giovanni Macchia* (Bari, 1986).
20 Forbes, op. cit., pp. 46–7.
21 Some similarities between the two are pointed out by P. Smith in *The Tenth Muse* (London, 1971), p. 167.
22 See G. Gronda, 'L'aria del catalogo: un precedente poetico del testo dapontiano', in the proceedings of the conference *Musica e spettacolo a Parma nel Settecento* (Parma, 1979); Goldin, 'In margine al catalogo di Leporello', in op. cit., pp. 149–63. Both articles trace the history of the catalogue aria and the occurrence of lists in eighteenth-century opera.
23 Goldin, op. cit., p. 112.
24 Daniela Goldin defines the content of the comedy in the following terms: 'la finzione elevata a sistema' ('pretence elevated to a system'), in ibid., p. 118.
25 N. Gerhart von Westerman, *Opera Guide* (London, 1964), p. 98.
26 For a discussion of the comic, intellectual and scientific aspects of the plot see Guido Paduano's illuminating chapter '*Così fan tutte* e la gaia scienza' in Guido Paduano, *Noi facemmo ambedue un sogno strano* (Palermo, 1982), pp. 118–51.

27 In the concluding words of Paduano, 'mettere in contraddizione l'individuo rispetto a sè stesso' (placing the individual in contradiction to itself) (ibid., p. 151), is the manner in which cold water is thrown on the pretensions of those who seek to live by love alone.

5 A CRY FOR FREEDOM: HIGH PRIESTS AND PATRIOTS

1 Ugo Foscolo was born in 1778 in Zante, at the time a Venetian possession. Following the death of his father, he came to live in Venice at the age of 14. In 1796, on account of his political affiliations, he was forced to retreat to the Euganean Hills, where he began the epistolary novel *Le ultime lettere di Jacopo Ortis*. Jacopo is a young student, and his letters are addressed to his friend Lorenzo Alderani. The novel is divided into two sections: Part One is devoted to his hopeless and idealized love for Teresa, which is expressed in Petrarcan and Dantesque terms; Part Two is more politically orientated, containing invective against the French, expressions of Italian nationalism and the protagonist's suicide. Significant is the letter from Milan, contained in Part Two and dated 11 November, in which he decries attempts to exclude the poet Vincenzo Monti from employment, and attacks the fashion in Italy for all things French. Foscolo died in exile in London in 1827. In 1871, by solemn decree of the Italian government, his body was taken to Florence, where he was reburied in the Church of Santa Croce. Often described as a Byronic spirit, a disciple of Alfieri and an admirer of Parini, he was not only a colourful writer of patriotic prose, but also composed poetic works, which include *I sepolcri* and *Le grazie*, together with odes and sonnets. Bibliography: E. R. Vincent, *An Italian in Regency England* (Cambridge, 1953); M. Fubini, *Ugo Foscolo* (Bari, 1962); D. Radcliff-Unstead, *Ugo Foscolo* (New York, 1970).

2 Alessandro Manzoni (Milan 1785–1873), the grandson of the Enlightenment philosopher and penal reformer Cesare Beccaria, applied his Enlightenment upbringing and interest in history to his novel *I promessi sposi*, first published 1825-7 and again, after a revision resulting from a sojourn in Florence, in 1840. The novel, besides tracing the misadventures of two peasants, Renzo and Lucia, can be regarded as a political document in favour of the exercise of personal, social, educational and political freedom. In addition, *I promessi sposi* (*The Betrothed*) can be interpreted as a treatise on the will, the significance of promise and its philosophical, psychological and theological implications. Bibliography: G. Petrocchi, *Manzoni: letteratura e vita* (Milan, 1971); S. B. Chandler, *Alessandro Manzoni: the Story of a Spiritual Quest* (Edinburgh, 1974); E. Caserta, *Manzoni's Christian Realism* (Florence, 1977); E. N. Girardi and G. Spada, *Manzoni e il Seicento lombardo* (Milan, 1977).

3 Tommaso Grossi (1790–1853), poet and prose writer, was a friend

NOTES

of Manzoni from whom he derived the inspiration for his historical novel *Marco Visconti*. Bibliography: G. Brognoligo, *Tommaso Grossi: la vita e le opere* (Messina, 1916); G. Bertacchi, 'Tra Grossi e Manzoni', in *Marco Visconti* (Milan, 1935); A. Bozzoli, *L'Arcadia all'incanto* (Milan, 1971).

4 Silvio Pellico (1789–1854) was born in Saluzzo (Piedmont) and at the age of 16 moved to Lyon, where he spent four years studying French literature. On his return to Italy he became acquainted with Monti and Foscolo. As editor of the patriotic newspaper *Il conciliatore*, he was arrested and imprisoned in Venice for two years. He was later transferred to the Spielberg prison, where he spent eight years. His memoirs of this period provide the material for his most famous work, the autobiographical *Le mie prigioni*. On his release from prison he played no further part in politics. He is also the author of twelve tragedies, of which only eight were published during his lifetime.

5 *Francesca da Rimini*, a tragedy by Pellico written before his imprisonment, dramatizing the marriage, infidelity and murder of Francesca, wife of Gianciotto Malatesta of Rimini, the story told in Canto 5 of Dante's *Inferno*. Pellico, in projecting Francesca's passion for her brother-in-law, develops the theme of brotherhood. In addition, he provides a psychological analysis of guilt, innocence and the relationship between them.

6 Felice Romani, an Italian librettist, was born in Genoa in 1788, and died in Moneglia in 1865. He was a lawyer by profession. After a classical education he moved to Milan and began writing librettos. An admirer of Metastasio and Monti, he published several books of verse. He attained the peak of his popularity at the time of his collaboration with Bellini, for whom he wrote the texts of *Norma* (1831), *Il pirata* (1827), *La straniera* (1829), *I Capuleti ed i Montecchi* (1830), *La sonnambula* (1831) and *Beatrice di Tenda* (1833). In 1834 he became editor of the Piedmontese *Gazzetta* in Turin, a post which he held until 1849. He also wrote texts for Rossini: *Il turco in Italia* (1813); and Donizetti: *Anna Bolena* (1830), *L'elisir d'amore* (1832) and *Lucrezia Borgia* (1833). Bibliography: E. Branca, *Felice Romani ed i più riputati maestri di musica del suo tempo* (Milan, 1882); Ermanno Loescher, *Romani, critico artistico scientifico* (Rome, 1884); F. L. Arruga, 'Alessandro Manzoni e "la lezione" del teatro musicale italiano', *Vita e pensiero* (May 1965): 369–76; M. Rinaldi, *Felice Romani* (Rome, 1965); P. Smith, *The Tenth Muse* (London, 1971), pp. 198–206; F. Cella, 'Prospettive della librettistica italiana nell'età romantica', in *Contributi dell'Instituto di Filologia Moderna: serie storia del teatro*, vol. 1 (Milan, 1968), pp. 217–34, and 'Indagini sulle fonti francesi dei libretti di Vincenzo Bellini', in *Contributi dell'Instituto di Filologia Moderna: serie francese*, vol. 5 (Milan, 1968), pp. 517–47; *Bellini a Milano* (Turin, 1985); F. Portinari, *Pari siamo* (Turin, 1981), pp. 51–9, 79–102; G. Tintori, *Bellini* (Milan, 1983); G. Paduano, '*Norma*, la crisi del modello

deliberativo', in *Noi facemmo ambedue un sogno strano* (Palermo, 1982), pp. 152–77.

7 Temistocle Solera, Italian librettist, born in Ferrara in 1825, and died in Milan in 1878. He played an active part in anti-Austrian propaganda and in the struggle for independence, his father had been imprisoned in the Spielberg with Pellico and Maroncelli. Educated at the Imperial College, Vienna, and at the University of Pavia, he produced a series of literary works in a Manzonian vein: *I miei primi canti, Lettere giocose* and the novel *Michelino*. In 1839 he began his collaboration with Verdi (*Oberto, Conte di San Bonifazio*), and continued with *Nabucco* (1842), *I lombardi alla prima crociata* (1843), *Giovanna d'Arco* (1845) and *Attila* (1846). The latter was left incomplete by Solera, but was finished at the composer's request by Francesco Maria Piave. Solera then left for Spain where he acted as impresario at the Royal Theatre, Madrid. In 1859 he returned to Milan where he engaged in further political activity. He was also a composer of opera. Bibliography: F. Regli, *Dizionario biografico dei più celebri poeti ed artisti melodrammatici che fiorirono in Italia dal 1800 al 1860* (Turin, 1860); R. Barbiera, *Figure e figurine del secolo che muore* (Milan, 1899); E. Cecchi, 'I librettisti di Giuseppe Verdi', *Nuova Antologia*, October 1913; T. Mantovani, 'Temistocle Solera', *Musica d'oggi*, October 1923; L. Miragoli, *Il melodramma italiano dell'Ottocento* (Rome, 1924); A. Cassi-Ramelli, *Libretti e librettisti* (Milan, 1973); M. Mila, *La giovinezza di Verdi* (Turin, 1974); F. Portinari, 'Introduzione' to *Il teatro italiano* V, vol. 2 (Turin, 1984), pp. xvii–xxv.

8 Francesco Maria Piave, Italian librettist, was born in Murano, Venice, in 1810, and died in Milan in 1876. He studied for the priesthood, but left the seminary in Venice in 1827. In 1828 he returned to Venice where he was employed as a proofreader at the Antonelli publishing group. As a member of the Accademia dei Concordi he made the acquaintance of Count Alvise Mocenigo, president of the Fenice Theatre, Venice, who in 1843 commissioned a libretto drawn from the text of *Cromwell* by Victor Hugo. The project did not materialize, but *Cromwell* was substituted by *Ernani* (1844) which marked the beginning of the Verdi/Piave collaboration. There followed *I due Foscari* (1844), *Macbeth* (1847), *Il corsaro* (1848), *Stiffelio* (1850) which in 1857 became *Aroldo*, *Rigoletto* (1851), *La traviata* (1853), *Simon Boccanegra* (1857) and *La forza del destino* (1862). In 1859 on the recommendation of Verdi and Massimo d'Azeglio, son-in-law of Alessandro Manzoni, he obtained the same position, that of official poet to theatre, at La Scala, Milan. In 1865 he applied for the Chair of Drama and Recitation at the Milan Conservatorio, but he failed to gain the position. In 1867 he suffered a stroke, and lived paralysed for a further nine years. Bibliography: A. Santi, 'Per il centenario della nascita di Francesco Maria Piave', *La voce di Murano*, 18 May 1910; T. Mantovani, 'F. M. Piave', *Musica d'oggi*, September 1924;

NOTES

V. Rolandi, *Libretti e librettisti verdiani* (Rome 1941), and 'Morbidità e patologia nei libretti delle opere verdiane', *L'Umbria medica* 20 (1941).

9   F. Cella, 'Indagini sulle fonti francesi dei libretti di Gaetano Donizetti' in *Contributi dell'Instituto di Filologia Moderna*, serie francese (Milan, 1966), pp. 342–590, and 'Il "Donizettismo" nei libretti donizettiani', in *Atti del primo convegno di studi donizettiani* (Bergamo, 1983), p. 43.

10 Vittorio Alfieri, Italian poet, dramatist and political thinker (1749–1803), was a native of Asti, Piedmont. He travelled extensively in Europe and absorbed French political ideology and English dramatic technique, which he brought to bear on his political and literary treatises (*Della tirannide*, *Del principe e delle lettere*). His twenty-two tragedies of 'Libertà' (Freedom) juxtaposing heroism and tyranny are contained in a classical framework and contain thematic and linguistic political symbolism. Dramatic creations such as Merope (*Merope*), Saul (*Saul*) and Clitennestra (*Agamennone*), among others, provide the basic theatrical sources for nineteenth-century melodramatic figures. The first great Italian writer of tragedies, Alfieri, in addition to reviving the classical drama, can be regarded as a significant contributor to Enlightenment thought. Bibliography: M. Fubini, *Alfieri, il pensiero, la tragedia* (Florence, 1937); V. Branca, *Alfieri e la ricerca dello stile* (Florence, 1947); A. Di Benedetto, *V. Alfieri, le passioni e il limite* (Naples, 1987). For the influence of Alfieri on the melodrama, see G. Confalonieri, *Storia della musica* (Milan, 1958), vol. 2, pp. 108–9; M. Apollonio, *Storia del teatro*, vol. 2 (Florence, 1954), p. 425 ss; and of greatest interest, F. L. Arruga, *Incontri fra poeti e musicisti nell'opera romantica italiana* (Milan, 1968), pp. 235–90. In this study Arruga refers to Alfieri's influence on Solera (*Nabucco*) and Piave (*Macbeth*) in the treatment of themes of delirium. See also V. Alfieri, *Vita* (Turin, 1967), Epoca II, Chapters IV-V.

11 Giacomo Leopardi, Italian lyric poet (1798–1836). Bibliography: I. Origo, *Leopardi, a Study in Solitude* (London, 1953); G. Carsaniga, *Giacomo Leopardi, the Unheeded Voice* (Edinburgh, 1977); U. Bosco, *Titanismo e pietà in Giacomo Leopardi* (Rome, 1980).

12 Smith, op. cit., p. 193.

13 Antonio Conti, an Italian poet, translator and tragedian, is best known in Britain for his translations into Italian of Alexander Pope's *The Rape of the Lock* and *Eloisa to Abelard*. See G. Gronda, *Antonio Conti, versioni poetiche* (Bari, 1966); D. O'Grady, *Alexander Pope and Eighteenth Century Italian Poetry* (Berne/New York, 1986), and 'La poesia di monacazione di A. Conti', *Testo* 13 (1987), pp. 38–51.

14 It has been noted that the work may have been hidden by Conti, as a result of his personal identification with the theme.

15 See O'Grady, 1987, op. cit.

16 Gerhart von Westerman, *Opera Guide* (London, 1964), p. 130.

17 Franca Cella's illuminating study of the libretto provides an analysis of the several versions of 'Casta Diva'. See also G. Pannain, *Ottocento musicale* (Milan, 1952), p. 39; M. Mila, *Cent'anni di musica moderna* (Milan, 1944), p. 38; O. Andolfi, *'Norma' di V. Bellini* (Rome, 1929), p. 21; Paduano, op. cit.

18 Romani's principal sources were: Gasparo Spontini, *La vestale* (1807, libretto Étienne de Jouy); Antonio Sacchini, *Arvire et Evelina* (1788, libretto Nicolas Guillard); Giovanni Pacini, *La sacerdotessa d'Irminsul* (1817, libretto F. Romani). As is apparent, Romani had treated the theme before his collaboration with Bellini. The principal dramatic, as opposed to melodramatic, source was A. Soumet, *Norma* (1831). For a comparison of Soumet and Romani, see G. Orrey, *Bellini* (London, 1969), p. iii; F. Pastura, *Bellini secondo la storia* (Milan, 1959), p. 288; H. Weinstock, *V. Bellini, his Life and his Operas* (New York, 1971), p. 275. Also worthy of note is the Italian bardic tradition and the poetry of M. Cesarotti and V. Monti.

19 The march became extremely popular in Italy during the Risorgimento. In opera it had been associated with political and social change since the eighteenth century, e.g. 'Non più andrai' in *Le nozze di Figaro*.

20 For a selection of the works of these poets, see Bruno Maier (ed.) *Lirici del Settecento* (Milan, 1959); *Lirici del secolo XVIII* (Milan, 1877); *Rime degli Arcadi*, 2 (Rome, 1816).

21 The complete translation of this work is in Gronda, op. cit., pp. 11–21.

22 Alexander Pope, *Collected Poems* (New York, 1965), pp. 97–8.

23 Smith, op. cit., p. 205.

24 Giacomo Leopardi, *Canti*, 2nd edn (Rizzoli, 1980), p. 96.

25 This point has been made by Pierluigi Petrobelli in his article 'Nabucco', in *Conferenze, 1966–7* (Associazione Amici della Scala, Milan). A further interesting source is Chateaubriand's *Les Martyrs*.

26 Charles Osborne, *The Complete Operas of Verdi* (London, 1969), p. 65.

27 'Una lettera di Giuseppe Verdi finora non pubblicata', ed. A. Bonaventura (Florence, 1948).

28 See John Black, *The Italian Romantic Libretto. A Study of Salvatore Cammarano* (Edinburgh, 1985), pp. 117–21.

29 A highly original analysis of the opera is included in G. Paduano's book *Noi facemmo ambedue un sogno strano* (op. cit.). Entitled 'Turbamenti del triangolo. Il sistema della autorità e delle tenerezze nell'*Ernani*', it also contains much bibliographical material.

6 OF REASON AND DELIRIUM

1 The Shakespearian influence on Alfieri is worthy of note. See V. Alfieri, *Vita* (Turin, 1968). Also significant is the influence of the Jesuit writers Granelli and Bettinelli.

2 Both Alfieri's *Saul* and *Agamennone* are influential in this respect.

NOTES

The delirium of the aged king (*Saul*) and the emotional conquest of Clitennestra by Egisto (*Agamennone*) are conveyed in terms of images of light and darkness. In addition, in *Agamennone*, images of blood project the transition from a state of lucidity to confusion and violence. The tragedies of Foscolo (*Tieste*, 1797, and *Aiace*, 1811) and Manzoni (*Adelchi*, 1822, and *Il conte di Carmagnola*, 1820) also owe much to Alfieri. In the case of Manzoni's work Enlightenment imagery is substituted by that of religious illumination and grace.

3 For an outline of the outstanding features of the romantic libretto, see Maria Grazia Accorsi, 'Il melodramma melodrammatico', *Sigma* 13, n. 1 (1980), pp. 109–27.
4 See H. Weinstock, *Vincenzo Bellini* (London, 1971), pp. 193–310; F. Portinari, *Pari Siamo* (Turin, 1981), pp. 79–82.
5 For a background study to the libretto of *Il pirata* see Leslie Orrey, *Bellini* (London, 1969), pp. 79–88; Andrew Porter, '*Il pirata*, an introduction', in *Wexford Festival 1972* (Wexford, 1972), p. 36.
6 Andrea della Corte and Guido Pannain, *Vincenzo Bellini: il carattere morale, i caratteri artistici* (Turin, 1935), pp. 54–6.
7 Giacomo Leopardi, *Canti*, 3rd edn (Milan, 1980), pp. 45, 46–7.
8 Ugo Foscolo, 'In morte del fratello Giovanni' in *Ugo Foscolo, Ultime lettere di Jacopo Ortis/Poesie*, ed. M. Puppo (Milan, 1965–88), p. 149.
9 For the text of Scenes 11 and 12, see Weinstock, op. cit., pp. 403–4.
10 Grossi's *Ildegonda* is the most singular influence on *Adelchi*. See *Ildegonda*, Part IV (conclusion), and Manzoni, *Adelchi*, Act 4, Scene 1.
11 The first 'romantic mad scene' can be said to take place in *Ildegonda*. It follows her enforced taking of the veil, and occurs at the conclusion of Part III and throughout Part IV. It can, for convenience, be divided into nine movements: (i) unhappiness; (ii) anxiety; (iii) fear; (iv) active imagination; (v) hallucination, in the guise of a horror story; (vi) recourse to violence; (vii) physical illness; (viii) calmness; (ix) death.
12 Described by Franco Lorenzo Arruga in *Incontri fra poeti e musicisti nell'opera romantica italiana* (Milan, 1968), p. 265, as 'il linguaggio della definizione morale, che risultò quindi assoluta, chiara e fidente' ('the language of moral definition, which established itself absolute, clear and trusting').
13 See Portinari, op. cit., p. 101. Portinari mentions only Ermengarda, the unfortunate heroine of *Adelchi* (1822).
14 Sir Henry Bishop lived in London, 1786–1855. At the age of 24 he had already been engaged to compose and direct music at Covent Garden. He became director of the King's Theatre, and for Drury Lane composed his *Aladdin*. He wrote nearly 60 operatic pieces, among them 11 adaptations of Scott's novels, and 15 arrangements of other operas. He was knighted in 1842.
15 In addition to his libretti for Donizetti, Cammarano also wrote texts for Mercadante (*La vestale* (1840), *Il proscritto* (1842), *Il*

reggente (1843), *Il vascello da Gama* (1845), *Orazi e Curiazi* (1846), *Medea* (1851) and *Virginia* (1866)), for Pacini (*Malvina di Scozia* (1851), *Saffo* (1840), *La fidanzata corsa* (1842), *Bondelmonte* (1845) and *Stella di Napoli* (1845)) and for Verdi (*Alzira* (1845), *La battaglia di Legnano* (1849), *Luisa Miller* (1849) and *Il trovatore* (1853)). He provided a libretto for Donizetti's *Poliuto* in 1848. See S. di Giacomo, 'Musica e librettisti: S. Cammarano, il librettista del "Trovatore" e G. Verdi', *Musica e musicisti* lix (1904), p. 81; T. Mantovani, 'Librettisti verdiani, S. Cammarano', *Musica d'oggi* viii (1926), p. 18; Gary Schmidgall, *Literature as Opera* (New York, 1977), pp. 137–47; John Black, *The Italian Romantic Libretto: A Study of Salvatore Cammarano* (Edinburgh, 1985).

16 Schmidgall, op. cit., p. 137.
17 See G. Agnoli, *Gli albori del romanzo storico in Italia e i primi imitatori di W. Scott* (Piacenza, 1906); A. Benedetti, *Le traduzioni italiane di Walter Scott* (Florence, 1974). The popularity of Scott in Italy is also treated by Mary Ambrose in *Atti dell XI Congresso Nazionale di Studi Manzoniani* (Lecco, 1982), pp. 363–76; Franca Ruggieri Punzo, *Scott in Italia* (Bari, 1975); Jerome Mitchell, *Operas of Sir Walter Scott* (Alabama, 1977).
18 The line in all Ricordi librettos and scores reads 'fronte' (forehead/brow). It has become customary, however, for some singers to sing 'fonte' (fountain), as it seems more in keeping with the content of the aria. However, the image of the fountain has already been established in the recitative.
19 During the nineteenth century an aria entitled 'Perchè non ho del vento' ('Since I have not the wings of the wind') was almost always substituted for 'Regnava nel silenzio'. This aria was composed by Donizetti for his opera *Rosamonda d'Inghilterra* (1834). Although extremely popular, since it was performed by the creator of Lucia, Fanny Tacchinardi Persiani, and prominent sopranos such as Jenny Lind, its inclusion robs the opera of its dramatic unity. The aria contains references to the fountain, which fills the heroine with foreboding, but there is no appearance of the bloodstained ghost. For this reason Lucia's identification with the hapless bride for a long time disappeared. Her reference to 'il fantasma' in the 'mad scene' loses its more subtle significance when the original 'Regnava' is not performed.
20 See Philip Gosett, *'Anna Bolena' and the Artistic Maturity of Gaetano Donizetti* (Oxford, 1985).

7 JESTER, TROUBADOUR AND COURTESAN

1 See Piero Weiss, 'Verdi e la fusione dei generi', in Lorenzo Bianconi (ed.) *La drammaturgia musicale* (Bologna, 1986), pp. 75–92.
2 F. Abbiati, *Verdi* (Milan, 1959), vol. 2, p. 62.
3 C. Osborne, *The Complete Operas of Verdi* (London, 1969), p. 259.
4 Letter to Piave in Abbiati, op. cit., p. 62.

NOTES

5 See A. Ubersfeld (ed.) *Victor Hugo, Théâtre*, vol. 1 (Paris, 1985), p. 829.
6 For the relevant documents, see ibid., pp. 839–45.
7 Free translation by the author of ibid., pp. 831–2.
8 A. Ubersfeld, *Le roi e le buffon: Étude sur le théâtre de Hugo de 1830 à 1839* (Paris, 1974), p. 156.
9 G. Verdi, *I copia-lettere di G. Verdi* (ed G. Cesari and A. Luzio) (Milan, 1913), p. 487.
10 See ibid., pp. 489–90.
11 For some historical information regarding the life and reputation of Francis I, see C. Osborne, *Rigoletto, a Guide to the Opera* (London, 1979), pp. 31–3.
12 For information on the censorship problems preceding the production of *Rigoletto*, see M. Lavagetto, *Un caso di censura: il 'Rigoletto'* (Milan, 1979).
13 See C. Dapino (ed.) *Il teatro italiano, V: Il libretto del melodramma dell'Ottocento*, vol. 2 (Turin, 1984), p. 288.
14 The text which Verdi already had in mind was the younger Dumas's tragic *La Dame aux camélias* which, with the aid of Piave, would later become *La traviata*. Although at the time of Verdi's writing to Cammarano it had not yet been performed dramatically, it had existed in novel form since 1848.
15 Patrick Smith, in *The Tenth Muse* (London, 1971), p. 237, makes this point when he states:

> Verdi must be treated as a librettist in any study of the form. He had such definite ideas about the dramatic shape of his works and insisted so strongly on obtaining what he desired that his influence, upon the libretto was almost as direct as his poets', and in most cases was more important.

16 See Tommaso Grossi, '*Marco Visconti*', aggiuntovi '*Ildegonda*', '*La fuggitiva*', '*Ulrico e Lida*' (Florence, 1849), p. 436:

> Era sereno il cielo, splendea la luna
> Ridente, a mezzo della sua carriera,
> Sicchè da lungi in armatura bruna
> Vedea un guerriero calata la visiera.
> Nessun fragor s'udia, voce nessuna.

> (The sky was clear, the moon was shining, smiling midway along the path. In the distance, in brown armour one beheld a warrior with face revealed. Not a sound was heard – no voice.)

Ildegonda, like Leonora, loves a chivalric warrior, successful at tournaments. She is placed in a convent on account of rejecting her family's choice of suitor. After a fruitless attempt on the part of her lover to rescue her from the cloister, she becomes mad and dies. The work contains some lines in the tradition of the poetry of the cloister, and the first nineteenth-century 'mad scene'.

17 F. L. Arruga (*Incontri fra poeti e musicisti italiane* (Milan, 1968),

p. 240) has stressed the importance of Alfieri in the study of the operatic libretto. 'Di quella pira' is an Alfierian line. The conflict between light and flame is nowhere more clearly demonstrated than in his tragedy *Agamennone*.

18 See A. Luzio, '*La traviata* e il dramma intimo personale di Verdi', in A. Luzio, *Carteggi verdiani*, vol. 4 (Rome, 1935–47), pp. 250–76; David R. B. Kimbell, *Verdi in the Age of Italian Romanticism* (Cambridge, 1981), pp. 647–9.

19 In his chapter on *La traviata*, '*La traviata* – a chamber opera', George R. Marek provides an account of the life and death of Alphonsine Plessis, the source of inspiration for Marguerite Gautier and Violetta Valéry. See G. R. Marek, *Opera as Theatre* (Westport, Conn., 1977), pp. 135–40.

20 See *Théâtre complet de Alexandre Dumas fils*, vol. 1 (Paris, 1867), p. 129.

21 This, by Piave, is a compressed form of Marguerite's longer speech.

22 Verdi, op. cit., p. 130.

23 It should be remembered that Giuseppina Strepponi was regarded as a 'fallen woman', as the mother of two illegitimate children from an earlier relationship with the tenor Napoleone Moriani. She also suffered from a consumptive disease, which during her early years with Verdi almost proved fatal. She lived, however, to the age of 82. For an account of her youth and sympathetic disposition, see F. Walker, *The Man Verdi* (London, 1962), Chapter 2, pp. 38–95 and 162–223.

24 Marek, op. cit., p. 135.

25 The 'horned creature', the symbol of the cuckold or betrayed husband.

8 DEVIL'S ADVOCATE: EVIL IN THE WORKS OF ARRIGO BOITO

1 For a critical approach to the *Scapigliatura*, see P. Nardi, *Scapigliatura* (Bologna, 1924); P. Madini, *La scapigliatura milanese* (Milan, 1929); A. Romanò, *Il secondo romanticismo lombardo* (Milan, 1958); M. Apollonio, 'Scapigliatura', in *Fondazioni della cultura italiana moderna* (Florence, 1961); M. Petrucciani and Neuro Bonifazi (eds) *Poeti della Scapigliatura* (Urbino, 1962), pp. 9–31.

2 Biography: A. Pompeati, *Arrigo Boito, poeta e musicista* (Florence, 1919); C. Ricci, *Arrigo Boito* (Milan, 1924); P. Nardi, *Vita di Arrigo Boito* (Milan, 1942); R. de Rensis, *Arrigo Boito, capitoli biografici* (Florence, 1942). For an account of Boito's achievement as a poet and librettist, see G. Scarsi, *Rapporto poesia–musica in Arrigo Boito* (Rome, 1972); J. Nicolaisen, *Italian Opera in Transition, 1871–1893* (Michigan, 1980), pp. 125–60.

3 A concise account of the significance of Boito's association with the *Scapigliatura* is given in Scarsi, op. cit., pp. 36–44. Pages 44–62 contain an analysis of the two versions of *Mefistofele*.

NOTES

4   See de Rensis, op. cit., pp. 28, 216.
5   Antonio Ghislanzoni (1824–93) was a poet, dramatist, librettist and singer. In addition to providing Verdi with his libretto for *Aida*, he also merits a place in literary history for his operatic adaptation of Manzoni's *I promessi sposi* (1869) for Petrella. As a result of his experiences as an operatic baritone, he wrote the entertaining novel *Gli artisti da teatro* (1856) and later was a successful editor (*Italia musicale, Gazzetta musicale*). Having founded in 1876–7 the *Rivista minima di scienze, lettere e arti*, he assumed its directorship. Bibliography: T. Mantovani, 'A. Ghislanzoni', *Musica d'oggi*, March–April 1929; A. della Corte, *Satire e grotteschi* (Turin, 1946); A. Luzio, 'Come fu composta l'*Aida*', *Nuova Antologia*, March 1935; P. Gossett, 'Verdi, Ghislanzoni and *Aida*: the users of convention', *Critical Enquiry*, 1 (1974–5), pp. 291–334; P. Petrobelli, 'La musica nel teatro: a proposito dell'atto III di *Aida*', in L. Bianconi (ed.) *La drammaturgia musicale* (Bologna, 1986), pp. 143–56.
6   This D'Annunzian concept of the artist is most clearly exposed, with all its attributes and side-effects, in *Il piacere* (1888).
7   See Scarsi, op. cit., p. 23.
8   In Petrucciani and Bonifazi, op. cit., p. 133.
9   Nicolaisen, op. cit., p. 149. For a synopsis of the principal differences between the two versions, see ibid., pp. 128–34.
10 See Leopardi, 'La ginestra', ll. 202–12, in G. Leopardi, *Canti* (Milan, 1949), p. 183; 'Dialogo di un folletto e uno gnomo', in *Operette morali* (Milan, 1976), pp. 100–5. By adopting a miniature scale both Leopardi and Boito bring human achievement to ridicule.
11 See Leopardi, 'Infinito', ll. 5–6 in Leopardi, 1949, op. cit., p. 93.
12 See F. Portinari, *Pari siamo* (Turin, 1981), pp. 215–18.
13 Boito had already provided the libretto for Faccio's Shakespeare opera *Amleto* (1865).
14 C. Osborne, *The Complete Operas of Verdi* (London, 1969), pp. 445–6.
15 A copy of *La tragédie d'Othello, Le Maure de Venise* in *Oeuvres complètes de W. Shakespeare*, vol. 5 (1860) belonging to Boito is now in the Museo teatrale alla Scala. This contains many notes, underlinings and comments, and is clearly the poet's principal working source.
16 James A. Hepokoski, *Giuseppe Verdi, Otello* (Cambridge, 1987), p. 25.
17 For some considerations on the libretto of *Simon Boccanegra*, see Portinari, op. cit., pp. 173–7; C. Dapino, *Il teatro italiano*, 5, *Il libretto del melodramma dell'Ottocento*, 2 (Turin, 1984), pp. 177–81; D. Goldin, *La vera fenice* (Turin, 1985), Chapter 8, pp. 283–314.
18 Boito did, however, use what he believed best from Act 1 and incorporated it in the 'love duet': 'E tu m'amavi per le mie sventure/Ed io t'amavo per la tua pietà' ('And you loved me on

account of my misfortune and I loved you on account of your pity') (*Otello*, Act 1, Scene 3). Cf. 'She lov'd me for the dangers I had pass'd,/And I lov'd her that she did pity them' (*Othello*, Act 1, Scene 3).

19 A. Alberti, *Carteggio di Giuseppe Verdi con il Conte Opprandino Arrivabene* (Milan, 1913), p. 201.

SELECT BIBLIOGRAPHY

Abbiati, F. (1959) *Verdi*, Milan: Ricordi.
Abert, A. A. (1970) 'Tasso, Guarini e l'opera', *Nuova rivista italiana* 4: 827–40.
Accorsi, M. G. (1980) 'Il melodramma melodrammatico', *Sigma* 13, no. 1: 109–27.
―――― (1984) 'Metastasio e l'idea dell'amore', *Italianistica* 13, no. 1–2: 71–123.
Alberti, L. (1977) 'I progressi attuali del dramma musicale', in *Il melodramma italiano dell'Ottocento: studi e ricerche per Massimo Mila*, Turin: Einaudi.
Apollonio, M. (1954) *Storia della letteratura italiana*, Brescia: La Scuola.
Arruga, F. L. (1965) 'Alessandro Manzoni e "la lezione" del teatro musicale italiano', *Vita e pensiero* (May 1965): 369–76.
―――― (1968) *Incontri fra poeti e musicisti nell'opera romantica italiana*, Milan: Vita e Pensiero.
Ashbrook, W. (1965) *Donizetti*, London: Cassell.
Austin, W. (1968) *New Looks at Italian Opera*, Westport, Conn.: Greenwood.
Baldacci, L. (1974) *Libretti d'opera*, Florence: Vallecchi.
Baratto, M. (1985) *La letteratura teatrale del Settecento: studi e letture su Carlo Goldoni*, Vicenza: Neri Pozza.
Bernardi, G. G. (1935) 'Contributo allo studio dell'elemento comico nell'opera seria veneziana del secolo XVII', *Musica d'oggi* 12: 53–61.
Bianconi, L. (ed.) (1986) *La drammaturgia musicale*, Bologna: Il Mulino.
Bianconi, L. and Bossa, R. (eds) (1983) *Musica e cultura a Napoli dal XV al XIX secolo*, Florence: Olschki.
Bjurstrom, P. (1966) *Feast and Theatre in Queen Christina's Rome*, Stockholm: Analecta Reginensis.
Black, J. (1985) *The Italian Romantic Libretto: A Study of Salvatore Cammarano*, Edinburgh: Edinburgh University Press.
Branca, E. (1882) *Felice Romani ed i più riputati maestri di musica del suo tempo*, Milan: Sonzogno.
Budden, J. (1973, 1978, 1981) *The Operas of Verdi*, 3 vols, London: Cassell.

Bukofzer, M. F. (1948) *Music in the Baroque Era*, London: Dent.
Busch, H. (1978) *The History of an Opera in Letters and Documents*, Minneapolis: University of Minnesota Press.
Busch, H. (ed.) (1987) *Verdi's 'Otello' and 'Simon Boccanegra' in Letters and Documents*, Oxford: Oxford University Press.
Busi, A. (1973) *Otello in Italia, 1777–1972*, Bari: Laterza.
Carutti, G. (1977) 'Musica e dramma nell'ultimo Verdi', unpublished degree thesis, University of Milan.
Cassi-Ramelli, A. (1973) *Libretti e librettisti*, Milan: Ceschina.
Cella, F. (1966) 'Indagini sulle fonti francesi dei libretti di Gaetano Donizetti', in *Contributi dell'Istituto di Filologia Moderna, serie francese*, Milan: Università Cattolica del Sacro Cuore.
—— (1968) 'Indagini sulle fonti francesi dei libretti di Vincenzo Bellini', in *Contributi dell'Istituto di Filologia Moderna, serie francese*, vol. 5, Milan: Università del Sacro Cuore.
—— (1968) 'Prospettive della librettistica italiana nell'età romantica', in *Contributi dell'Istituto di Filologia Moderna, serie storia del teatro*, vol. 1, Milan: Università Cattolica del Sacro Cuore.
—— (1985) *Bellini a Milano*, Turin: Einaudi.
Cella, F. and Petrobelli, P. (eds) (1982) *Giuseppe Verdi–Giulio Ricordi: corrispondenza e immagini, 1881/1890*, Milan: Ricordi.
Cervaro, L. (1967) 'Il linguaggio melodrammatico di Ottavio Rinuccini', unpublished degree thesis, University of Padua.
Chiarelli, A. (1974) '*L'incoronazione di Poppea* o *Il Nerone*: problemi di filologia', *Rivista italiana di musicologia* 9: 117–51.
Coe, D. (1978–9) 'The original production book for *Otello*: an introduction', *Nineteenth-Century Music* 2: 148–58.
Conrad, P. (1977) *Romantic Opera and Literary Form*, Berkeley: University of California Press.
Cox, C. (1962) *The Real Figaro*, London: Longman.
Da Mosto, A. (1899) 'Il teatro a Venezia nel secolo XVII', *Revista politica e letteraria* (August 1899): 10–12.
Dapino, C. (ed.) (1984) *Il libretto del melodramma dell'Ottocento*, vol. 2, Turin: Einaudi.
De Grada, F. (1968) 'G. F. Busenello e il libretto dell'*Incoronazione di Poppea*', in *Claudio Monteverdi e il suo tempo*, Venice-Mantua-Cremona: Monterosso.
—— (1979) *Il palazzo incantato: studi sulla tradizione del melodramma dal Barocco al Romanticismo*, Fiesole: Discanto.
Della Corte, A. (1923) *L'opera comica italiana nel Settecento*, Bari: Laterza.
—— (1958) *Drammi per musica dal Rinuccini allo Zeno*, Turin: Einaudi.
Descotes, M. (1982) 'Du drame à l'opéra: les transpositions lyriques du théâtre de Victor Hugo', *Revue d'histoire du théâtre* 34: 103–56.
Dumas (fils), A. (1867) *Théâtre*, vol. 1, Paris: Calmann Lévy.
Einstein, A. (1950–1) '*Orlando furioso* and *La Gerusalemme liberata* as set to music during the sixteenth and seventeenth centuries', *Notes* 8: 623–30.

BIBLIOGRAPHY

Fido, F. (1977) *Guida a Goldoni: teatro e società nel Settecento*, Turin: Einaudi.
Folena, G. (1981) 'Goldoni librettista comico', in *Venezia e il melodramma*, Florence: Olschki.
―――― (1982) 'Cesarotti, Monti e il melodramma fra Sette e Ottocento', *Analecta musicologica* 21: 236–62.
―――― (1982) *L'italiano in Europa: esperienze linguistiche del Settecento*, Turin: Einaudi.
Franceschetti, G. (1961) 'La fortuna di Hugo nel melodramma italiano dell'Ottocento', in *Contributi dell'Istituto di Filologia Moderna, serie francese*, vol. 2, Milan: Università Cattolica del Sacro Cuore.
Gallarati, P. (1984) *Musica e maschera*, Turin: Einaudi.
Gavazzani, F. (1964) 'Le disuguaglianze stilistiche del *Didone*', in *Studi metastasiani*, Padua: Liviana.
Goldin, D. (1985) *La vera fenice*, Turin: Einaudi.
Goldoni, C. (1946) *Mémoires*, Paris: Editions du Verger.
Gossett, P. (1985) *'Anna Bolena' and the Artistic Maturity of Gaetano Donizetti*, Oxford: Clarendon Press.
Gravina, G. A. (1973) *Scritti critici e teorici*, ed. A Quondam, Bari: Laterza.
Gronda, G. (1984) 'Metastasiana', *Rivista italiana di musicologia* 19: 314–39.
Hepokoski, J. A. (1987) *Giuseppe Verdi's 'Otello'*, Cambridge: Cambridge University Press.
Hodges, S. (1985) *Lorenzo da Ponte: the Life and Times of Mozart's Librettist*, London: Granada.
Jeuland-Meynaud, M. (1976) 'Légitimité de la librettologie', *Revue des études italiennes* 22: 60–101.
Kimbell, D. R. B. (1981) *Verdi in the Age of Italian Romanticism*, Cambridge: Cambridge University Press.
Lavagetto, M. (1979) *Quei più modesti romanzi: il libretto del melodramma di Verdi*, Milan: Garzanti.
―――― (1979) *Un caso di censura: il 'Rigoletto'*, Milan: Il Formichiere.
Lindenberger, H. (1984) *Opera, the Extravagant Art*, Ithaca: Cornell University Press.
Lippmann, F. (1986) *Versificazione italiana e ritmo musicale: i rapporti tra versi e musica nell'opera italiana dell'Ottocento*, Naples: Liguori.
Luzio, A. (ed.) (1935–47) *Carteggi verdiani*, 4 vols, Rome: Reale Accademia d'Italia.
Macchia, G. (1978) *Vita, avventure e morte di Don Giovanni*, Turin: Einaudi.
Manzoni, A. (1980) *I promessi sposi*, ed E. Noè Girardi, 4th edn, Turin: Petrini.
Marek, G. R. (1977) *Opera as Theatre*, Westport, Conn.: Greenwood.
Merrill Knapp, J. (1975) *The Magic of Opera*, London: Hale.
Mila, M. (1974) *La giovinezza di Verdi*, Turin: ERI.
―――― (1979) *Lettura delle 'Nozze di Figaro'*, Turin: Einaudi.
―――― (1980) *L'arte di Verdi*, Turin: Einaudi.

Miragoli, L. (1924) *Il melodramma italiano nell'Ottocento*, Rome: Tipografia delle Mantellate.
Muraro, M. T. (ed.) (1986) *Metastasio e il mondo musicale*, Florence: Olschki.
—— (1976) *Venezia e il melodramma nel Seicento*, Florence: Olschki.
—— (1978) *Venezia e il melodramma nel Settecento*, vol. 1, Florence: Olschki.
—— (1981) *Venezia e il melodramma nel Settecento*, vol. 2, Florence: Olschki.
Murata, M. (1981) *Operas for the Papal Court*, Michigan: UMI Research Press.
Muresu, G. (1982) *La parola cantata*, Rome: Bulzoni.
Nardi, P. (1942) *Vita di Arrigo Boito*, Milan: Mondadori.
Nicastro, G. (1973) *Metastasio e il teatro del primo Settecento*, Bari: Laterza.
—— (1974) *Goldoni e il teatro del secondo Settecento*, Bari: Laterza.
Nicolaisen, J. (1980) *Italian Opera in Transition 1871–1893*, Michigan: UMI Research Press.
Noske, F. (1977) *The Signifier and the Signified: Studies in the Operas of Mozart and Verdi*, The Hague: Nijhoff.
O'Brien, G. (n.d.) *The Golden Age of Italian Music*, London: Jarrods.
Orrey, L. (1969) *Bellini*, London: Dent.
Osborne, C. (1969) *The Complete Operas of Verdi*, London: Pan.
—— (1979) *Rigoletto, a Guide to the Opera*, London: Barrie & Jenkins.
Osthoff, W. (1956) 'Zu den Quellen von Monteverdi's *Ritorno di Ulisse in patria*', *Studien zur Musikwissenschaft* 23: 67–78.
Paduano, G. (1982) *Noi facemmo ambedue un sogno strano*, Palermo: Sellerio.
Pagnini, G. (1971) *Memorie ed altri scritti di Lorenzo da Ponte*, Milan: Longanesi.
Palisca, C. V. (ed.) (1960) *Girolamo Mei: Letters on Ancient and Modern Music to Vincenzo Galilei and Giovanni Bardi*, New York: American Institute of Musicology.
—— (1963) 'Musical aids in the diplomatic correspondence of Emilio de' Cavalieri', *Musical Quarterly*, 49: 339–55.
Parker, R. and Brown, M. (1985–6) ' "Ancora un bacio": three scenes from Verdi's *Otello*', *Nineteenth-Century Music* 9: 50–62.
Pendell, W. B. (1947) *Victor Hugo's Acted Dramas and the Contemporary Press*, Baltimore: Johns Hopkins Studies in Romance Literature and Languages.
Petrucciani, M. and Bonifazi, N. (eds) (1962) *La poesia della Scapigliatura*, Urbino: Argalia.
Pirrotta, N. (1954) 'Temperaments and tendencies in the Florentine Camerata', *Musical Quarterly* 40: 169–89.
—— (1969) *Li due Orfei: da Poliziano a Monteverdi*, Turin: Einaudi.
—— (1971) 'Monteverdi e i problemi dell'opera', in *Studi sul teatro veneto fra Rinascimento e età barocca*, Florence: Olschki.
Pompeati, A. (1919) *Arrigo Boito, poeta e musicista*, Florence: Battistelli.

BIBLIOGRAPHY

Porter, W. V. (1965) 'Peri and Corsi's *Dafne*: some new discoveries and observations', *Journal of the American Musicological Society* 17: 170–96.
Portinari, F. (1981) *Pari siamo*, Turin: Einaudi.
Ricci, C. (1924) *Arrigo Boito*, Milan: Treves.
Robinson, M. F. (1972) *Naples and Neapolitan Opera*, Oxford: Clarendon Press.
Robinson, P. (1985) *Opera and Ideas: from Mozart to Strauss*, New York: Harper & Row.
Rolandi, U. (1940) *Libretti e librettisti verdiani*, Rome: Istituto Grafico Tiberino.
_____ (1941) 'Morbidità e patologia nei libretti delle opere verdiane', *L'Umbria medica* 20.
_____ (1951) *Il libretto per musica attraverso i tempi*, Rome: Edizioni dell'Ateneo.
Roncaglia, G. (1928) *La rivoluzione musicale italiana: secolo XVII*, Milan: Magnani.
Sala di Felice, E. (1985) *Metastasio e il melodramma*, Padua: Sannia Nose.
Scarsi, G. (1972) *Rapporto poesia–musica in Arrigo Boito*, Rome: Istituto per le Lettere, la Musica e il Teatro.
Schmidgall, G. (1977) *Literature as Opera*, New York: Oxford University Press.
Smith, P. (1971) *The Tenth Muse*, London: Gollancz.
Solerti, A. (1976) *Gli albori del melodramma*, Bologna: Forni.
Steele, E. (1981) *Goldoni: Life, Works and Times*, Ravenna: Longo.
Tintori, G. (1958) *L'opera napolitana*, Milan: Ricordi.
_____ (1983) *Bellini*, Milan: Rusconi.
Ubersfeld, A. (ed.) (1985) *Victor Hugo: Théâtre*, vol. 1, Paris: Laffont.
Vatielli, F. (1939) 'Operisti–librettisti dei secoli XVII e XVIII', *Rivista musicale italiana* 43: 1–16, 315–32, 605–21.
Verdi, G. (1913) *I coppialettere di Giuseppe Verdi*, ed G. Cesari and A. Luzio, Milan: Stucchi Ceretti.
Von Westerman, N. G. (1964) *Opera Guide*, London: Thames & Hudson.
Walker, F. (1962) *The Man Verdi*, London: Dent.
Weinstock, H. (1971) *V. Bellini, his Life and his Operas*, London: Weidenfeld & Nicolson.

INDEX

Accademia degli Alterati 5
Accademia degli Incogniti 37
Accademia dell'Arcadia 42, 44–5, 50, 58–9
Accorsi, Maria Grazia, 'Metastasio e l'idea dell'amore' 53–4
Adam, Adolf, *Giselle* 130
Aldobrandini, Cardinal Pietro 25
Alfieri, Vittorio 46, 49, 58, 103, 128; *Agamennone* 55; *Saul* 130
Ambrogini, Angelo (Il Poliziano), *Favola d'Orfeo* 6–7
Anderson, H. Ch. and I. F. Breda, *Bruden fra Lammermoor* 143
Anelli, Angelo, *L'italiana in Algieri* 102
Anicet-Bourgeois and Cornu, Francis, *Nabuchodonsor* 120
Apolloni, *La Dori* 40
Apollonio, Mario 6
Arcadia, Accademia dell' 42, 44–5, 50, 58–9
Archilei, Vittoria 11
arias 43, 46, 53, 133; in Busenello's *Gli amori di Apollo di Dafne* 33–4; *da capo* aria 46–7, 54, 60, 72; in Piave–Verdi's *La traviata* ('addio del passato bei sogni ridenti') 178–9; in Romani's *Norma* ('Casta Diva') 116; Zeno's use of 46–8

Badaoro, Giacomo 29, 31, 37; *Helena rapita da Theseo* 37; *Il ritorno di Ulisse in patria* 37, 40; *L'Ulisse errante* 37
Balbo 120, 127
Balzac, Honoré de 170
Barbarossa, Frederick 126
Barberini, Antonio 26
Barberini, Prince 25
Barbieri, G. 143; *Il talismano* 143
Bardare, Leone Emmanuele, *Il trovatore* (libretto) 154, 160
Bardi, Count Giovanni 4, 5
Barezzi, Antonio 167, 168
baroque style, reaction against 42–3, 44–6
Barry, Madame du 77
Beaumarchais, Caron de 66, 76–7, 80, 82; *Le Barbier de Seville* 76, 83–4; *Le Mariage de Figaro* 76; *La Mère coupable* 76
Bellini brothers 28
Bellini, Vincenzo 28, 103, 106, 134, 152; *Norma* 102; *Il pirata* 130, 132–8; *I puritani (e i cavalieri) di Scozia* 130, 143, 150–1; *La sonnambula* 130; *La straniera* 138
Belmonte, Countess Marianna Pignatelli 51
Beltrame, P. and A. Mazzucato, *La fidanzata di Lammermoor* 143
Benini, Gian-Vincenzo 105
Benti Bulgarelli, Marianna 50
Berchet, Giovanni 101
Berni 45

INDEX

Bernini, Gian Lorenzo 8, 26–7
Bertati, Giovanni 77, 85–7
Bettinelli, Saverio, *Serse re di Persia* 130
Bettinelli, Zaverio 112
Bianchi, Barbara 30–1
Bianchi, Sebastiano (Domenico Lalli) 44
Bidera, Giovanni Emanuele, *Marin Faliero* (libretto) 129
Bis, I, 101
Bishop, Sir Henry, *Clari, the Maid of Milan* 142
Boccaccio, Giovanni 48
Boito, Arrigo 157, 159, 180, 181, 182–201; *Falstaff* (libretto) 201; *La Gioconda* (libretto) 184, 194–5; *Il libro dei versi – Re orso* 181, 184; *Mefistofele* 180, 181, 182–3, 184, 188–94, 196; *Nerone* 201; *Otello* (libretto) 181, 184, 196–201; *Re orso* 181, 184; *Simon Boccanegra* (libretto revision) 196; 'Dualismo' 186; 'Lezione d'anatomia' 187–8
Bonarelli, *Solimano* 37
Bonlini, Giovanni Carlo, *Le glorie della poesia e della musica* 30
Bononcini, Giovanni Battista 43, 46
Brizi, Professor Bruno 29
Busenello, Faustina 31
Busenello, Gian Francesco 29, 30–7; *La Didone* 31, 38; *La discesa d'Enea all'Inferno* 31; *Gli amori di Apollo e di Dafne* 31, 32–5; *L'incoronazione di Poppea* 31, 35–7; *La prosperita infelice di Giulio Cesare dittatore* 31; *La Statira, principessa di Persia* 31, 35
Byron, Lord 152, 159

cabaletta 104, 117
Caccini, Giulio 4, 6, 7, 11
Caccini, Pompeo 25
Callas, Maria 179
Caloprese, Gregorio 50
Calzabigi, Ranieri di' 43, 59–63; *Alceste* 60, 61, 62–3; *Iphigenie en Tauride* 60, 63; *Orfeo ed Euridice* 60–3; *Paride ed Elena* 63
Camerana, Giovanni 181
Camerata dei Bardi 4, 4–5
Cammarano, Salvatore 126, 142–3, 152; *L'assedio di Calais* (libretto) 143; *Belisario* (libretto) 143; *Lucia di Lammermoor* (libretto) 129, 130, 133, 138, 143, 144–51, 163; *Maria di Rudenz* (libretto) 129, 143; *Pia de' Tolomei* (libretto) 143; *Roberto Devereux* (libretto) 129, 143; *Il trovatore* (libretto) 129, 154, 159–66
Carbonari 100
Carner, Mosco 178
Carpaccio 28
Casanova de Seinfalt, Giacomo 78
Casti, Giovanni Battista 63, 77–8
Catalani 188
Caterino, Pier 46, 49
Cavalieri, Emilio de' 6; *La rappresentazione di Anima e di Corpo* 25
Cavalli, Francesco 31, 37, 38
cavatina 104, 134
Cavicchi, Adriano 35
Cavour, Camilio Benso di 126
Cella, Franca 103; *Indagini sulle fonti francesi dei libretti di Vincenzo Bellini* 106
censorship 123, 154–6
Ceroni, Giuseppe, *Lettere di sei donne ai lori sposi ed amanti* 105
Cerretti, Luigi, *Il chiostro* 105
Cesti, Antonio 37, 38, 40; *Cesare amante* 38; *La Dori* 38; *Orontea* 38–9, 40; *Il pomo d'oro* 38
Charles III, King of Spain 76
Charles V 127
Charles VI of Austria 52
Cherubini, *Médée* 100
Chiabrera, Gabriello 5; *Il pianto d'Orfeo* 8, 10
Chiari, Pietro 105
chorus, role of 61

INDEX

Christina, Queen of Sweden 27, 44, 85
cicisbeismo (concept of service) 44, 71–2
Cicognini, Giacinto Andrea 37, 38; *Celia* 38; *Giasone* 38; *Gl'amori di Alessandro Magno* 38; *Orontea* 38
Cinthio, Giraldi, *Hecartommihi* 196
Clement IX, Pope, *see* Rospigliosi, Cardinal Giulio
Coleridge, S. T., *Biographia Literaria* 132
Colobrano, Carafa di, *Le nozze di Lammermoor* 143
comic opera 43, 64–96; *commedia lacrimosa* 72; and demands of popular audience 65; introduction of comic elements 24, 27, 39–41, 60, 64; 'moral comedy' 89–90; and work of Beaumarchais 76–7
commedia dell'arte 24, 27, 40, 43, 63–9, 81, 86; Goldoni's reform of 63, 69–76
commedia lacrimosa 72
Conti, Antonio 105, 112–13; *Lettera di Abelardo a Eloisa* 105
Corsi, Jacopo 4, 5, 7, 8
Crescimbeni, G. M. 45; *Dell'istoria della volgar poesia* 38

Dalrympyle, Janet 144
D'Annunzio, Gabriele 180, 182
Dante (Dante Alighieri) 11; *Divina commedia* 16, 21; *Inferno* 4, 21
Da Ponte, Lorenzo (Emmanuele Conegliano) 63, 66, 76, 77; *Così fan tutte* 77, 90–6, 128; *Don Giovanni* 77, 78, 85, 86, 87–90; *Le nozze de Figaro* 39–40, 67, 74–6, 78–85, 89–91, 95–6
De Grada 31
De Sanctis 50
Della Corte, Andrea 134
Della Valle, Federigo, *Reina di Scozia* 37
Donizetti, Gaetano 103, 129, 138–51, 152; *Anna Bolena* 124, 129, 130, 138; *L'assedio di Calais* 143; *Belisario* 143; *Il castello di Kenilworth* 129; *Don Pasquale* 69; *Elisabetta al castello di Kenilworth* 143; *L'elisir d'amore* 69, 138; *Lucia di Lammermoor* 129, 130–1, 133, 138, 143; *Lucrezia Borgia* 129, 138; *Maria di Rudenz* (libretto) 129, 143; *Maria Stuarda* 138; *Marin Faliero* 129, 138; *Parisina* 138; *Pia de' Tolomei* 143; *Roberto Devereux* 129, 143; *Ugo, conte di Paris* 138
Dumas, Alexandre (fils) 170; *La Dame aux camelias* 154, 166–74
Dunbar, David 144

Enlightenment thought, Da Ponte's appraisal of 80–96; and natural philosophy 73–4; and work of Metastasio 52–9
ensemble, growing importance of 152
Euripides, *Medea* 106
evil, as theme in opera 124, 158–9, 184, 194–5, 196–201

Faccio, Franco 182, 196
Federico, G. A., *La serva padrona* 67–9
Ferdinand, Archduke of Austria 38
Ferrari, Benedetto 28, 29
Figaro (newspaper) 182, 196
Florence, as opera centre 4–14, 25
Folena, Professor Gianfranco 29, 68
Follino, Federico 22
Forbes, Elizabeth 85
Foscolo, Ugo 100, 101; *Dei sepolcri* 135–6; *Le ultime lettere di Jacopo Ortis* 100, 101; 'In morte del fratello Giovanni' 135, 136
Francis II, Emperor of Austria 78
Frederick II of Italy 3
Frescobaldi 25

Gabrieli, Giovanni 28

INDEX

Gagliano, Marco da 7, 8
Galilei, Vincenzo 4; *Dialogo sulla musica antica e moderna* 4; *Lamentations of Jeremiah* 4
Gallarati, Paolo, *Musica e maschera, il libretto italiano del Settecento* 72
Galuppi 71, 72
Galvani, Livio Niso (Giovanni Salvioli) 30
Garcia, Manuel 78
Garibaldi, Giuseppe 126, 182
Gavazzeni, Franco 56
Gazzaniga, Giuseppe 85
Germi, Pietro 7
Ghislanzoni, Antonio, *Aida* (libretto) 181
Giacosa 180
Gianni, Francesco, *Eloisa ed Abelardo* 105
Gilardoni, D., *I fidanzati* 143
Gioberti, Vincenzo 100, 101, 120, 127; *Del primato morale e civile degli Italiani* 101
Giusti, Giuseppe 125, 126
Gluck, Christoph Willibald 59–63; *Alceste* 60, 61, 62–3; *Iphigenie en Tauride* 60, 63; *Orfeo ed Euridice* 60–3; *Paride ed Elena* 63
Goldin, Daniela, *La vera fenice* 89
Goldoni, Carlo 43, 63, 64, 66, 68, 69–76, 78; *L'amante cabala* 71; *L'Arcadia in Brenta* 72; *Birba* 71; *La bottega del caffe* 71; *Il bugiardo* 71; *La buona figliuola* 72; *Il cavaliere e la dama* 72; *Il Conte Caramella* 72; *La contessina* 75; *Don Giovanni Tenorio, o sia il dissoluto* 85; *La donna di garbo* 71; *La femmine puntigliose* 71; *Il filofoso di campagna* 72–5; *Filosofo* 71; *La locandiera* 67, 71; *Momolo courtesan* 72; *Momolo sulla Brenta* 72; *Il mondo della luna* 72; *Monsieur Petiton* 71; *La Pamela* 71; *Pupilla* 71
Gonzaga, Cardinal of Mantua 7
Gonzaga, Vincenzo, Duke of Mantua 6, 14, 22–3
Gorrio, Tobia, *see* Boito, Arrigo
Granelli, Giovanni, *Sedecia, ultima re di Giuda* 130
Gravina, Gian Vincenzo 45, 50; *Ragion poetica* 45
Gray, Thomas, 'Elegy in a Country Churchyard' 135
Greatti, Giuseppe 105
Grisi, Giulia 106
Groppo, Antonio 30
Grossi, Tommaso 103, 131, 138; *Ildegonda* 124, 139, 163; *I lombardi alla prima crociata* 124; *Marco Visconti* 100
Guillard, François 63
Guitti, Francesco 29
Gutierrez, Antonio Garcia, 159; *El trovador* 154, 159–60

Haydn, Franz Joseph 72
Henry III, King of France 67
Henry IV, King of France 7
Hepokoski, James A. 196
heroic opera (*opera seria*) 43–64, 100, 104, 152
historical drama 37, 129–51
Hoffman, F. B. 100
Holmes, William J. 37, 38
Homer 11
Hugo, Victor 152, 155–6, 159; *Angelo, tyran de Padoue* 194; *Marion de Lorme* 170; *Le roi s'amuse* 153–4, 154–6, 158, 166, 181; translation of Shakespeare 196

Ingegneri, Marcantonio 14
insanity 129–51; in Bellini's *Il pirata* 132–8; in Bellini's *I puritani* 150–1; in Donizetti's *Anna Bolena* 138–42; in Donizetti's *Lucia di Lammermoor* 143–51; in Manzoni's *Adelchi* 138–42
Instituti della Ragunanza degli Arcadi 42
Isabella, Queen of Spain 126

INDEX

Italian Federation (1818–20) 101
Italian unification 99–127
Ivanovich, Cristoforo, *La Minerva al tavolino* 29, 30

Jomelli, Niccolo 43
Joseph II, Emperor of Austria 77, 78, 80
Jouy, Etienne de 100
Jouy, S. de 101

Lalli, Domenico (Sebastiano Bianchi) 44; *Cambise* 44; *Il gran Mogol* 44; *Tigrane* 44
laments, in Calzabigi's *Orfeo ed Euridice* 61–3; in Rinuccini's *Arianna* ('lasciatemi morire') 22, 24; in Rinuccini's *Euridice* 13–14
Landi, Stefano, *La morte d'Orfeo* 8, 25, 39; *Sant'Alessio* 40
Lauzieres, de 181
Lentini, Jacobo da 3
Leopardi, Giacomo 103, 150; *Idylls* 114; *L'infinito* 114; 'Canzone all'Italia' 136; 'Sopra il monumento di Dante' 136
Leopold II, Emperor of Austria 77
libretto, as classical drama 43; and philosophical instruction 25–7, 43; place of 29–30, 42–4, 129–30
Lombardy 99, 101, 128
Louis Philippe, King of France 156
Louis XV, King of France 76
love, as theme in opera 110–14, 129–51, 160–1, 165–6
Lucilla, D., *La bella fanciulla di Perth* 144

Maffei, Scipione 46
Magalotti 45
Maggi 45
Mancini, Carlo 44, 182
Manfredi, Eustachio 112
Manni, Agostino 25
Mantua, as opera centre 4, 14–24
Manzi 46
Manzoni, Alessandro 100, 101, 103, 131, 138; *Adelchi* 124, 138–40; *I promessi sposi* 100, 105–6, 140, 149–50
Marazzoli, Marco 27
Marek, George R., *La traviata* – a chamber opera' 176; *Opera as Theatre* 80
Marenzio 25
Maria Teresa of Austria 52
Marini, G. B. *Il templario* 144
Marino, Giovanni Battista 31, 36; *Adone* 31
Maroncelli, Pietro 125
marriage festivities, operas performed for 3, 6
Maturin, Rev. R. C., *Bertram, or The Castle of Saint Aldebrand* 132
Mazza, Angelo 112
Mazzini, Giuseppe 100, 120, 126, 127; *Le speranze d'Italia* 127
Mazzocchi, Domenico 25; *La catene di Adone* 25–6
Mazzocchi, Virgilio 27
Medici, Catherine dei 6
Medici, Don Giovanni dei 5
Medici, Duke Cosimo I 5
Medici, Eleanora dei 6
Medici, Maria dei 7, 11
Melani, Alessandro, *L'empio punito* 85
melodramma (early opera) 3–4, 7–24, 28, 35–7, 153; reforms of 42–3, 44–64, 128–9
Menzini 45
Méric-Lalande 132
Mérimée 161
Merulo, Claudio 28
Metastasio, Pietro (Pietro Trapassi) 43, 46, 48, 49–59, 72, 77, 78, 129; *Adriano in Siria* 51, 56; *Alessandro nelle Indie* 50; *Artaserse* 50; *Attilio Regolo* 51, 53, 56–8, 128; *Catone in Utica* 50; *La clemenza di Tito* 56; *Demetrio* 51; *Demofoonte* 51; *Didone abbandonata* 50, 53–6; *Ezio* 50, 56; *Giustiniano* 50; *Olimpiade* 53; *Il re pastore* 56; *Semiramide riconosciuta* 50;

INDEX

Siroe 50; *La strada della gloria* 50; *Temistocle* 56; *Estratto della 'poetica' d'Aristotle* 52; *Note all'arte poetica di Orazio* 52; *Osservazioni sul teatro greco* 52
middle classes, emergence of 99; values of depicted in opera 153
Milton, John 27
Molière (Jean-Baptiste Poquelin) 64, 67; *Don Juan, ou le festin de pierre* 85
Molina, Tirso de, *El burlador de Sevilla y Convidado de Pietra* 85
Monteverdi, Claudio 14, 23, 37; *Arianna* 7, 8, 15–16, 22, 22–4; *Il ballo delle ingrate* 7, 22; *La favola d'Orfeo* 6, 8, 14, 15–22; *L'incoronazione di Poppea* 31
Monti, Vincenzo 101
Mozart, Wolfgang Amadeus 66, 76; *Don Giovanni* 84
Muratori 45

Naples, as centre of opera 41, 43–4, 50
Napoleon III 126
neo-classical revival 59–64
Newton, Isaac 59
Niccolini, Giovanni Battista, *Nabucco* 122
Nicolai, C. O. E., *Il templario* 144
nun/priestess figure, popularity of 104–14

Obizzi, Pio Enea, Marquis of Padua 31
opera, influence on Italian nationalism 127; literary basis of 5–6, 16; see also libretto; origins of 3–6, 11
opera houses, San Cassiano Theatre (Venice) 28; Teatro alla Scala (Milan) 100
opera seria (heroic opera) 43–64, 100, 104, 152
Orologio, Lucrezia 31
Osborne, Charles 124, 154, 196
Osthoff, Wolfgang 29
Ovid, *Metamorphoses* 8–9

Pacini, *Allen Cameron* 144; *I fidanzati* 143; *Il talismano* 143; *Vallace o L'eroe* 143
Paduano, Guido, *Norma: la crisi del modello deliberativo* 106
Palestrina, Giovanni Pierluigi de 25
Palisca, Claude V. 4, 5
Pariatri, Pietro 46
Parini, *Il giorno* 72
Pasta, Giuditta 106
pastoral drama 6–17, 31–7
patriotism, reflected in nineteenth-century opera 99–127; and religion 102–27; as theme in heroic opera 56–8
Paul V, Pope 25
Pavesi, S., *La dama bianca d'Avenello* 143
Pellico, Silvio 100, 101, 125; *Francesca da Rimini* 101; *Le mie prigoni* 125
Pepoli, Carlo, *I puritani (e i cavalieri) di Scozia* (libretto) 130, 143, 150–1
Pergolesi, Giovanni Battista 43, 67
Peri, Jacopo 4, 6, 7, 11, 14
Perrucci, Andrea 44
Petrarch, Francesco, influence of 8–10, 45, 105; *Rerum vulgarum fragmenta (Canzoniere)* 3
Piave, Francesco Maria 101, 103, 126, 152, 180; *Allen Cameron* 144; *I due Foscari* (libretto) 154; *Ernani* (libretto) 102, 154; *I fidanzati* 144; *La forza del destino* (libretto) 130; *Macbeth* (libretto) 130; *Rebecca* 144; *Rigoletto* (libretto) 154, 156–9, 181; *Simon Boccanegra* (libretto) 181; *Stiffelio* (libretto) 154; *La traviata* (libretto) 129, 154, 166–79, 181; 'A Carlo Quinto siagloria ed onor' 127
Piazzano, G. F., *Carlo il temerario* 144
Piccini, *La buona figliuola* 72
Pindemonte, Ippolito, *Lettera di una monaca a Federico IV re di Danimarca* 105

INDEX

Pirrotta, Nino 6, 7, 8, 29
Pisani, B., *I fidanzati* 144; *Rebecca* 144
Pius IX, Pope 127
Plautus 64
poesia di monacazione 105
political comment, in Da Ponte's work 75–96; in Goldoni's work 75
political conflict, as theme in opera 99–127
Poliziano, *Orfeo* 16
Ponchielli 180; *La Gioconda* 181, 184, 194–5
Pope, Alexander, *Eloisa to Abelard* 104–5, 112–13; *The Rape of the Lock* 44
Portinari, Folco 140
Praga, Emilio 181, 182; and Arrigo Boito, *Le madri galanti* 182
Prévost d'Exiles, Antoine, *Manon Lescaut* 170
Puccini, Giacomo 188
Purcell, Henry 85; 'Mad Bess' aria 130

Raimond, Hippolyte 132
realism 170; psychological 147–50, 152–3; in Boito's *Mefistofele* 181, 184; in *Il trovatore* 166; in *Otello* 181, 196–201; in *Rigoletto* 156, 181; in *La traviata* 171–9, 181
reason, role of in theatre 128–9; in romantic opera 128–51; in Romani's *Norma* 112–14
recitativo secco 27, 60
Redi 45
religion, and patriotism 102–27; *poesia di monacazione* 105; as subject of opera 4, 25–7
Ricci, F., *Le prignoni di Edimburgo* 143
Ricordo, Giulio 196
Rinuccini, Alessandro 5
Rinuccini, Ottavio 5, 22; *Arianna* 22–4; *Dafne* 6, 7, 8–10, 11, 17, 32, 33; *Euridice* 7, 8, 10–14, 17, 18–19; *Il Narciso* 7, 8, 24

Risorgimento 100, 125–7, 139, 152
Rolandi, Ulderico 8
Romani, Felice 103, 132; *Anna Bolena* (libretto) 124, 129, 130, 135, 138–42, 151; *Il castello di Woodstock* (libretto) 144; *L'elisir d'amore* (libretto) 69, 138; *Gianni di Parigi* (libretto) 138; *Lucrezia Borgia* (libretto) 129, 138; *Matilde di Scozia* (libretto) 144; *Norma* (libretto) 102–4, 106–14, 116–19, 122–3, 125, 133–6; *Parasina* (libretto) 138; *Il pirata* (libretto) 130, 132–8, 145; *La sonnambula* (libretto) 130; *Ugo, conte di Paris* (libretto) 138; *Vallace o L'eroe* (libretto) 143
romantic opera, development of 103–27; role of reason 128–51
romanticism 100, 152; decline of 170; and political orientation 128; reaction against 180–1
Rome, as opera centre 4, 25–7
Rospigliosi, Cardinal Giulio (later Pope Clement IX) 39; *Chi soffre speri* 27; *Dal male al bene* 27; *Saint'Alessio* 26, 27, 40; *San Bonifatio* 26; *Santa Teodora* 26
Rossi, Gaetano 138; *La dama bianca d'Avenello* 143; *Le prignoni di Edimburgo* 143; *Tancredi* 101
Rossini, Gioacchino Antonio 76; *Il barbiere di Siviglia* 69, 78; *La donna del lago* 143; *Guglielmo Tell* 101; *L'italiana in Algieri* 102; *Mosè* 102, 103–4, 118, 119–20, 127; *Tancredi* 101, 127
Rousseau, Jean-Jacques 59
Royer 138
Rubini 132
Ruff, M. A. 132
Ruffini 138; *Don Pasquale* 69
Ruggeri, *Reina di Scozia* 37
Rutherford, Lord 144

Sacrati 37
St. Cloud, Edict of 135

INDEX

Sala, Marco 182
Salle, Jouslin de la 155
Scapigliatura milanese 180, 181–2, 184, 191, 193
Scarlatti, Alessandro 43, 44, 46
Scarsi 184
Schiller, Johann von 152; *Don Carlo* (libretto) 181
Schira, F. V., *Kenilworth* 144
Schmidgall, Gary 143
Scott, Sir Walter 131; *The Bride of Lammermoor* 143, 146–7; *Rokeby* 132
sensuality, place of in opera 34–5
settings for opera 15–16, 26–7, 177, 195
Shadwell, Thomas, *The Libertine* 85
Shakespeare, William 64; *Hamlet* 130; *King Lear* 130; *Macbeth* 152; *The Merchant of Venice* 66; *Othello* 196–9
Smith, Patrick 114; *The Tenth Muse* 104
Solera, Temistocle 103, 119, 125–6, 152; *I lombardi alla prima crociata* (libretto) 102, 124–6; *Nabucco* (libretto) 102, 103–4, 120–4, 129
Solerti, Angelo 24
Somma, Antonio, *Un ballo in maschera* (libretto) 129
soprano, emergence of 120; and 'mad scenes' 130, 150–1
Spontini, *La vestale* 100, 105–6
Stair family 144
Stampiglia, Silvio 43, 45, 59; *La caduta dei decemviri* 46; *Eraclea* 46; *Partenope* 46; *Tito Sempronio Gracco* 46; *Il trionfo di Camilla* 46
Stendhal (Marie Henri Beyle), *La Chartreuse de Parme* 170; *Le Rouge et le Noir* 170
Sterbini 76; *Il barbiere di Siviglia* 69
stilo recitativo 5
Strepponi, F., *I contestabili di Chester* 143

Strepponi, Giuseppina 167–8
Striggio, Alessandro, *La favola d'Orfeo* 8, 10, 14, 15–22
Strozzi, Pietro 4
Sullivan, Sir Arthur, *Ruddigore* 130

Tamburini 132
Tarchetti, Ugo 181
Tasso, Torquato, *Aminta* 7, 32; *La Gerusalemme liberata* 26, 124
Tellez, Gabriel 85
Terence 64
themes, insanity 129–51; love 46, 54–6, 80, 90–6, 110–14, 129–51, 153, 160–1, 165–6; moral strength 48–9, 52–9; Nature 114–16; patriotism 56–8; political conflict 99–127; problem of evil 124, 158–9, 184, 194–5, 196–201
Thomas, Ambroise, *Hamlet* 130
tomb, cult of in pre-romantic poetry 135–7
Tommasini 201
Tonasso, T. and P. Collavo, *Il castello di Woodstock* 144
Toscanini, Arturo 201
Tottola, Leone Andrea 119; *La donna del lago* 143; *Elisabetta al castello di Kenilworth* (libretto) 129, 143
Townley-Worsthorne, Simon 29
Traetta, Tommaso 43
Trapassi, Pietro *see* Metastasio
Trissino, *Italia liberata dai goti* 50
Tuscany, Grand Duke of 6

Ubersfield 156
United States, introduction of opera to 78
Urban VIII, Pope 26, 27

Vallisnieri, Antonio 46
Venice, as opera centre 15, 28–41, 43, 101
Verdi, Giuseppe 123–4, 152, 167, 180, 182, 188, 195–6, 201; *Aida* 181, 188, 195; *Alzira* 152; *Attila* 120, 154; *Un ballo in maschera*

129, 166; *La battaglia di Legnano* 126–7; *Don Carlo* 181, 188, 196; *I due Foscari* 152; *Ernani* 101, 102, 120, 152, 154; *Falstaff* 153, 201; *La forza del destino* 124, 159, 181, 196; *Giovanna d'Arco* 124, 152; *I lombardi alla prima crociata* 102, 124–6; *Luisa Miller* 152, 153; *Macbeth* 120, 129, 130, 152; *I masnadieri* 152; *Nabucco* 102, 103, 118, 119, 120–4, 129, 167; *Oberto* 167; *Otello* 124, 153, 158, 159, 166, 181, 184, 196–201; *Rigoletto* 153, 154, 156–9, 166, 181, 196; *Simon Boccanegra* 181, 196; *La traviata* 129, 153, 154, 156, 166–79; *Il trovatore* 129, 153, 154, 159–66
Verga, Giovanni 161, 180; *Vita dei campi* 170
Victor Emmanuel, King of Italy 123–4

Vienna, as opera centre 46, 51–2, 59–64, 77–8, 100
Vinci, Leonardo da 43
Vitali, Filippo, *Aretusa* 25
Voltaire (François Marie Arouet) 152
Von Possant, Ernst 91

Wagner, Richard 153
Walker, Thomas 29, 30
Westerman, Gerhart von 106
Winter, G., *Matilde di Scozia* 144

Young Italy movement 100

Zanardini 181
Zeffirelli, Franco 179
Zeno, Apostolo 43, 46, 50, 51, 53, 59; *Andromaca* 47–8; *Gli inganni felici* 46; *Griselda* 46, 48–9
Zola, Emile 170

For Product Safety Concerns and Information please contact our EU representative GPSR@taylorandfrancis.com
Taylor & Francis Verlag GmbH, Kaufingerstraße 24, 80331 München, Germany

www.ingramcontent.com/pod-product-compliance
Lightning Source LLC
Chambersburg PA
CBHW052031300426
44116CB00024B/1432